PRAISE FOR
HOW TO FIND YOUR IDEAL COUNTRY HOME

"Wise, wise-acre (so to speak), and a hoot to read.... Includes economics, demographics...instructions for playing the country realty game, and checklists to ensure your own honesty—all stuff you need to know if contemplating a move to the country."

—J. BALDWIN, *Whole Earth Review*

"If urban life has worn you out and you yearn for life on a small town or on a farm, this is the one book you need to read."

—ALAN CARUBA, *Bookviews*

"Here it all is, in One Big Book. I shall keep it handy for would-be homesteaders who stop by for earthy information and for those who don't know what's facing them in the way of work to be done."

—HELEN NEARING, author, *Loving & Leaving the Good Life*

"[A] wonderful book...just plain fun to read."

—LYNDA DAHL, author of
Ten Thousand Whispers: A Guide to Conscious Creation

"Thorough, clearly-written, up-to-date. I will certainly recommend it to my readers."

—CARLA EMERY, author, *The Encyclopedia of Country Living*

more . . .

How to Find Your Ideal Country Home

❧ A Comprehensive Guide ❧

Gene GeRue

WARNER BOOKS

A Time Warner Company

Copyright © 1994, 1996, 1999 by Gene GeRue

All rights reserved.

Warner Books, Inc., 1271 Avenue of the Americas,

New York, NY 10020

Visit our Web site at www.warnerbooks.com

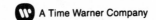 A Time Warner Company

Printed in the United States of America

First Warner Books Printing: July 1999

10 9 8 7 6 5 4 3 2

Library of Congress Cataloging-in-Publication Data

GeRue, Gene.

How to find your ideal country home : a comprehensive guide / Gene GeRue.

p.   cm.

Originally published: 2nd ed. Zanoni, Mo. : Heartwood Publications, c1996.

With a new preface and introduction. Includes index.

ISBN 0-446-67454-0

1. Country homes—United States—Purchasing.

2. Vacation homes—United States—Purchasing. I. Title.

HD256.G47   1999

643.12—dc21   98-50858

CIP

Book design by Bernadette Evangelist

Cover design by Cathy Saksa

Cover illustration by David McCall Johnston

For Christina,
without whom, an
unfulfilled dream

Contents

Preface

I was reared in rural Wisconsin, first at the edge of Beloit in the 1940s, later on a farm in Marquette County. In 1963, a G.I. loan bought my first home, in Concord, California—a two-bedroom bungalow on a large lot for $11,200, payments $72 per month. I still remember feeling the natural high. I walked around my kingdom touching trees and admiring how well the grass grew. My next-door neighbor appeared in his front yard. "Good morning, neighbor," I beamed. No answer. Thinking that he had not heard me, I raised my beam several decibels and repeated. He turned, looked at me—turned his back—and walked away. I was dumbfounded.

In the two decades following that bittersweet Saturday morning I found that city living is "some different" from country life. In twenty-five years of California city living I went to college, raised a family, grew a business, bought several houses—and I never, ever, felt *at home.*

As a teenage farm boy, inspired by Louis Bromfield's *Malabar Farm,* I developed a naive dream of one day owning 1,000 acres and having my friends all live nearby, each of us contributing an essential skill. With great romantic idealism that dream stayed with me.

In 1975 I took a TV course titled *Ready or Not,* designed to help individuals prepare for retirement. (I was thirty-nine at the time but rather full of myself. I later realized that almost anyone could do well in the 1970s California real estate market.) The final assignment was a written retirement plan, including an answer to the big question: where to live? I wrote a five-year plan.

To find my ideal home, I devised a method. First I made a list of the features of my ideal home place. Taking this list to the local library, I initially identified seven states as possibles. After much research I chose one area, part of what I now know to be a bioregion, 2,000 miles away. I made contact with a large number of real estate agents and asked them to send information on any listings that fit my criteria. In August 1976 I took a two-week vacation/exploration trip to look at properties in my chosen area, a band approximately 60 miles wide and over 100 miles long.

The third day of viewing revealed a property in a small valley with a year-round stream babbling along 200 feet in front of a humble old farmhouse. It looked wonderful, but I still had over a week of appointments with agents who had properties for me to examine. A week and a half later I looked at the valley place a second time. Back in California, I wrote and mailed an offer. It was accepted.

For tax reasons, the sellers deferred the closing until 1977. On January 3, I owned my permanent place, my ideal country home. In 1983 I moved to that place in southern Missouri, many hundreds of miles south of my growing-up place. I immediately felt at home.

Are your motivations to move to the country pragmatic or romantic? Mine were both. I'm a pragmatic romantic, very serious about romance. Living in the country provides more freedom to express myself, helps me be more creative, allows me communion with nature, which I find essential for my well-being. City life seems abnormal, a denial of natural laws and factors of geography. My parents always gardened and each of the three places where we lived while I was growing up was progressively larger in acreage. My home place is 130 acres of real Midwest country. My wife and I raise a good proportion of our food and have the option of heating and cooking with wood from our forest.

Many would find our place too remote. One city visitor who slept here remarked, "It's awfully quiet at night." Too bad he wasn't here on one of the nights when the coyotes partied. The yipping, yapping, squealing, yowling, and howling competes with the very highest attainment of punk rockers. But he wasn't and it was normal—very quiet. Not everyone likes that degree of quiet. To me, the city is outrageously noisy, an ever-present din. The coyote parties only happen a few times a year. Truth be told, I enjoy them.

How much sound do you like? How close do you need to be to a shopping mall, building supply center, sports arena, opera house? As we explore these questions, you may find that what would please you most will be a place on a large lot at the edge of a small town. Or you may find that you want to be in a remote place, where malls are nonexistent, where the nearest fast food palace is a two-hour drive.

This book was written for a wide range of people. It will be useful to retirees who have attained the secure status of knowing that a monthly check will follow them wherever they live and who have decided that they will plant their mailbox in front of a country home; to parents who want their children to know where food really comes from and to learn the power of community; to people of all ages who are simply disenchanted with city life and seek simpler but sounder lives in places where values are held in greater esteem than economic achievement.

Moving to the country may not create instant joy. After all, when we move, we take ourselves with us. Country living can be wonderful and it can be awful. Many people make life-altering moves based on emotional passion without due regard for commonsense considerations and practical knowledge. Such moves are seldom satisfactory, often very expensive. This book will assist you in making a sound, lasting decision. Your joy of country living will be ever so much greater for having made the effort to acquire the knowledge and having done the planning.

The premise behind this book can be stated in four lines:

- If you carefully identify how and where you most want to live, and
- If you accordingly locate a property using those criteria, and
- If you acquire and live on that property, then
- Your life will be greatly enriched.

Somebody, joking I think, called me "the man who would empty the cities." Not true. Polls show that 19 percent of Americans want to live in cities and 25 percent prefer suburbs. I sincerely hope they stay there. Think crowding. Think safety. Think Woody Allen with a chainsaw.

I believe that part of my life purpose is to help others get what they want by sharing what I have learned. This book is one attempt to fulfill that purpose. Here I have endeavored to bring together the knowledge of these various subjects that I have gained from personal experience and from ongoing research. The torrent of fresh information and changing conditions makes this a challenging but enriching experience. For the first edition I subjected myself to the countryman's pain of city life by living and writing near the great libraries of Los Angeles

County. Computer technology plus online services and the Internet have allowed this edition to be made here at Heartwood in the very rural Missouri Ozarks. A miracle.

Most of what I feel sure about has been learned by making many mistakes and enjoying some successes. Much of the information in this book comes from my experience as a real estate broker and teacher, from the successful personal quest for my ideal place, and from living in the country for over three decades. Much comes from talking to countless others who have made successful city breaks.

I am indebted to my former real estate clients and students who collectively helped me learn much of what I know about real estate, and to the friends, neighbors, and authors who have enhanced my knowledge and joy of country life.

Craig J. Crawford is much more than my computer bailout guy, but that aspect is critical. Whenever I become befuddled by hardware or software challenges, Craig comes to the rescue. His expertise as a geographer and planner makes him most valuable as a consultant. In between bailouts and consultations he keeps my wife, Chris, and me up to date on how our daughter-in-law Susan and grandsons Colin and James are doing way up in Canada. This is crucial to the author's contentment.

Sandra Bellinger continues to be my local proofreader/editor and she and her husband, Ron, have become close friends. Sandra is an ideal lay editor for this book, as she knows the subject from a personal perspective. She also knows the author, so she can help Chris keep him focused.

Christina GeRue is the research assistant, head proofreader, and most importantly, the author's primary muse. She should in her spare time write a guide for wives on how to keep imperfect husbands perfectly happy.

The two self-published editions were successful experiments; thousands bought the book, necessitating four printings. I am most grateful for input from readers who have written and those who have attended book signings across the country.

I continue to be indebted to readers-in-my-mind who will become readers-in-reality. As I write I try to visualize you, who are now reading these words. Your fears and dreams give me motivation and energy to make this book a useful tool that will help you find a lower-cost but higher-quality life. Thanks for being out there and in here.

Notes on Using This Book

This is not a book for posterity—it is a tool to be used now. I strongly urge you to read with pen in hand. Circle or underline points you wish to be able to easily return to. Write key words and make notes in the margins. If you have borrowed this book or you simply cannot bring yourself to mark in it, use a pad of paper for both a bookmark and note journal. Perhaps like you, I used to keep book pages unmarked, unfolded, unused. It's a symptom of the same dis-ease that keeps some from walking on grass.

Throughout this book "you" should be understood to include you, your spouse/significant other/partner/companion/friend/children or others you consider your family. Maximum involvement of all family members will generally result in the most agreeable choices. Parents know of the exceptions.

The gender-neutral challenge can often be handled by using "we," "our," "they," and other substitutes. Occasionally these do not work well. I respect women and men equally. I've done the best I can. If my use of "he" or "she" offends someone, I am truly sorry.

Before beginning to read, make a preliminary list of all the features and conditions of your ideal home place as you now envision them. This will get your brain operating in the right realm. Try hard to be open-minded. There will not be a test but there will be challenges.

> *"From the feeling that there must be many like me, who wanted a vantage point from which they could survey the whole battlefield before deciding where they would stand the best chance of survival, I came to believe that there must be many veterans who would see what an outsider has to make of them. That is an author's job: to weigh the options, clarify the objectives, balance the physical facts against the convention and tradition. Above all it is to identify the principles: to reach the nub of the matter. It is not easy to remain an outsider from such an enthralling subject for long."*
>
> —Hugh Johnson, *The Principles of Gardening*

> *"On an occasion of this kind it becomes more than a moral duty to speak one's mind; it becomes a pleasure."*
>
> —Oscar Wilde

Introduction

The patchwork quilt that is America is being resewn even before it has been completed. Overwhelmingly rural for centuries, predominantly urban since 1920, the urban cloth is coming unstitched and population pieces are moving back to rural fields. It is one of the great stories of our time.

The exodus of urbanites to the countryside that began in the 1960s and 1970s is growing. Those disconnecting from urban and suburban life are part of a quiet revolution, a rejection of social, economic, and environmental conditions resulting from inattentiveness to traditional values. The beatniks, the hippies, the soppies (semi-old professional persons—yuppies used to think we were all wet but now they're following our lead), and now the yuppies have found material success a hollow house. The return to lower costs and higher values has become the province of the educated, the aware, the sensitive, the demanding—many of whom are turning to rural life as both a reaction against insane urban conditions and an attraction toward a lifestyle where community is more important than big houses and big wheels. As a nation we're starting to *get it*.

Three decades ago, in *Future Shock*, Alvin Toffler suggested we are imagining the future so we may shape our present. What we are now imagining is community meltdown—clearly evidenced by violent crime and attendant widespread fear. "Drive-by shooting" has become part of our lexicon. More cops and more prisons are prescribed because honest diagnosis is overwhelming, and the treatment—real solutions that address the cause—requires us to confront unpleasant facts about our way of life.

We are imagining losing control of our health. We are revolting against increased longevity that comes only at huge financial cost. We are revolting against poisoned food, poisoned air, impure water.

We are imagining environmental loss. Evidence clearly shows that we are destroying our earth, our air, our water—facts so alarming that environmentalism has become an international unifying force, a common goal.

We are imagining traditional values as more sound than modern materialism. We are rejecting the madness that modern city life has become and the worse hell it seems headed for. In 1970 Toffler wrote: "We have set the stage for a completely new society and we are now racing toward it. . . . Can we adapt to its imperatives?" Toffler's future new society has become the present and for a majority of Americans the answer to his question is: We don't want to.

American commerce and culture are rapidly decentralizing. People and businesses are fleeing cities and suburbs with their high prices, pollution, crime, and crowding and are spreading out to small towns and rural areas with clean air, low prices, real community. New concepts are imprinted on our consciousness: cities are sick—country is healthy—wilderness is safer than cities.

It is not just that cities have become unlivable, although many have. Cities have become unnecessary. Widespread roads, electricity, telephones, and the technology of satellites, computers, and fax modems have made cities cumbersome, vestigial remnants of a society that for the first time in human history is free to live anywhere and be instantly connectable to nearly any part of the world. In his 1980 book *The Third Wave*, Toffler noted: "While millions of people continue to pour into urban areas in the still-industrializing parts of the world, all the high-technology countries are already experiencing a reversal of this flow. Tokyo, London, Zurich, Glasgow, and dozens of other major cities are all losing population. . . . The American Council of Life Insurance declares: 'Some urban experts believe that the major U.S. city is a thing of the past.'" New York City is the only major American city that within its nineteenth-century boundaries has as many inhabitants today as fifty years ago.

Commercial enterprises are following the crowd. Land prices and taxes are lower in rural areas. Lower wages are acceptable to workers with lower family overhead. And—no surprise—company executives and their families also want to live away from city conditions. Even New York City is losing businesses. In 1960, 27 percent of Fortune 500 companies were located there; by 1990, only 9 percent.

Computers with fax modems enable millions to work at home, whether that home is on a mountaintop or deep in the woods. The completed national highway system and economical cars allow many more to move quickly from a country cottage to high-paying employment within a thirty-minute drive. Living in the country is not only psychologically desirable, it is economically feasible.

The Modern American Migration

The small-town and rural renaissance is not just the stuff of writers' imaginations. In the late 1960s, U.S. Department of Agriculture senior demographer Calvin L.

Beale first noticed that more people were leaving some metropolitan areas than moving there. His fellow demographers were skeptical. Not until the 1980 census was the national trend measured, confirmed, and finally accepted as fact. That census showed huge losses in city populations. For the first time since 1820, small-town and rural-area population was growing ahead of cities. In the 1970s, small towns and rural areas grew 15.5 percent faster than urban areas.

The 1990 census seemed to show that the flow from city to country had slightly reversed. If so, the condition was short-lived. Kenneth M. Johnson and Calvin Beale presented a paper to the Southern Demographic Association in New Orleans, Louisiana, on October 22, 1993, titled *Nonmetropolitan Demographic Trends Since 1990*. They reported: "In a reversal of the trend of the 1980s, population growth was widespread in nonmetropolitan areas of the United States during the early 1990s. More than 67 percent of the 2,288 counties classified as nonmetropolitan in 1992 gained population between 1990 and 1991, compared to only 46 percent in the 1980s. In all, 500 more nonmetropolitan counties gained population than in the 1980s."

In *Megatrends 2000*, John Naisbitt and Patricia Aburdene spot the trends and predict the future: "In the United States, for the first time in 200 years, more people are moving to rural areas than urban—many more. In the Northeast, West, Great Plains, and Southwest, everywhere, people are moving from cities and suburbs to rural areas. They are abandoning cities for quality-of-life reasons: low crime rates, comparatively low housing costs, recreational opportunities, and, perhaps most of all, a return to community values."

Naisbitt and Aburdene moved to Telluride, population 1,200, in southwest Colorado. "Although we are six hours from Denver, with our computers, telephones, fax machine, and Federal Express we are as in touch with the rest of the world as if we were in downtown London or Tokyo."

During the 1980s as in the 1970s the population of most of the major central cities continued to fall, reported professor Jon C. Teaford in *Cities of the Heartland*. According to Jack Lessinger, professor emeritus at the University of Washington, between one third and one half of the American and Canadian middle class will live outside metropolitan and suburban areas by 2010.

The historical westward movement has also reversed. United Van Lines and U-Haul figures show more native-born Americans leaving California than entering. For the first time ever, California's adult population is growing only because of legal and illegal immigration from other countries. Between 1990 and 1995, California lost 1.1 million more residents than it gained from other states. According to John Mehalic of the American Movers Conference, which represents ten of the largest moving companies, 64 percent of California moves are out-bound.

What Is This Thing Called Country?

A study by Yankelovich Partners found that almost half of all Americans identify themselves as part of the "country universe." Yet more than 70 percent of that group live in places with populations of over 150,000. Country music, country-style dancing, country clothing, country cookbooks, country decorating maga-zines, four-wheel-drive vehicles—for many, "country" is evidently as much lifestyle as physical location.

Webster's Ninth New Collegiate defines *country* as "rural as distinguished from urban areas." Under *urban* we find "of, relating to, characteristic of, or con-stituting a city." *City* gives us "an inhabited place of greater size, population, or importance than a town or village." *Town*, we find, is "usually larger than a village but smaller than a city." *Village* is "a settlement usually larger than a hamlet and smaller than a town." Onward; I feel we are closing in on the elusive thing. Here we are: a *hamlet* is "a small village." Gee, thanks a lot, Noah.

Sometimes the politics of place create unique definitions. Cities in Wyoming are communities with a population of at least 4,000. Those with between 150 and 3,999 are classified as towns. Everything else is country.

One definition of country, or rural, is "sparsely populated and not directly influenced by a city." But even *sparsely* elicits diverse reactions. It is fair to say that each of us has a personal vision of country, and like "good" paintings, we know it when we see it.

For me, country means low-density areas lacking evidence of a nearby city. A home in the country may therefore be an old farmhouse on a large acreage with the nearest neighbor miles away or it may be a house on a lot in a town/village/hamlet, far enough from the nearest city that urban atmosphere, attitudes, culture, and problems, even nighttime "sky glow" are not in evidence. In this book, country does not include suburbs, edge cities, master-planned communi-ties. It is beyond what *The Last Landscape* author William H. Whyte referred to as the *greed line*, where the value of land has been reduced to its ability to create profit. By definition that leaves out agribusiness land, which you will learn to avoid.

The American quilt still has hundreds of low-density patches with ten to fifty persons per square mile. At fifty per square mile, that gives each person 12.8 acres. Take out space for roads and public places and we still have about 12.5, or twenty-five acres of elbow room for a couple, fifty acres for a family of four. That's a bit more than the 8.64 acres available for each citizen if the entire U.S. land mass were equally apportioned, but most urbanites and suburbanites live in apartments, condos, or on postage-stamp lots, so don't feel guilty if you buy a place with more than your "fair share" of acres.

The dictionary is but one reason for the definitional uncertainty of country. Towns and small cities have lobbied for the metropolitan designation to impress commercial interests and to tap federal programs. The federal designation "metropolitan area" was changed to mean a densely populated area that contains at least 50,000 people. These areas often include much land that is rural or semirural, not urban. In fact, by Census Bureau manipulations that boggle the brain, "*39 percent of the rural population is metropolitan*" (my emphasis) (Glenn Fuguitt, David L. Brown, and Calvin L. Beale, *Rural and Small Town America, 1989*). As an example, the St. Louis metropolitan area now includes eleven counties, many of which exhibit bona fide wilderness. Go figure.

John Fraser Hart, in " 'Rural' and 'Farm' No Longer Mean the Same," in *The Changing American Countryside*, explains that the Census Bureau expanded its definition of urban to include the urban fringe: "The urban fringe is the densely settled (1,000 or more persons per square mile) area contiguous to a city of 50,000 persons or more. The entire built-up area, including both the city and its urban fringe, is designated the urbanized area. It keeps expanding as the city grows. . . . It is a poor unit for statistical comparisons over time because it grows larger at every census."

Metropolitan areas currently have such ballooned boundaries that they encompass approximately one fifth of the total U.S. land area. In my view, these artificial designations are why 1990 census figures are unreliable concerning the reported stall-out of city-to-country migration during the 1980s. Apparently many people moved from city or suburb to true country yet were included in the metro count.

The Census Bureau reported in late 1997 that from March 1995 to March

1996, there were 275,000 more urbanites who moved to rural areas than ruralites who moved to urban areas. *USA Today*, 12-4-97, noted that "the recent shift is more dramatic because it is the first time the Census Bureau has used a broader definition of a metro area. The change expanded the size and the number of metro areas and was expected to boost metro population. But the opposite occurred."

Such census shenanigans strengthen my belief that urban-to-rural migration is stronger than reported and rural population numbers are greater than the official count. I also believe that as soon as the intelligence of telecommuting penetrates corporate fog, the current steady city exodus will become a stampede to the hills.

A major population shift back to the country will tear and resew the American quilt. North Carolina is often held up as the shape of the future. The tenth most populous state, North Carolina has seven million people but no large cities—at about 400,000, Charlotte is the largest, with no other city over 200,000. With an extensive paved road system, a state university spread over sixteen campuses, and textile mills, furniture factories, and other manufacturing facilities scattered throughout the countryside, North Carolina today is the result of purposeful planning and shaping by a succession of visionary leaders. As a result, the majority of the state is essentially rural in character.

Sick cities: dirty air, undependable water, crime, failing schools and other social systems, high prices, overcrowding, crumbling infrastructure. These are the apparent reasons why so many of us are moving back to the country. I believe the reasons are deeper, hidden within, sublimated for decades. I believe that our quest to understand our world and our human condition is more difficult the more removed we are from nature. I believe we instinctively know that truth and beauty are more likely to be found in a natural environment.

The quest for quality of life, peace of mind, personal growth, living in harmony with one another is now combined with a growing understanding of our interconnectedness through nature. Awareness of the many environmental crises and the damage each of us contributes to those problems is compelling us to reexamine values, to seek to become part of the solution.

I have lived in cities and I have lived in country. Cities still provide greater economic opportunity, greater cultural offerings, a greater number of services. Country living is less expensive, cleaner, quieter, healthier, has less crime and less stress, is more independent, closer to nature, and, I believe, more conducive to personal growth.

Solid value systems are derived from living close to nature. It is not by chance that the majority of our most successful leaders have come from low-population areas. Upon retirement from public service, these leaders have often returned to rural homes.

Those who study migration ponder the question: Are Americans repelled by cities or drawn to country? Both seem true. Rural vacations are historically popular. Rural retirement is common. Now that employers are figuring out what workers want, we don't have to wait for vacation or retirement time to be where we most desire. Now we can ruralize our dreams.

Surveys on national trends by the Gallup organization show an increasing preference for country living. A 1985 Gallup poll disclosed that "almost half of American adults would move to towns with fewer than 10,000 inhabitants or to rural areas." Nineteen ninety results showed an even stronger desire for rural life: 34 percent wanted a home in a small town; 24 percent picked a suburb; 22 percent desired a farm; and only 19 percent preferred a city. Over twenty years of Gallup polls show that an average of 56 percent of Americans would prefer to live in a small town or on a farm.

But only about 25 percent of us do live in the country. What holds the rest of us back? Likely answers are jobs, friends, family, fear.

My stepson, Craig J. Crawford, observes that all change is unnerving, "the more dramatic, the more traumatic." He notes that change means opening the wall of our comfort zone. "We lose some of our security deposit." Fear often comes from lack of knowledge. This book is an attempt to allay that fear.

Truly, as Pogo said, we are "confronted with insurmountable opportunities." And, as Robert Frost said, "You come, too."

*"My point of view is, of course, that of the countryman,
and no doubt it has the countryman's bias."*

—LIBERTY HYDE BAILEY

First Things

~ 1 ~

The Importance of Place

"Perhaps the most psychologically significant kind of movement that an individual can make is geographical relocation of his home."

—ALVIN TOFFLER, *Future Shock*

The importance of the place where we choose to live is beyond the kisses or kicks that climate delivers, more than the landform that shapes us, greater than the soil that feeds us and the water that washes us and replenishes our vital fluids, more than the natural and human community. It is all this but more. Our place grounds us, steadies our posture to the world; it nurtures our body and spirit; it gives us the strength to be what we would be.

Simone Weil felt that "to be rooted is perhaps the most important and least recognized need of the human soul." Terry Tempest Williams says "if you know where you are, you know who you are." And Scott Russell Sanders states that "I cannot have a spiritual center without having a geographical one; I cannot live a grounded life without being grounded in a place."

"Try to live . . . deep in nature. Be native as trees to the wood, as grass to the floor of the valley. Only then can the democratic spirit of man, individual, rise out of the confusion of communal life in the city to a creative civilization of the ground."

—FRANK LLOYD WRIGHT

The importance of place is overlooked, underestimated, and insufficiently acted upon. Living in the wrong place is a self-inflicted life handicap. Living in one's right place is the foundation of a fulfilling life. And for each of us, there is an ideal place.

My bias toward rural living derives from decades spent in both cities and country. I find that a natural setting with much open space inflicts fewer falsehoods; in such a place I make fewer mistakes. I am calmed. I absorb truth. In *Community of the Future and the Future of Community*, Arthur Morgan wrote: "Mediocrity is at home in the crowd. The discriminating mind and spirit make their best growths when they have opportunity for periods of quiet and solitude."

> *"This return to nature is by no means a cure-all for the ills of civilization, but it is one of the means of restoring the proper balance and proportion in our lives."*
>
> —LIBERTY HYDE BAILEY, *The Outlook to Nature*

In rural places we are compelled to observe and understand the dynamic connections between ourselves and Earth. Truth, beauty, and natural laws become self-evident.

There is something else. Cities nurture the impression that all things, including Earth itself, belong to humans, rather than humans belonging to Earth. Living with this anthropocentric mind-set stunts personal growth. The cultures of place, community, and family are most sound when they reflect natural conditions. Children who help to produce family food, maintain household systems, and play within a natural environment not only have a strong sense of personal worth—they know to whom and to what they belong.

> *"Self-fulfillment comes more easily at the foot of a blue-gray mountain and a few strides from a creek."*
>
> —JACK LESSINGER, *Regions of Opportunity*

Water shortages, high prices, crime, bad schools, noise pollution, and community disintegration result from too many people living too close together. Congestion creates tension. Human rules try to maintain order. Goodbye freedom. *No parking here. Stay off the grass.* Want to build a tree house? Get a permit. Quadruplicate forms. *I'm sorry, sir, you're in the wrong line.* The wrong lane, say I—a lane where quality of life has become a euphemism, where freedom is no longer appreciated because it cannot be achieved.

> *"Our relationship with the places we know is a close bond, intricate in nature, and not abstract, not remote at all. . . . The danger . . . is that whenever we make changes in our surroundings, we can all too easily shortchange ourselves. . . . The way to avoid the danger is to start doing three things at once: Make sure that when we change a place, the change agreed upon nurtures our growth as capable and responsible people, while also protecting the natural environment, and developing jobs and homes enough for all."*

> —Tony Hiss, *The Experience of Place*

Rural living encourages us to be in charge of our lives. We feel good about ourselves and have less anxiety when our activities are free and when we control basic needs—food production, utilities, safety.

The air smells sweet and pure. Background sounds are bird songs and rustling leaves. Skylight is stars and moon.

In *The Soul's Code*, James Hillman finds commonality in love of person and love of place. "A similar sense of destiny, if less sudden and less heated, and a similar devotion can mark falling for a place . . . as well as for a person. You can't leave it, you must stay with it until it's over, you perform ritual magic devotions to keep it going."

In the movie *Enchanted April*, four *dis*-enchanted English ladies pool their resources to rent a villa in Italy for one month. The beauty of the place—the trees, shrubs, flowers, views—vanquishes their unhappiness. The theme is timeless and persevering because it is a truism: whatever our psychological state, we are improved by the influence of a natural environment.

*"The place where a person lives dramatically affects his happiness
and success in life. Living in a place which is not right for you can be
incredibly handicapping."*

—THOMAS F. BOWMAN, GEORGE A. GIULIANI, M. RONALD MINGE,
Finding Your Best Place to Live in America

Beyond psychological nurture, a good natural environment raises intelligence. Um, really. Researchers at the University of California at Berkeley verified that rat brains grow larger when the animals are placed in an enriched environment. The brains of rats raised in a seminatural outdoor environment grow larger still. So our quest is for a place where rat brains grow like crazy. Onward!

Essential Country Skills #87 and #93

Instructions for Skill #87—Chasing bears away: Always keep the pointed end of the spear in the bear's face. Tell the bear to go away. If the bear slaps the spear out of your hands, pick up the spear and again point it at the bear's face. Repeat this procedure as long as necessary to impress the bear with your sincerity. Some bears are stubborn and require prolonged training.

Instructions for Skill #93—Shooting birds for dinner: Point the gun at a bird and pull the trigger. If the bird keeps flying, repeat the procedure. Continue shooting birds until you have as many birds as people coming to dinner. Have an alternative menu.

— 2 —

The Ideal
Country Home

". . . a little nest that nestles where the roses bloom . . ."

—George Whiting (and Walter Donaldson), "My Blue Heaven"

Except in the 1516 work by Sir Thomas More, Utopia is said to be impossible. That is probably a blessing—it would be terribly boring after a week or three. No challenges. For each of us, though, there is an ideal place—one that embodies most of our wants and needs and fewest of our dislikes. One that soothes us and excites us, makes us feel secure but gives us energy for life's explorations. With clarification, focus, and persistence we each can find the place that is ideal for us.

In our mind, we can create any world we choose. Our finest achievements often begin with dreams. So dream. Daydream or nightdream, but dream. Emerson said: "The ancestor of every action is a thought." George Bernard Shaw wrote: "You see things; and you say, 'Why?' But I dream things that never were; and I say, 'Why not?'" With a poet's conciseness, Carl Sandburg cut right to it: "Nothing happens unless first a dream."

One's imagined ideal place is often a blend of dreams and chance: lingering memories of childhood camps and visits to grandparents, vacations, books or movies, college or job experiences. I recently recalled an emotional connection with place that I made in January of 1970. My paternal grandmother had died, and my brother and I were driving our "won't fly" parents and sister nonstop from California to Wisconsin for the funeral.

As we sped through the Missouri Ozarks I found myself captivated by the scenery. I spotted a cabin on a hill, just visible through the leafless trees, gray smoke twisting skyward from a stone chimney. In only a few moments an indelible connection was apparently made. Seven years later, after considering all forty-eight contiguous states and carefully researching many specific ones, never consciously remembering that cabin in the trees, I bought my ideal country place—smack dab in the middle of the Ozarks.

> *" 'Mid pleasures and palaces though we may roam,*
> *Be it ever so humble, there's no place like home."*
>
> —JOHN HOWARD PAYNE

"Country home" typically defines a house, a somewhat controlled area around the house, and a larger, more natural, perhaps wild area expanding beyond—whether majestic mountains, undulating sands, shimmering waves of grasses, or the quiet, cool green of forest. It is often more, the sum of house, garden, and landscape plus the magical, mystical aura common to a natural place. The whole can only be improved by working with instead of against nature.

The ideal country home place provides necessities: healthful air, water, and soil, climate in which we thrive, and those utilities and services necessary to our chosen lifestyle. It provides space and conditions for our buildings and activities, including food production and recreation and, increasingly, our commercial work. Located amidst chosen natural beauty, the ideal home provides mental and psychological well-being and it stimulates and nurtures our spiritual explorations. The ideal home place inspires us to become more than we are. It elicits light, truth, joy.

> *"The happiness of the domestic fireside is*
> *the first boon of heaven."*
>
> —THOMAS JEFFERSON

Location is paramount. The reason for the cliché "The three most important elements of value are location, location, and location" is that almost anything about a place can be changed except its location. Terrain can be graded, trees and shrubs cut down or planted, and a house can be built, rebuilt, altered, razed, or moved. Only location and the attendant climate are unchangeable.

The ideal country home is located in an area that is stable. The income base is broad, not dependent on a single industry. In many ideal rural counties, the three strongest sources of income are transfer payments (such as retirement checks), agriculture, and tourism. Stability derives not only from economics but from social conditions. The ideal home is located within a fair and nurturing community.

It is a deeply personal decision whether the ideal country home is in a tiny hamlet, a small town, near a town, or out in the boondocks. Each has advantages; each has unique challenges.

The ideal home site (in the United States) faces in a southerly direction with maximum solar exposure for lighting, gardening, and vegetative growth. Whether it is in a valley or on a ridgetop will partly depend on whether you wish to look up or down at soaring birds—the kind of view you prefer.

Without leaving the contiguous forty-eight states you can find virtually any type of house, climate, topography, and demographics you prefer. An A-frame in the mountains; a cottage at the beach; a cabin in the woods; an adobe casa in the desert. Two hours from the nearest neighbor or tucked against a small town. On a thousand acres, a hundred acres, ten acres, an acre, or a large lot. Skiing country, fishing country, farming country. But country.

Obtain as much land as you can afford to purchase and pay taxes on. Nothing will guarantee your future peace and privacy more than ownership of a substantial land buffer around your home. Extra land provides the kind of privacy that makes window coverings redundant and the volume of Luciano Pavarotti or Willie Nelson while gardening strictly a matter of personal choice. And owning extra acreage allows one to be a land steward, an honorable calling on our distressed planet-home.

If buying a large acreage seems beyond your means, you can look for a place that has characteristics undesirable to developers: remoteness, bad roads, rough terrain, steep access, parcels too small to develop. Such land will usually be low-priced.

Like-minded persons can combine their dollars to buy a large acreage, deed a house site to each owner, and hold the rest of the land as common area to be enjoyed by all and to be a buffer against intrusive development. If five buyers purchase an old 200-acre farm, and each uses five acres for house, outbuildings, garden, and orchard, that leaves 175 acres to ensure peace, quiet, and firewood forever. We have friends who did this. At first they had trouble getting bank financing for house construction because of legal questions regarding foreclosure and resale in case of default. They hired a lawyer who drafted an ownership agreement acceptable to their banks. Our friends each now enjoy the use of a large, beautiful acreage that none of them could have purchased alone.

Now that is my viewpoint. There is another: buy only as much land as you need and wish to care for. This view comes from city people who treat country land like city land, busting their butts to prune forests and manicure meadows. Forget it. Manicure to your mind's content around the house, mow meadows a few times a year to thicken the grass and prevent erosion, and cut firewood judiciously, taking dead, dying, and crooked trees. Let the rest of your land be natural. If the natural landscape offends you, you would probably be unhappy living in real country. Consider a small town.

There is in fact a great need for land to be protected from further human meddling. Forests, wetlands, grasslands, meadows, glades, and fens left in their natural states maintain biodiversity, protect watersheds, consume carbon dioxide, and preserve this bountiful and beautiful planet for our children. That such land can also be a buffer for serene living is a bonus.

In the next section we will explore the various factors that will help you identify your ideal country home place. As you choose your criteria, stretch your horizons. While considering climate, for instance, keep an open mind about areas extending beyond the edge of your first choice.

Now look at the preliminary list you made when you finished "Notes on Using This Book." Does it include your fondest dreams, no matter how unrealistic they may seem? Write them down. Make any other additions you have thought of.

> *"The home idea is clearly dying out in the cities. Homes seem to be incompatible with compact city life; [the] consequence is that the serious-minded middle class is constantly working out and out toward the suburbs and the adjacent towns, in the effort to secure the greatest possible proximity to nature consistent with business prudence. This transfer of domicile at once raises far-reaching questions. The political philosopher*

sees danger because this movement removes a large class of voters and is
likely to leave the city, or the congested parts of it, in the hands
of politicians. The social philosopher finds a new breed of citizen developing—not
country-bred nor city-bred, but suburban-bred, product of neither extreme.
Will this citizen have the prejudices of either extreme? And will he be a more
useful social factor because of his intermediate origin?"

—LIBERTY HYDE BAILEY, *The Outlook to Nature*

Essential Country Equipment #1: the horse
This is the original 4 X 4. Model shown comes with four speeds, runs on renewable fuels. Models
suitable for children drivers are available. Can often be held for ransom from teenagers.

— 3 —

Buy Your Land as Soon as You Can

"Buy land. They ain't makin' any more of the stuff."

—WILL ROGERS

Those scheming a city break would do well to acquire their land soon. Diminishing supply and increasing demand are pumping up prices of desirable country property. While stratospheric city prices max out their markets, rural prices are often refreshingly low—but are escalating, especially in areas near cities.

In country-chic places prices are moving like leaves in a storm. Ron Powers, in *Far from Home: Life and Loss in Two American Towns*, shows how dollar-burdened buyers such as Henry Kissinger have disfranchised natives from Kent, a small town in northwestern Connecticut.

Wily Will's wry observation was made more than sixty years ago. (Many of Will's observations were wry. Some were pure corn. Few were whole wheat.) Not only is there a finite amount of land, but the most desirable rural land is being gobbled up like ice cream at an August picnic. Cropland, pastures, woods, and Civil War battlefields have been targeted for or are already becoming roads, shopping centers, office buildings, factories, airports, and theme parks. Penturbia (Jack Lessinger's word for America's fifth area of development) replaced suburbia as the home choice of Americans in the 1970s, and as we approach the new millennium the migration is growing stronger.

Demand for rural homes is accelerating due to both urban conditions and rural opportunities. The quest for ideal life in the information overload age finds many Americans desperate for basic peace and safety. Natural and man-made disasters are reported ad nauseam by mainstream media. Each earthquake, fire, riot, bombing, murder, or rape sends more moving vans heading to the hills.

Gold fever has been replaced by green fever. Baby boomers are rejecting corporate servitude and "incityous" frenzy for country home businesses in scenic vistas. Burned-out corporate climbers of all ages are planting themselves in small towns and small acreages. For many, the current consciousness is: phooey on big incomes with high price tags—let's live better on less where the financial and psychological costs are sane. Property beyond the sidewalks is increasingly seen as a superior scene.

Many inconveniences of rural life have been overcome. The interstate highway system is finished. Electric and telephone services reach into the boondocks. Beyond the power poles, affordable independent home energy systems, cellular telephones, and satellite receivers make even mountaintops habitable and those living there in touch with the world. Communication clouds have evaporated. This is being written in a wild Ozarks hollow and can zip through phone wires to a New York editor's computer far faster than snail mail—unless a thunderstorm threatens to zap the fax modem, in which case I will unplug, read a book, and transmit tomorrow.

Boards of directors have moved factories and corporate headquarters to rural settings where land prices, taxes, regulations, and wages favor profits. And that's where CEOs, managers, workers, and their families increasingly want to live.

Celebrities are often trendsetters. High-profile country property owners include Robert Redford, Ted Turner and Jane Fonda, Oprah Winfrey, Paul Newman. Robert James Waller made enough on *The Bridges of Madison County* to live anywhere he likes—he chose a thousand acres in West Texas. Of stargrazers, only Barbra seems stymied—Manhattan refuses to sell Central Park and large acreage is tough to find in Yonkers.

For many rural wannabes the dilemma is financial timing—when to sell the rancher for gold and buy a cabin for copper. In some regions, city prices have become so high they are unaffordable for most. It is certain that such city prices will plateau and fall while adjacent rural prices will rise. Local economic and social conditions create price movement. Have some fun. Call a real estate agent and ask if it's a good time to sell. Have a friend call the same agent and ask if it's a good time to buy.

Is your house more important to you as an investment or as a home? Urban refugees typically judge money less important than clean air and water, safety, community, low stress levels, and freedom.

One plan is to buy a second home in the country now and ride out city conditions as long as you can. Buy now, make payments, and move after your property is paid for or when city prices appear to have peaked. City pay averages about 20 percent higher than rural income, so land payments are less strain with city bucks.

The message here is: identify your ideal place and buy land as soon as you can. They ain't makin' any more of the stuff—and city conditions ain't gettin' any better.

Essential Country Equipment #3: the pig
The pig is the original breakfast food production unit. This is the high-cholesterol model. Pigs are very intelligent and make good companions but can be an embarrassment at formal dinners, as they are unable to hold a wineglass.

— 4 —
Who Are You?

*"Development of character consists solely in
moving toward self-sufficiency."*

—QUENTIN CRISP

Most of us feel pretty confident that we know who we are. In fact we proudly disclose ourselves to the world—to total strangers we meet in stores, bars, and especially at parties. Less willingly we reveal all (well, nearly all) to employment agencies, credit agencies, and the IRS. Extended city living dampens such enthusiasm. In the city world of crime and incessant, aggressive marketing we retreat behind security doors and answering machines. From a state of willingly proclaiming ourselves to all who ask, we have evolved to using defensive screening techniques. "Who are you with?" "How do you know her?" "What is your business with him?" "I'm very busy; is this important?"

Knowing who we are and acknowledging the truth, if only to ourselves, is of critical value in determining which country conditions will make us happiest. People who move from city to country generally fall into definable groups, rather like subspecies. For some, moving from city to country is like mutating—for others, simply reverting to type. I don't particularly like labels but in this case using them will be helpful to our quest. Categories of those repotting themselves in country soil, in no particular order, are back-to-the-landers/homesteaders, boomer burnouts/urban refugees, concerned parents, environmentalists, retirees and cashing-outers, and survivalists.

Back-to-the-Landers / Homesteaders

The back-to-the-land movement is correctly named only in that all of our ancestors once lived on the land. (If Eve and the snake had not collaborated on the apple thing we all might still be living—tightly—in the original garden.)

Some writers label all who move from city to country as back-to-the-landers. This is a gross generalization. True BTTLs—who may or may not be rock 'n' rollers—are those who were born in the country, moved to bright lights for fun, fame, and fortunes, burned out on city heat, remembered rural serenity, and moved back—typically either to their growing-up place or another like it. Those who desperately desire to belong to this group but were city-reared are hereby allowed ancestral exemption, the grandfather clause for BTTLs. Reach back as far as necessary.

Back-to-the-landers and homesteaders lead very similar lifestyles. Homesteading is a self-reliant way of life on the land. There is tremendous satisfaction and security to be derived from eating homegrown food, staying warm with our own wood fuel, and building and maintaining buildings and support systems.

It is not possible to be entirely self-sufficient and still live a high-quality life—such an effort quickly becomes long-hour drudgery. It does make sense, however, to become self-reliant. Using current technology, it is now possible to enjoy long-term, secure, lower-cost living largely independent of public systems. A wind or photovoltaic system with generator backup provides independence from the electric company. A ram pump will supply gravity-fed water. Freezers and canners extend homegrown food availability year-round. An energy-efficient house, owner-built and -maintained, can keep us warm in the winter with only solar gain, a stove, and (homegrown) wood for heat. We can even cook with wood—new wood-burning kitchen stoves are available (but, boy, are they hot; an alternative stove for summertime use is indicated). All of these things and more are possible right now.

One factor against being totally self-sufficient is that most of us want to use as many labor-saving devices as we can afford. My father taught me to make firewood with an axe and a crosscut saw; trust me when I say that a chainsaw is more humane. Abe Lincoln is but the most well known of those who quickly tired of working wood with an axe.

As with rearing children, there is one area—home food production—where the results are worth almost any effort. Growing food takes more time than earning dollars and buying it. But the quality of homegrown food far surpasses the best food in the best stores of the best food-growing regions in the country. Homegrown vegetables and fruits are fresher, more nutritious, and are safe from chemical residue. Eating poisoned food is courting an early demise—we might as well take up do-it-yourself bungee jumping. Home gardeners can look their potatoes in the eye and feel good about what they see there.

Homesteading with modern tools and technology can be a very high-quality lifestyle. Becoming self-reliant and independent from "the system" are worthwhile and enriching goals. Our body, our family, and our planet benefit.

Boomer Burnouts / Urban Refugees

"Solitude is impracticable, and society fatal. We must keep our head in the one and our hands in the other. The conditions are met, if we keep our independence, yet do not lose our sympathy."

—RALPH WALDO EMERSON

America's baby boomers have met middle age—and they are not ecstatic about the introduction, never mind the relationship. Boomer burnouts are rejecting corporate ladders and choosing fruit-picking ladders. They're talking health, longevity, ecology, sustainability. They're reconsidering family, community, safety, security, the purpose of life. Many of the 76 million boomers have boarded the wagon train leaving metropolis for the boondocks.

Urban refugees are moving to the country as well as away from the city. Often unequipped with country skills, many move to fringe areas and small towns rather than real country. In the aftermath of mass layoffs many have redefined their work ethic. Working to live is accepted—living to work is passé.

This group's collective profile is: married, above-average education, affluent, zero to two children, homeowner, long-distance commuter, sixty-hour workweek, fantasizer of better quality life with more time to spend with family. Those couples who have ever thought, "We just had sex, so it must be Saturday," may fit into this group.

Concerned Parents

Plummeting academic standards and achievements, schoolyard drug dealers, guns, graffiti, and hoodlumism pervade all but the top city schools. Concerned parents are homeschooling or moving to carefully selected rural school districts with high standards. The introduction to rural school discipline can be shocking to city kids accustomed to rowdy classrooms.

If you fit into this category, be aware that many rural school boards have budget challenges as serious as those of their city counterparts. Also, not all country communities place a premium on education. Identify several areas you like, then contact school principals with questions regarding class size, curriculum, gifted and special education programs, percentage of dropouts, and percentage of graduates who go on to college. Query county clerks on voter response to school bond issues and taxes. Shorten your list, then visit schools and observe the attitudes of teachers and students. Don't be put off by modest physical facilities; although few one-room schools still exist, they often do a superior job of educating up to the high school level. No wonder—by the time students reach the eighth grade, they've already heard the material seven times!

Environmentalists

"Seventy-six percent of all Americans describe themselves as environmentalists. There is precious little else about which we so thoroughly agree."

—Joel Garreau, *Edge City*

Conservationists, ecologists, environmentalists, Greens—however we label ourselves—constitute the surging swell of citizens who understand that Spaceship Earth is suffering from bad management. We are informed people who believe in taking greater responsibility for our conduct, who understand that we are in fact "all in this together."

Environmentalists cite cities as inefficient and wasteful of energy resources, generators of greenhouse gasses, acid rain, toxic waste, and enormous accumulations of garbage. Some stay in the city to effect change from within. Many move to the country to lead simpler lives in tune with natural laws.

This group has the greatest age spread, the highest idealism, and perhaps the greatest potential for rural life disaster. If you identify most strongly with this group, I recommend you spend substantial time in your chosen area before buying. Rent or caretake for a year. Learn country skills. Live with farm families, perhaps with alternative communities. And do not expect to change the attitudes of the natives. Show beliefs by actions, not words. You will find similar souls who have preceded you.

Retirees and Cashing-Outers

Once the gold encircles the wrist (what—they don't do that anymore?) and the long-dreamed-about check appears in the mailbox, there is the challenge of what to do between naps. There is also the freedom to live wherever that check will cover expenses. The usual scenario is to sell the city house for big bucks, buy a country cottage for a third as much, then fish, golf, garden, and entertain city friends who come to vacation rent-free. Today, many retirees are breaking the Sunbelt syndrome and moving to the so-called Cloudbelt—places of spectacular scenery with moderate-to-cold winters where they find low prices and taxes, no crowding, and satisfying lifestyles.

> *"Retirement destinations are no longer limited to the popular*
> *stereotypes of Florida and the Southwest. Widespread in-migration has*
> *occurred in the Ozarks, the New England coast, the southern Blue Ridge, the*
> *Texas Hill Country, the Puget Sound area, the Upper Great Lakes,*
> *the Sierra Nevada foothills, western Oregon, east Texas, and the*
> *Tidewater areas of Maryland and Virginia. All of these locations involve*
> *dispersed settlement, and not merely aggregations of people in towns."*
>
> —CALVIN BEALE

The term *cashing-outers* was coined by Faith Popcorn, who wrote in *The Popcorn Report* that cashing out "is a dream as old as America itself: give me a piece of land to call my own, a little town where everyone knows my name. It's a dream we are dreaming with a new heart-and-gut-felt urgency. More than the romance of the country, it's a promise of safety, of comfort, and of old-fashioned values."

Cashing-outers buy or create bed-and-breakfast inns, ink small-town news-papers, mix goat milk ice cream, raise sheep and weave wool products, operate fishing resorts, throw pottery, craft furniture, consult. They often work harder than they did for the corporate cats, but they don't commute, they don't wear suits, they don't lug briefcases, and they call their own shots.

Survivalists

So-called survivalists (aren't we all?) deserve better press. While a few seem to suffer from a Rambo complex, most are level-headed citizens, and many are sincere passivists. What all share is a fear that senseless crime, riots, bombings, and the fragility of urban food and utility systems are precursors to chaos—and that when city systems collapse there will be a mob exodus to the countryside. Alvin Toffler wrote in *Future Shock* that "Great cities are paralyzed by strikes, power failures, riots." The New York garbage collectors' strike, the 1965 Watts riots, the 1992 L.A. riots, the 1994 L.A. earthquake, and the Blizzard of '96 were examples of near paralysis that illustrated the dependence and vulnerability of city dwellers when systems break down. It is at such times that the social condition of a place is magnified and clarified. In the first thirty minutes of the 1977 New York power blackout, looters had stolen $150 million in goods.

A dramatic example of a national paralysis began November 24, 1995, in France with a strike by civil servants. Railroad workers, mass-transit workers, mail sorters, and utility workers nearly shut down the country for a week. Cities were choked with traffic jams and millions of people were forced to walk, bicycle, or hitchhike to work. The economic cost was hundreds of millions of dollars per day.

Survivalists buy land far from highways, strive for self-sufficiency, often homeschool. The more militant arm themselves heavily, but they usually make peaceful neighbors. Their complaints typically focus on federal and state government, not on locally elected officials.

In addition to one or more of the above you may find yourself labeled urban dropout, urban flighter, rat race escapee, yupneck, or new American pioneer. The diversity of labels shows that the wagon train is composed of diverse, unique types. The common quest is high-quality life. Welcome aboard.

Pop Quiz

So now, do you know who you are? Did you quickly identify with one of the above groups or, more likely, did you find something of yourself in two or more? That's fine, of course. You pass. What this chapter is about is getting you thinking about your basic and vital motivations, your needs and your wants.

Final Thought

Country living is conducive to fresh thinking about values. Donald McCaig, in *An American Homeplace*, quotes Scott Nearing: "The only thing more cowardly than a million dollars is two million dollars." Nearing lived his words: he and wife, Helen, refused inheritances and when they left Vermont for less-crowded Maine they sold their homestead for only the value of the cash and labor they had invested in it, one fourth of its market value. That says a lot for who *they* were.

Essential Country Equipment #7: the turkey

This is the original model much favored by Ben Franklin as the finest example of American qualities: keen eyesight, superb hearing, and so smart it could tutor Harvard Law School students. (The currently favored dim-witted, chesty model was developed by breast-fetish bio-engineers.) Specimens of this classic design may be found in wooded areas around homesteads except from mid-November to early January (during this period they vacation in Puerto Vallarta).

— 5 —
Do You Have What It Takes?

"Men are born to succeed, not to fail."

—HENRY DAVID THOREAU

More people fantasize about living in the country than actually move there, nearly one third of Americans. Nostalgia plays a role, but the primary factor separating wannabes from ruralites seems to be fear—fear of being unable to make a living, fear of independence, fear of losing known social conditions. Call it comfort zone clutch—cocoon life—staying with the known even when it is emotionally stultifying, even when health and life are endangered.

In *You Can't Grow Tomatoes in Central Park: The Urban Dropouts Guide to Rural Relocation*, Frank Ruegg and Paul Bianchina report that respondents to their survey of those who had moved agreed on two success factors: perseverance and a positive attitude. The survey also found the majority of respondents had, as children, "dreamed about living in a special, less densely populated spot."

In my experience, those who have triumphantly transplanted themselves are independent types not much concerned with approval ratings. They are self-directed. While often gregarious, they treasure peace, quiet, privacy.

Surprisingly, most who make the city-to-sanity move are not strongly concerned about making a living. Most move with at least a small stash to back them, easy to accomplish when selling sky-priced city caves and buying country cottages. Most overcome financial challenges and, in three to five years, are making as much as before while enjoying lower overhead.

The following listing of human characteristics is appropriate to many matters more mundane than finding our ideal country home. But here, regarding this essential enterprise, they are critical and worthy of review. As greater minds than mine have already expounded on these topics, this chapter consists primarily of quotes.

A Dream

*"You've got to create a dream. You've got to
uphold the dream. If you can't, go back to the
factory or go back to the desk."*

—ERIC BURDON

Yes, I know this is redundant. But I believe that the importance of dreaming cannot be overstated.

Passion

*"The essential conditions of everything you do
must be choice, love, passion."*

—NADIA BOULANGER

A Plan

*"The journey of ten thousand miles begins
with a single phone call."*

—CONFUCIUS BELL

Hopefully you will have a plan by the time you finish this book. Perhaps you already do. Making a plan is simply gathering information, investigating possibilities, and choosing alternatives. The more information, the sounder the resulting plan.

Positive Focusing

*"Keeping your mind on the goal and moving toward the
goal is the essence of positive focusing. All the rest is fun, but not
essential. Unless, of course, you consider fun to be essential."*

—PETER MCWILLIAMS

Positive thinking by itself rarely gets us what we want except positive thoughts. Positive focusing helps move us toward our goal, even if we have negative thoughts about it. Together, positive thinking and positive focusing help move us happily to our goal.

Open-mindedness

"Minds are like parachutes. They only function when open."

—JAMES DEWAR

*"The only means of strengthening one's intellect is to
make up one's mind about nothing—to let the mind
be a thoroughfare for all thoughts."*

—JOHN KEATS

"Where there is an open mind, there will always be a frontier."

—CHARLES F. KETTERING

*"The beautiful souls are they that are universal, open,
and ready for all things."*

—MONTAIGNE

The quality of open-mindedness is essential to learning. Never fear to be open to new ideas. Nothing new or useful ever results from a closed mind. Specifically, consider all the country, not just those areas to which you presently feel drawn. Once in your new place, let your brain be like a sponge.

Persistence

> *"Writing is easy. All you do is stare at a blank sheet of paper*
> *until drops of blood form on your forehead."*
>
> —GENE FOWLER

Stay with it until you get what you want. Few have said it as well as cool Calvin Coolidge: "Nothing in the world can take the place of persistence. Talent will not; nothing is more common than unsuccessful men with talent. Genius will not; unrewarded genius is almost a proverb. Education alone will not; the world is full of educated derelicts. Persistence and determination alone are omnipotent."

Here's one by Lucretius that will make a picture: "The drops of rain make a hole in the stone not by violence, but by oft falling."

Ability to Make Decisions

> *"When you have to make a choice and don't make it,*
> *that is in itself a choice."*
>
> —WILLIAM JAMES

By picking up this book you've already made a decision. We'll get back to this one later, when we need it most.

Willingness to Take a Chance

"Be bold —and mighty forces will come to your aid."

—BASIL KING

Willingness to take a chance derives from passion and confidence—knowing that we're ready because we've accumulated adequate information. This book provides the recipe for the ideal country place. That will contribute to your confidence level. Add passion and stir.

Tolerance

*"Truth resides in every human heart, and one has to search
for it there, and to be guided by truth as one sees it. But no one has
a right to coerce others to act according to his own view of truth."*

—MOHANDAS K. GANDHI

*"We are all full of weakness and errors, let us mutually
pardon each other our follies—it is the first law of nature."*

—VOLTAIRE

*"Let us forget such words, and all they mean, as Hatred,
Bitterness and Rancor, Greed, Intolerance, Bigotry. Let us renew our
faith and pledge to Man, his right to be Himself, and free."*

—EDNA ST. VINCENT MILLAY

— 6 —
Wants, Needs, and Fantasies

"The great question . . . which I have not been able to answer, despite my thirty years of research into the feminine soul, is 'What does a woman want?'"

—SIGMUND FREUD

"You have to know what you want to get."

—GERTRUDE STEIN

Compared to needs, wants are a boundless quagmire. Wants require choices. As teens we anguish over career decisions; as young adults we choose beauty over substance; as parents we project our desires onto pure minds. Later, unless life turns out, uh, perfect, we second-guess our choices. Throughout life we grope for self-actualization, whatever that means. We know we should at least attempt to achieve it because our favorite friends, authors, personalities say so.

Our needs are air, water, food, shelter, clothing, socialization. Nudists nix clothing. Skeptics question socialization as essential. Yet, in a time when attaining the first five is generally certain, social isolation has become a common problem. We are alone in our crowds.

Our time is unique. Genetically equipped as hunters, gatherers, farmers, we barter our servitude for Styrofoam food, transport ourselves in computer-controlled sport-utility fuel hogs, and program VCRs lest we miss a favorite television program as we race through our day. Occasionally we converse with each other.

Robert Wright wrote in *Time* of "the mismatch between our genetic makeup and the modern world." A new breed of scientists, "evolutionary psychologists," posit that our ancestral environment is incongruous with our modern environment. We are programmed by survival for social cooperation yet live lives devoid of meaningful social intercourse. Wright cites social isolation, along with capitalism, technology, and information overload, as the cause of high levels of insecurity, depression, clinical anxiety disorder, suicide.

No doubt this new science looks to cities for data. In fact, lack of community has been repeatedly identified through polls as a primary source of urban discontent. Social service and support was essential for tribal survival and that genetic programming remains vital, demands attention.

Blink evolution? In fact we have evolved neither too fast nor too far, but we have forgotten too much. We put our social needs on a waiting list while we follow the direction of strangers. Erich Fromm wrote in *Escape from Freedom*: "Modern man lives under the illusion that he knows what he wants, while he actually wants what he is supposed to want."

We have turned our backs on the natural landscape. Americans crowd parks and other natural environments as an antidote to the stress and sterility of the city landscape—a way to restore psychological balance by returning to the ancestral home. And the absence of conversation beside a babbling brook is more natural than in city din. The current migration from cities to rural communities partly reflects the primal urge to regain the ancestral environment. Soon yet another branch of science will no doubt suggest that aspects of rural life are basic to human happiness. And the naked ape will marvel at the insight.

As a rural Wisconsin teen I was taken by Louis Bromfield's *Pleasant Valley* and *Malabar Farm*. In 1939, with Hitler's invasion imminent, Bromfield left France and returned to Ohio, to the valley of his youth. There he created Malabar Farm, which became the most famous experimental farm in America.

Earlier he had written *The Farm*, a fictionalized family biography which proved to be a forecasting of Malabar. His writings from Malabar were strong with love of the land and a desire to create a personal Utopia.

Bromfield's books seeded my dream of one day owning a self-sufficient home place among trees and hills and fields, with a stream running through it all. My dream included a community of good people who gave and received service. After twenty-five years making choices about military service, college, marriage, children, jobs, business, and divorce, the dream matured, became insistent, became reality. Life has never been better.

"I feel that if one follows what I call one's bliss—the thing that really gets you deep in the gut and that you feel is your life—doors will open up. They do!"

—Joseph Campbell

Are you consciously living or seeking your ideal life? Do you rise when you naturally awake, eat as you choose, work and play your passions? Do you feel important? Do you feel that you are in charge of your life? Do you enjoy self-knowledge and self-expression? Do you fulfill your social needs?

Treat yourself to a fantasy. No restrictions. No rules. No one is peeking. Make a huge effort to ignore the Madison Avenue menu. Imagine that you are living in your ideal place, with your ideal family situation, engaged in satisfying work and play, pursuing all your passions.

What are you doing? What's the weather like? What's the scenery? Are there lots of trees? Big or small? Mountains? A stream, river, pond, lake? Make notes. Do you see a garden? How many friends do you have? What do you do with them?

Our quest here is no less than the ideal life. An essential part of that life is living in one's ideal place. One's place affects all parts of life and we must know what we want of life before we can choose that special place. It's worth the effort. Keep working on that fantasy.

Are You Seeking a Permanent, Temporary, or Second Home?

This is a fundamental question. If you are seeking a permanent home you have the luxury to ignore investment considerations. But do be concerned about growth direction, as nothing can so annihilate peace and quiet as nearby development.

If you need a temporary home you will do well to buy where values are rising, so that you can make maximum profit when you sell. The optimum investment location is where rapid growth is imminent. Read Jack Lessinger's book *Regions of Opportunity: A Bold New Strategy for Real Estate Investment with Forecasts to the Year 2010.* If you must be able to sell quickly when the time comes, buy something that is in high demand—not too big, not too small, and within a short distance of school, shopping, highway. Try for assumable financing and high loan-to-sale price ratio—invest as little cash as possible. Sellers are more likely to make an assumable loan than institutional lenders.

A second home used for long weekends and vacations often eventually becomes more desirable than the primary residence. It would be wise to treat the search for a second home as if it were for a permanent home, as it may turn out to be. If you want a second home that may become a permanent home, then do not compromise—look for your ideal place. Spending enjoyable holidays and vacations at a second home is seductive—you may soon find that life is better there than "back home." Welcome to the country.

Wants and Needs

What are your true needs and wants, your hot buttons—what turns you on? Do you want to garden, landscape, conduct a business, farm commercially? Find a traditional school for your children? Have your fishing boat tied up to a dock in front of the house? Ski out the back door? Hunt and trap? Park your plane on your own landing strip near your house? Answers to these questions will begin to shape your requirements. Write them down.

How Much Land Do You Want?

This decision not only has a dollar value—in many ways it affects quality of life. One of the reasons most of us move to the country is to experience openness and quiet not possible with close neighbors. Larger parcels create more privacy—our activities remain only ours unless we choose to share them. Later, if children or grandchildren are drawn to join us living on the land, a larger acreage will allow each a measure of privacy.

Securing a high level of privacy derives from two qualities: location and size of acreage. Other than climate, location is the only factor that cannot be changed about a piece of land. Area population change is inevitable but we can go a long way toward ensuring stable tranquillity by choosing a home place with attention to certain factors.

Desirability of place is a double-edged sword; if we find an area highly desirable, others will find it to be so also. The result can be a phenomenon, or dis-ease, sometimes indelicately called "Californication." There are two solutions: choose a place that has a feature others find objectionable (economically depressed, poor accessibility, remoteness, occasional flooding); or get there first and buy enough land to buffer the inevitable invasion. Note: when the invasion comes, taxes will rise.

Beyond privacy, there are other considerations for owning more land than needed for personal use. My wife and I presently own 130 acres but use only about five on a regular basis other than for cutting firewood and taking walks. We feel good about the remaining land being protected in its natural state, the trees helping to ameliorate global warming, all vegetation protecting the watershed and providing a home to a multitude of flora and fauna, the natural world essentially untouched. And there is deep pleasure gained from walking on and observing one's own land, knowing that it is safeguarded and will not be damaged during our lifetime. Or just sitting on a rock and absorbing. It is a better church than any building.

The how-much-land decision must be a very personal choice for each of us, but the following is offered as a guide:

- Space for house and other buildings: garage, workshop, barn, other outbuildings.
- Space for activities for yourself and your animals: crops, pastures, gardens, orchard, woodlot, pond, landscaping, leisure activities.
- Extra acres to ensure the desired degree of privacy and quiet.
- Land for natural, undisturbed space.

JED CLAMPETT: *Pearl, what d'ya think? Think I oughta move?*

COUSIN PEARL: *Jed, how can ya even ask? Look around ya. Yer eight miles from yer nearest neighbor. Yor overrun with skunks, possums, coyotes, bobcats. Ya use kerosene lamps fer light and ya cook on a wood stove summer and winter. Yer drinkin' homemade moonshine and washin' with homemade lye soap. And yor bathroom is fifty feet from the house and you ask "Should I move?"*

JED: *I reckon yor right. A man'd be a dang fool to leave all this!*

—THE BEVERLY HILLBILLIES

PART II

Criteria
and
Considerations

$-7-$
Developing a Criteria List

"It is a funny thing about life . . . If you refuse to accept anything but the best, you very often get it."

—SOMERSET MAUGHAM

Transplanting oneself from city to country can produce flower or wilt. At ubiquitous summer volleyball-and-potluck parties here in the Ozarks I have often discussed with fellow immigrant hillbillies their successes and trials since arriving from various cities. Certain recommendations commonly result. Pay cash for your land. Stay out of debt. Bring a business or skill that will provide at least basic needs. If you have children, check out the schools very carefully. Expect social opportunities to be further and fewer between. Don't be in a hurry. Before you decide where to go, make a list of what you want and be true to it.

When we embark on a trip we consult a map. Making a criteria list is a technique to map the direction of our life. Think of your list not only as a map but as a self-written prescription for health and happiness. Discover your preferences, put them on paper, then purposefully find the place that meets them best. Include your values, interests, wants, and needs regarding lifestyle, climate, topography, vegetation, soil, acreage, water, health, community, demographics (density, political, ethnic, social, economic conditions), employment, taxes, services, utilities, structures, price, financing.

The criteria worksheet offered here can help you identify all important considerations for your move from an urban to a rural home. The worksheet is an evolving plan that will emerge as each chapter subject is explored and your wants and needs become clarified. After the worksheet is completed you can use it to write your criteria list.

This is the criteria list I wrote in the mid-1970s as part of a five-year plan to leave city life in the San Francisco Bay Area for country life—somewhere:

1. Four seasons but milder winters than those I grew up with in Wisconsin.
2. An area of hills and valleys.
3. Primarily wooded.
4. Clean air.
5. Clean flowing water.
6. Land prices low enough to allow purchase of at least forty acres.
7. Low population density.
8. Low property taxes.
9. Background bureaucracy—minimal local regulations re: zoning, building codes, permits, and so forth, to maximize personal freedom.
10. Within one hour of a city with a four-year college or university.
11. At least twenty miles away from railroads, major highways, and cities, and not contiguous to national forests—to minimize chances of development or eminent domain proceedings.
12. I don't care if there is a house or not.

I applied my criteria to the contiguous forty-eight states, initially chose seven, did further research, decided on one area, and told a large number of real estate agents in that area exactly what I wanted and when I would arrive to look. I drove nearly 2,000 miles to the area and spent the next two weeks looking at dozens of properties in a band about 60 miles wide and more than 100 miles long.

How did it work out? Wonderful! I got everything I wanted except No. 10, but, with one exception about which I will write later, everything else is so great that I have no regrets. In fact, because some areas are growing so rapidly, I'm glad I landed farther out in the boondocks than I had planned. Our nearest four-year college is in Springfield, Missouri, nearly two hours away. Had I uncompromisingly bought land within one hour of Springfield, I might now find my tranquillity threatened by the phenomenal growth of Branson, predicted to become the country music center of America. If heavy summer traffic is a good indicator, it already is. We hillbillies prefer to visit during the more relaxing off season—unless we entertain visitors who insist on the summer experience.

You will have noticed that my list did not include an income source. My five-year plan extrapolated my real estate investment equities into a totally reasonable financial formula for supporting an idyllic country life. Alas, divorce and recession later required major adjustments. As Pansy Penner said: "Just about the time you think you can make both ends meet, somebody moves the ends." Oh well, we all need to learn humility—some of us, ahem, more than others.

With the 20/20 vision of hindsight, I realize how many criteria I did not think of back in 1976 and how lucky I was to find a place that, for instance, continues to have clean water and soil and is far upwind and upstream from toxic pollution.

Eleven keys to successful city-to-country migration:

1. Verify that you truly wish to live in the country.
2. Determine who you are and what you want to do.
3. Identify the characteristics of your ideal property.
4. Locate regions that have the climatic, topographic, demographic, economic, and other characteristics that fit your wants and needs.
5. Narrow your list down to two or three areas to investigate.
6. Determine your ideal area.
7. Look at all appropriate properties in your ideal area, measure them against your criteria, and choose the best one.
8. Obtain a fair-price contract on your chosen property, with adequate protection to allow withdrawal if you discover a challenge that is larger than you can live with.
9. Satisfy yourself, through inspections and investigations, that the property has no hidden flaws, and you will be able to do with it as you wish.
10. Close the sale and take possession.
11. Enjoy living on your country property. If you took care of the first ten steps and have an income, this one is a natural.

The criteria worksheet includes the subjects we will be considering. Make a copy and use it to make notes as you continue to read Part II. Look at the notes you have made thus far and transfer your priorities to the worksheet.

A final thought: while the purpose of this book is to help you find your ideal country home, a certain reality must be faced—namely, that perfection is, well, impossible. As expressed by Peter McWilliams in *You Can't Afford the Luxury of a Negative Thought*, "You can have anything you want—you just can't have everything you want." I vacillate on whether that is best considered wisdom or challenge. You choose.

CRITERIA WORKSHEET

Lifestyle

Current activities I want to keep

1. _____
2. _____
3. _____
4. _____
5. _____
6. _____
7. _____
8. _____
9. _____
10. _____

New activities I would like to adopt

1. _____
2. _____
3. _____
4. _____
5. _____
6. _____
7. _____
8. _____
9. _____
10. _____

SO: Potential states for my lifestyle: _____

Climate

What climate conditions best suit my lifestyle preferences? _____

_____

SO: These states might be suitable: _____

Land characteristics

How many acres do I want? Minimum _____ *Maximum* _____

What kind of topography? Flat ___ *Rolling* ___ *Hills* ___ *Mountains* ___
Water's edge ___

What kind of vegetation? _____

What type of trees? Hardwoods ___ *Softwoods* ___ *For lumber?* ___
  For woodworking? ___ *For firewood?* ___

Soil quality requirements: Garden ___ *Pasture* ___ *Cropland* ___

SO: These states are appropriate: _____

Making a living

What is my current financial status?

Ready to retire ___ *Need to replace present income* ___
Want/need to develop income within ___ *months* ___ *years*

SO: These states might be best: _____

Farming/market gardening
If appropriate, note needs in climate, land characteristics (soil quality), acreage, water quantity, market demographics: _____

_____

Water
*These are the water features I want: Well ___ Spring ___ Stream ___
River ___ Pond ___ Lake ___ Ocean ___*

Health considerations
My health conditions that are affected by climate: _____
How close do I want/need to be to a doctor? ___ Hospital? ___

Community
How important is it to me? _____

Demographics
My ethnic-grouping preferences: _____
Cultural/social preferences: _____
Political values: _____
Other considerations: _____

Services vs. taxes
What services do I want to pay for?
*Schools ___ Libraries ___ Police/fire departments
Municipal water supply ___ Municipal sewage disposal ___
Trash pickup ___ Cable TV ___ Multiple private phone lines ___
Paved roads ___ Planning/zoning department ___
Building department ___ Other ___*

To build or not
Prefer to build my own home ___
Prefer to buy property with a house already built ___

Price
Total maximum _____ Per acre _____
Pay cash ___ Financing ___ Type ___

Narrowing the choices
Regions, bioregions, states: _____
*Small town? ___ Ecovillage? ___ Intentional community? ___
Subdivision? ___ Old farm? ___ Boondocks? ___*

Notes: _____

_____

_____

_____

_____

_____

~ 8 ~
Lifestyle

*"A man who has spent much time and money in dreary
restaurants moodily chewing filet of sole on the special
luncheon is bound to become unmanageable when
he discovers that he can produce the main fish course directly,
at the edge of his own pasture, by a bit of trickery
on a fine morning."*

—E. B. WHITE, *One Man's Meat*

Lifestyle is the things we do, which comes from our needs and wants, our values, and the influence of our place. In Chapter 4, "Who Are You?," we began to explore needs and values. First on our criteria worksheet is preferred activities. What we wish to do may dictate where we do it. Gardening in the desert, skiing on the plains, golfing on a mountain peak are unreasonable expectations.

Country lifestyle is the result of needs, wants, habits, values, the land's influence, the size of the place, the tools, and the skills we have.

In the country we get our exercise preparing soil, planting, tending animals, harvesting crops, making firewood, building stone walls, walking, playing. In the city exercise is accomplished at "fitness centers" where the fitness seekers pay for the privilege of using machines to work muscles. What a waste. Why *hasn't* someone developed a way to convert all that running, climbing, pedaling, lifting into electricity? Maybe public utilities should own those places and pay exercisers for expending their calories to generate Btus.

The fact that you are considering moving to the country means that you want to change at least some of your activities. The ideal life includes doing those things we most enjoy. Being in control. Having maximum free choice and maximum independence.

Besides Your Vocation, What Do You Do?

Identify all of your preferred activities that require certain conditions: weather, water, snow, space, mountains, woods, facilities, equipment, and so forth.

Here is a list of place-related activities to bump your brain: swimming, diving, fishing, floating, boating, water skiing; hunting, trapping; snow skiing, ice skating, making snowpeople, having white Christmases; golfing; attending the symphony, concerts, music shows, plays, opera, ballet, baseball, football, basketball; hang gliding; rock climbing; bird watching; beekeeping. Some activities may be practiced nearly anywhere, but climate, topography, raw materials, or local conditions may make them more enjoyable in certain places. These include gardening, hiking, horseback riding, running, woodworking, nature photography, camping.

To Thine Own Self Be True

One ridge to the north of us lived a lady who brought a fur opera jacket with her when she and her husband moved from the city. Each year she took the jacket out of its protective case, shook it, aired it, and brushed it. But only once did she and her husband make the many-hour round trip to attend the opera. Just before they moved, in the midst of explaining why they were leaving, she showed me the coat and spoke of how important opera was to her. She explained that their modest budget did not allow the expense of a long drive, overnight accommodations, meals, and tickets.

If part of you will die if you can't attend musical or sports events, then your ideal place criteria list will include easy driving distance to those facilities.

Homesteading

As a noun, *homestead* is a home, outbuildings, and the adjoining land. As a verb, *homestead* is to settle on a property and to gain sustenance from it. In this country the concept evolved from the Pilgrims' early subsistence patches. The phrase came into public usage with the Homestead Act of 1862, which gave 160 acres of public land to any adult who could live on it for five years. By 1900 about 600,000 had said yes. Considering conditions in the late 1800s, today's option of buying land may be easier.

Some feel that homesteading is synonymous with family farming. It once may have been but in current usage it is not. Homesteading implies that substantial sustenance comes from one's land. Many modern family farmers grow cash crops only, then buy their food at the supermarket. Use of the word nowadays is pretty loose—anyone who moves from city to country and grows a garden is in peril of being labeled a homesteader. There are worse things. It's a great tradition and can be a high-quality lifestyle.

In *The Owner-Built Homestead* Barbara and Ken Kern offer: "Reduced to its simplest terms, a homestead is an ecosystem in which humans evolve in mutual association and coexistence with plants, animals, and other life forces. In this cohabitation the various components of the homestead germinate, develop, and mature at varying rates for varying purposes, all interdependent and individually supportive of life therein."

Most modern homesteaders have these things in common: they believe that life is better in the country; they believe that self-sufficiency is a right goal; they believe that humans are destroying Earth; they want to make the transition from being part of the problem to being part of the solution. Modern homesteaders striving for self-sufficiency are working environmentalists, not only committed to being part of the solution, but living their truth. They walk their talk. They are value-fueled.

Self-reliance

"There is a time in every man's education when he arrives at the conviction that envy is ignorance; that imitation is suicide; that he must take himself for better, for worse, as his portion; that though the wide universe is full of good, no kernel of nourishing corn can come to him but through his toil bestowed on that plot of ground which is given him to till. The power which resides in him is new in nature, and none but he knows what that is which he can do, nor does he know, until he has tried."

—RALPH WALDO EMERSON, *Self Reliance*

Self-reliance. There is a resonance to it—it evokes security, holds hands with words like home and harvest and wood heat. It implies working with, instead of against nature.

It can indeed provide security. Available information and technology allow substantial control of one's basic needs. Wind or photovoltaic generation of electricity now permits use of a full array of tools and appliances independent of an electric company. Good soil and an adequate growing season can produce a large percentage of a family's food needs. With a tight house and a wood stove, a woodlot can provide heat. *Five Acres and Independence* has evolved from a book title to a dream, a challenge, a rallying cry, a reality.

Yes, five good acres is enough. My parents, brother, sister, and I ate very well from one bountiful acre until we moved to our farm. But more land provides pasture, cropland, firewood, wild game if you want it, less chance of bothering your neighbors or your neighbors annoying you, and a condition to allow part of the world to heal itself.

Having It All

The ideal life includes access to what we value. It is now reasonably possible to live in a rural place, surrounded by nature, and use and enjoy the latest creations of technology. More easily than ever we can have the peace of the country and the products of the city. We can live, work, and grow our food in the midst of nature, using space-age tools, and access knowledge and entertainment at will through the magic of technology.

We have portable culture. With tapes and CDs we have the world's finest music. With satellite antennas we receive news and programming from around the globe. After a dinner of homegrown food we can watch the latest movie, then take a safe moon-and-starlit walk in the parklike setting of our own property.

Reflections

> *"I often think today of what a difference it would make if children believed they were contributing to a family's survival and happiness.*
> *In the transformation from a rural to an urban society, children are robbed of the opportunity to do genuinely responsible work."*
>
> —Dwight D. Eisenhower

Politicians, sociologists, and writers spout infobytes on what is wrong with our lives and how we might be "fixed." What they rarely suggest is the importance of consciously choosing a lifestyle based on current conditions. The information age both allows and requires lifestyle adjustment. We have enormous opportunity to transcend the mundane. To stay in place is to reject the gift, to deny our heritage.

Way back in 1970, in *The Greening of America*, Charles A. Reich noted: "What is the central idea of America, unless each man's ability to create his own life? The dream was deferred for many generations in order to create a technology that could raise life to a higher level." That technology arrived yesterday. Embrace it.

For each of us, our individual life is our most creative endeavor. Rooted in the soil of our genetic heritage, shaped by our experiences, nourished by our values, directed by our dreams, we choose from all and make ourselves the best we can. We create our lifestyle, changing it to fit our experiences. Knowledge, experience, success give us the courage to evolve, to grow beyond yesterday. We take ourselves with us no matter where we go, but moving to a new place allows reevaluation of our values. Our lifestyle, as a reflection of our evolving values, must often change for us to grow. For some, city activities become vague country memories. For others, rural barriers to social and cultural activities can be intolerable.

Where you decide to plant yourself will come partly from how you want to live each day. Living in a small town allows you to walk to the coffee shop to compare sage observations with cronies. Living just outside of town probably dictates a bicycle, motorcycle or car trip, or perhaps on a pony. Living in the boonies means sipping coffee on the front porch with yourself, your partner, or your cat or dog for company.

Old bad habits are easier to break in the country. New habits, true to your values, will give you greater pleasure. They will also make you healthier.

A helpful technique is to make a list of all the things you most like to do and then add those things you don't or can't do now that you really want to do. Then go back and rate the items. Do this in private so you will not be inhibited in writing down anything. You can burn the list later if you like.

So now, after lifestyle on your criteria worksheet, write those activities you wish to keep and new ones you wish to adopt. Your ideal place will have appropriate weather, enough space, and will be close enough to needed facilities for you to enjoy those activities.

"You don't get to choose how you're going to die.
Or when. You can decide how you're going to live now."

—JOAN BAEZ

Essential Country Equipment #4: chickens

Chickens come in designer colors and models. The ones with shorter rear plumage are hens. Hens are hard workers. They are sweet, gentle things that produce the main ingredient in omelettes and angel food cake, and the second most important ingredient in eggnog.

Male models are the orginal design alarm clock, which require no electricity, batteries, or winding. Fuel with corn and stones. Alarm goes off about 4 A.M. and continues until midmorning, strangulation, or axing, whichever comes first. No models known available with snooze button. Other than providing alarm service, males—also called cocks, roosters, and several unprintable names—are best known for being oversexed macho terrorists.

— 9 —

Choose Your Climate

"The first day of spring was once the time for taking the young virgins
into the fields, there in dalliance to set an example in fertility for Nature to follow.
Now we just set the clock an hour ahead and change the oil in the crankcase."

—E. B. WHITE

Climate Is Predictable Weather Patterns

Climate is the general state of atmospheric conditions over a long period of time—a composite of averages and extremes during a number of years. Weather is the expression of day-to-day conditions. In short, climate is a large amount of weather averaged out. Climate affects patterns of vegetation and water resources and every human endeavor. Mounting evidence shows that human impact on the environment is causing climatic changes.

The following maps show average conditions over many years. Conditions for any given year will differ significantly from long-term averages. Sharp changes may occur within short distances, particularly in mountainous areas, due to differences in elevation, slope of terrain, type of soil, vegetative cover, bodies of water, air drainage, and human activity.

The Value of Weather

The main value of weather is conversation. As "Kin" Hubbard pointed out, "Don't knock the weather; nine-tenths of the people couldn't start a conversation if it didn't change once in a while." Coastal Californians don't have real weather so they use riots and earthquakes for the purpose.

We humans are fascinated by anything that we can't control. Actually, we're embarrassed by our failure. That's why there are so many weather jokes. (City slicker: "Think it'll rain?" Farmer: "Always has.")

So-called perfect climate isn't. It's predictable, it's boring, it's expensive to live

51

where it occurs. Seasons bring continual change and delight the senses. Cold is refreshing. Gardeners know that many plants need a cold dormancy period before they produce—like politicians between elections. That's why apples grow better up north.

Nonetheless, some folks prefer dependable warmth. My mother and father, who grew up in Wisconsin and northern Michigan, now live in Arizona. They've evolved from snowbirds to roadrunners, though at eighty-five and ninety-two there's not much running going on. They love the warm winters. But what an awful spot to garden! Their place is a tiny oasis in the desert but the ovenlike summer heat challenges even my mother's formidable gardening skills.

Many others who seek predictable comfort without effort have moved to the subtropical climate of the Sunbelt. But Florida in summer is awfully hot and humid, and southern California has so many problems it's losing natives as fast as it is gaining immigrants.

Climate is important for much more than just the quality of temperature comfort. If your greatest passion is skiing then your ideal home will be in or near a snow area. If gardening is your highest priority you will choose a climate with a long growing season and ample rainfall.

In Praise of Seasons

> *"Interest in the changing seasons is a much happier state of mind*
> *than being hopelessly in love with spring."*

—GEORGE SANTAYANA

When I visualize four seasons I think of a rainy warming spring, grasses appearing, flowers exploding into view, the burgeoning, multigreen panorama of budding trees, birds building nests, spotted fawns on wobbly legs; a summer of waking to sunlight, lushly clothed trees, heat, thunderstorms, occasional humidity, meals straight from the garden, straw hats, the smell of new-mown grass, sitting in the porch swing until 9 P.M., sleeping with just a sheet; a glorious autumn, my favorite season, with vines, shrubs, trees offering yellows, oranges, reds, nature's big palette, each day a new hue, cool days and cooler nights; then a winter of resting plants, gray, somber days, my beard full of frost after the mile mailbox walk, and of course snow, although in our part of the world it usually lasts for only a few days; and then, finally, impatience for spring to begin again.

Like the seasons of human life, the seasons of weather move us, invigorate us, inspire us to taste of life to the fullest. Changing temperatures are elixirs for human vigor. Four seasons show off nature. Those who refuse winter give up the glory of spring and autumn. The energy of the cycling natural world makes boredom an unlikely condition.

Preference may simply be conditioning. I grew up in Wisconsin. If you grew up, say, in Florida or southern California, you may have different feelings. And feelings are always correct. So visualize your ideal climatic conditions.

"We decided in favor of the north-east, for various reasons. Aesthetically, we enjoy the procession of the seasons. In any other part of the country we would have missed the perpetual surprises and delights to which New England weather treats its devotees: the snow piled high in winter and the black and white coloring from December to March; the long lingering spring with its hesitant burgeoning into green; the gorgeous burst of hot summer beauty combined with cool nights; and the crisp snap of autumn with its sudden flare of color in the most beautiful of all the seasons. The land that has four well-defined seasons cannot lack beauty, or pall with monotony."

—Helen and Scott Nearing, *Living the Good Life*

Climate Change

Conventional thinking is that almost anything about a piece of land can be changed except the climate and, usually, the topography, although bulldozer operators working for determined developers sometimes make even large hills disappear. For us more sensitive types, topography pretty much stays intact.

Climate and topography are wedded together; in fact, they shape each other. A billion or so years of rain and freezing turn rock into soil. Flat terrain becomes hills and hollows. Birds drop seeds, trees and grasses grow and cause water to linger where it falls before it begins its insistent descent. Hills cause warm wind currents to rise, dropping their gift of water as they meet higher, cooler air. Evaporation reloads the water machine and the cycle continues.

If we cut down enough trees we can create a desert; some feel that if we grow enough trees, we can reclaim arid regions. There is reason to believe that the Sahara desert was once the Sahara forest. Archaeological evidence proves the Sahara had extensive settlement during prehistoric times. Much of its land is fertile—only 20 percent of Saharan soil is sand—but natural regeneration is thwarted by overgrazing and firewood gathering. Scientists now fear further desertification will occur in both Africa and South America where tropical rain forests are being systematically destroyed. According to Worldwatch Institute's *State of the World 1994*, Earth's forests cover 24 percent less land than in 1700 and just between 1980 and 1990 decreased by an area twice the size of Texas. *State of the World 1996* explains how global warming will force forests to move north or die from disease and fires, further exacerbating CO_2 (carbon dioxide) buildup. And *State of the World 1998* reports that 16 million hectares (39.52 million acres) of forests are disappearing each year.

We now know that humans are changing the weather, indeed, the temperature of our planetary home. The 1995 Intergovernmental Panel on Climate Change (U.N. scientists) in Berlin concluded that "a pattern of climatic response to human activities is identifiable in the climatological record." The scientific focus today is on how fast it is happening. The burning of fossil fuels has increased almost fivefold since 1980. Atmospheric concentrations of CO_2 are at the highest level in 150,000 years.

United States Climate

Most of the forty-eight contiguous states have substantial seasonal climate variability. Coastal areas moderated by the oceans or land near large lakes have less variability. The eastern U.S. is humid, with annual precipitation averaging about 40 inches. The northwestern coast receives more than 100 inches per year, but the rest of the West is mostly semiarid, with 10 to 20 inches per year.

The forty-eight states have been divided into four major climatic regions, shown below. "Cool" areas experience a wide range of temperatures, from -30

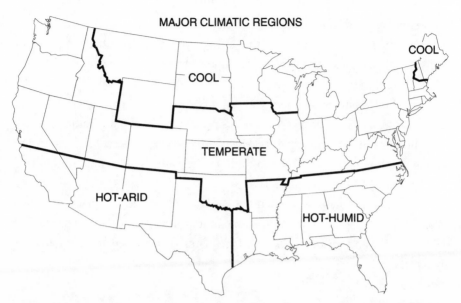

degrees to 100+ degrees. These areas typically have cold winters and hot summers with winds year-round, generally out of the northwest and the southeast. "Temperate" denotes an equal distribution of overheated and underheated periods, with seasonal winds from the northwest and south together with periods of high humidity and large amounts of precipitation in the east but much less in the west, except in the far northwest. "Hot-Arid" is a region of clear, dry atmosphere, extended periods of overheating, and large daily temperature range. Wind is usually along an east–west axis with variations between day and evening. "Hot-Humid" is a region of high temperatures and consistent vapor pressure. Wind velocities and direction vary throughout the year, with velocities of up to 120 miles per hour accompanying hurricanes, which usually come from the east-southeast.

Climate has a profound influence on human experience. With the exception of love, weather has arguably appeared in more songs than any other subject. Well, okay, old songs. As I don't mind dating myself, I'll let words from songs introduce most of the various features of weather, which with seasonal occurrence we call climate.

"Everything's coming up roses for you and for me . . ."

If your activity criteria include gardening, you'll want a climate that cooperates.

All ornamental and food plants have natural climatic preferences: citrus thrives in the south and apples do best in the north; if you must have fresh mangoes or die, you will not move to Maine. Growing tomatoes is a far greater challenge in North Dakota than in Tennessee.

Pick the climate zone where you can grow what you most want to look at and to eat fresh. The Northwest, with lots of rain and cool temperatures, is lush with rhododendrons, azaleas, ferns. Much of the lower Midwest has a six-month growing season, from mid-April to mid-October, which allows cultivation of a wide variety of fruits and vegetables.

The United States Department of Agriculture developed plant hardiness zones based on average minimum temperatures. These zones are often referred to by nurseries and gardening books where plants are classified according to their ability to survive cold.

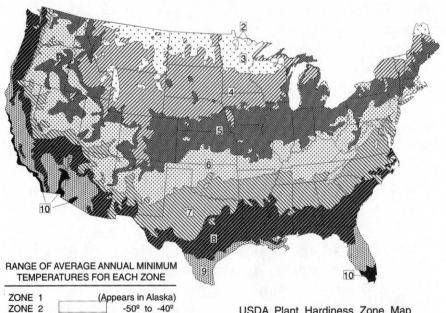

RANGE OF AVERAGE ANNUAL MINIMUM
TEMPERATURES FOR EACH ZONE

ZONE 1	(Appears in Alaska)
ZONE 2	-50º to -40º
ZONE 3	-40º to -30º
ZONE 4	-30º to -20º
ZONE 5	-20º to -10º
ZONE 6	-10º to 0º
ZONE 7	0º to 10º
ZONE 8	10º to 20º
ZONE 9	20º to 30º
ZONE 10	30º to 40º

USDA Plant Hardiness Zone Map

Shows the lowest temperatures that can be expected each year. These temperatures are referred to as "average annual minimum temperatures" and are based on the lowest temperatures recorded for each of the years 1974 to 1986.

The minimum temperature often determines whether a plant will survive in a given spot. The problems faced by southern gardeners are often the opposite of those in the north. Southerners are unable to grow some plants common in northern landscapes because of too much heat or too little winter cold. Azaleas won't make it in hot, dry Arizona.

Whether garden plants will fail, or whether they will grow to maturity and fruit depends in great part on the length of the growing season, for most garden plants the period between the last spring freeze and the first fall freeze. A long growing season may allow two crops of certain vegetables, for instance brassica and various salad plants. A growing season can be too long; constant heat and warmth precludes growing certain plants, although botanists regularly introduce new varieties tolerant of diverse conditions.

Microclimates

Small areas on the sunny or shady, upwind or downwind side of a hill or mountain, protected valleys, and other spots often exhibit climatic conditions substantially different from those in the surrounding area. Water warms and cools more slowly than land masses, so areas near large bodies of water tend to exhibit more stable climatic conditions. These microclimatic areas are sought by those who wish to raise certain crops which might be damaged by late frost, or which thrive on certain temperatures, air-movement patterns, or precipitation. Well-known microclimates include New York's Finger Lakes region below Lake Ontario and California's Napa Valley. Microclimates abound in mountainous areas.

"It's too darn hot . . ."

> "It was so hot here that I found there was nothing left for it but to take off my flesh and sit in my bones."
>
> —SYDNEY SMITH

The retiree flight from northeast states to Florida is propelled by the lure of escape from cold, windy, snowy winters. Once there, many find the sultry summers unbearable. Snowbirds from Montana spend winters in Arizona, then flee north before the summer sun starts sizzling. But today even northern spots get hot; in Chicago on July 13, 1995, the mercury reached an all-time high of 106 degrees—536 deaths were attributed to the heat.

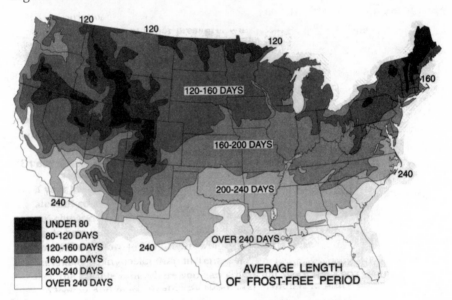

AVERAGE LENGTH OF FROST-FREE PERIOD

MEAN ANNUAL NUMBER OF DAYS WITH MAXIMUM TEMPERATURE 90°F AND ABOVE

Data source: U.S. Dept. of Commerce Nat'l Oceanic & Atmospheric Administration (After H. McKinley Conway, Jr., and Linda L. Liston, "The Weather Handbook.")

Note: Sharp changes in number of days 90° and above may occur within short distances due to differences in altitude, slope of land, type of soil, vegetative cover, bodies of water, air drainage, etc.

"Let it snow, let it snow, let it snow" 'cause "Baby, it's cold outside"

"In the range of inorganic nature, I doubt if any
object can be found more perfectly beautiful than a fresh,
deep snowdrift, seen under warm light."

—JOHN RUSKIN

Those who experienced the record-setting Blizzard of '96 may disagree with Mr. Ruskin. Philadelphians found thirty inches of the white stuff a bit much and New Yorkers were housebound for several days. Such climatic anomalies appear to be increasing. Scientists say that more extreme weather will occur as global warming accelerates.

Cold and snow are not constant companions but they often hold hands. To me, cold without some snow is rather like eating pizza without wine or beer. Winter heaven is awakening to a fresh snow, walking in a white wonderland, taking pictures for Christmas cards, following animal tracks, and seeing the world perfectly clean. Skiing and ice skating are optional. Sitting in front of a crackling fire is a perfect end to an exhilarating day.

MEAN ANNUAL SNOWFALL (INCHES)

Note:
Large differences may occur within short distances, particularly in mountainous areas.
Data source: U.S. Dept. of Commerce Nat'l Oceanic & Atmospheric Administration
(After H. McKinley Conway, Jr., and Linda L. Liston, "The Weather Handbook.")

While a foot of fresh snow is a skier's paradise, it is bad news to someone who has to drive to work. Even with snowblowers, getting out to a cleared road can be a major challenge. If you want to live in snow country and must commute to work, you will want to have short, level access to a county road. County road crews typically are out plowing the roads first thing in the morning. And employers in snow country are aware of how road conditions affect commuters.

The map on page 59 shows where the cheeks are rosy, the skiing is great, and Christmas is almost guaranteed to be white.

The Effect of Elevation (Altitude)

Temperature in the atmosphere drops with increasing elevation. Some writers state that the rate of decrease is 3.3 degrees Fahrenheit per 1,000 feet. Others say one degree Fahrenheit for every 250 feet. Your choice.

"The Iceman Cometh"

Yeah, I know, it's a play, not a song. We don't think too much about ice unless we ice-skate, or unless we find ourselves suddenly lying on it wincing at the sky, or unless our car slides into a ditch. If you choose an area with four distinct seasons but have not lived with ice, practice driving in a large, empty parking lot covered with hard snow or ice. Accelerate, brake, and turn increasingly smaller figure-eights until you know what to expect and how to handle it. Plan ahead—it's like driving a boat. Expect other drivers to make mistakes. They will.

The Great Ice Storm of 1998 demolished trees and power lines in northern New England. Thousands of Maine, Vermont, New Hampshire, and Quebec residents were without power for weeks. If you choose to live in an area with a history of ice storms, consider installing backup systems for water pumps and heating systems that blow or pump the heat medium. When the electricity goes out, our modern world shuts down.

"I'm singing in the rain . . ."

> *"When it rains we'll laugh at the weather."*
>
> —Lorenz Hart (and Richard Rodgers), "Mountain Greenery"

Precipitation usually, but certainly not dependably, equates to available water for human use. In many populated areas water demand far exceeds water supply. That condition is worsening, most strongly in the West, where population continues to grow even as droughts regularly occur and even as critical water shortages have become widely acknowledged. Arizona, California, and Colorado are three notable examples of states where water demand exceeds water supply. Areas of the West are currently experiencing heavy population growth, which will cause even deadlier water wars than those already experienced between cattle and sheep ranchers. While the battles may be fought in the courts, make no mistake about the outcome. Individual lives will be uplifted or crushed by the verdicts.

Water has always been valued; now it is fast becoming a high-priced commodity. It is prudent to expect that politically powerful cities will continue to rob farmers and other rural residents of water. We would do well to put ourselves where precipitation and groundwater are dependably abundant.

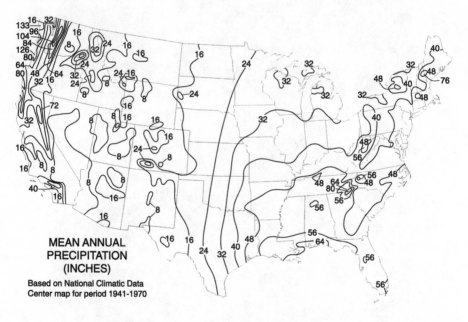

**MEAN ANNUAL
PRECIPITATION
(INCHES)**

Based on National Climatic Data
Center map for period 1941-1970

As shown on the map above, levels of precipitation can be far different within short distances, most dramatically in the Northwest, but also in many places subject to the microclimate phenomena. In Washington and Oregon, depending on which side of the Cascade Range you are on, you may receive a stingy six inches or an awesome 100-plus inches of rainfall. Desert or deluge, take your pick.

Effect of Mountains on Rainfall

The reason that mountains collect rain on their windward side is the orographic effect—the rain shadow of a mountain—shown in the drawing here. Warm, moisture-laden air currents are forced upward by mountains; as they rise they collide with cooler air, which precipitates the moisture. Once past the peak, the now-dry air slides down the leeward slope, evaporating ground moisture, which makes the moisture difference between the west and east sides even more dramatic, as illustrated by the lush growth on the west slope and the relative lack of tree growth on the east slope.

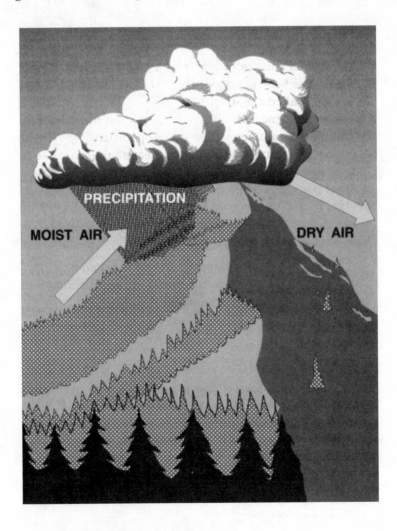

"*I just finished drying off from my shower and I'm already dripping with sweat*"

Well, that's not from a song (although singing and showers do go well together), but we've all heard the expression, especially if we have friends living in Florida or what is often called the Deep South.

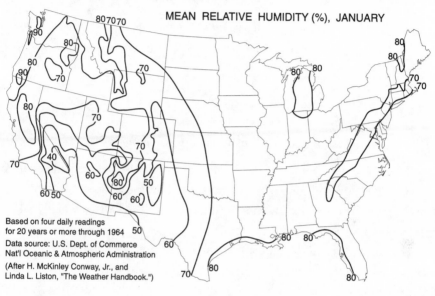

MEAN RELATIVE HUMIDITY (%), JANUARY

Based on four daily readings
for 20 years or more through 1964
Data source: U.S. Dept. of Commerce
Nat'l Oceanic & Atmospheric Administration
(After H. McKinley Conway, Jr., and
Linda L. Liston, "The Weather Handbook.")

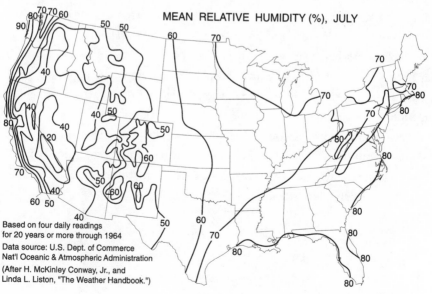

MEAN RELATIVE HUMIDITY (%), JULY

Based on four daily readings
for 20 years or more through 1964
Data source: U.S. Dept. of Commerce
Nat'l Oceanic & Atmospheric Administration
(After H. McKinley Conway, Jr., and
Linda L. Liston, "The Weather Handbook.")

Humidity is water suspended in air, like fog. It's not much of a nuisance except when high humidity combines with high temperatures. High relative humidity is uncomfortable, energy-draining, and may be detrimental to some health conditions. Either high or low humidity may feel uncomfortable. Dry desert air dries one's skin and nasal passages. High humidity thwarts perspiration and intensifies heat discomfort. It also makes cold feel colder.

> *"What men call gallantry, and gods adultery,*
> *Is much more common where the climate's sultry."*
>
> —LORD BYRON

❧

"I'll huff and I'll puff, and I'll blow your house down"

Okay, that's also not from a song. It's from a nursery rhyme, but it should be from a song. Why *hasn't* someone written a musical about the three swine architects? Miss Piggy is the obvious choice for narrator and Jack Nicholson would make a great huffer. I wonder if he can sing.

The January and July wind maps are produced from ground data gathered at local weather stations, most often airports. The direction of the arrows indicates the prevailing wind direction during those two months, indicative of both winter and summer conditions. At first glance, these maps seem to indicate that U.S. winds have little order and are in fact rather helter-skelter.

While local low-level winds may come from many different directions depending on constantly changing atmospheric conditions, the prevailing winds and weather movements in the U.S. generally move from west to east. This is shown on the map "Major Climatological Storm Tracks."

The following maps are useful not only for understanding weather movement but for determining the potential for acid rain and other airborne pollution for a given site. They are also useful for planning the placement of buildings, gardens, landscaping, and windbreaks.

JANUARY WINDS
Source: National Weather Service

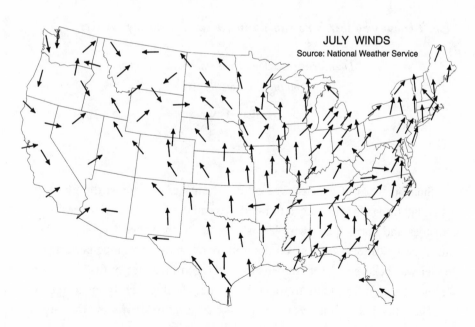

JULY WINDS
Source: National Weather Service

MAJOR CLIMATOLOGICAL STORM TRACKS

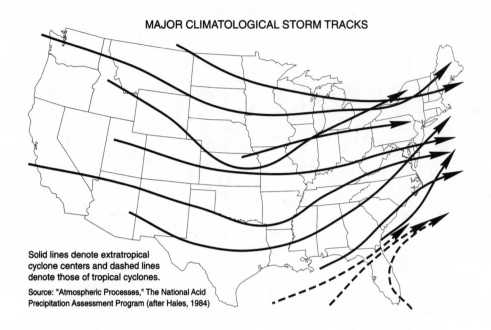

Solid lines denote extratropical
cyclone centers and dashed lines
denote those of tropical cyclones.

Source: "Atmospheric Processes," The National Acid
Precipitation Assessment Program (after Hales, 1984)

"Don't know why there's no sun up in the sky . . . stormy weather . . ."

*"Thunder is good, thunder is impressive; but it is
lightning that does the work."*

—MARK TWAIN

Smart man, Mr. Clemens. One of the advantages of summer thunderstorms is that lightning affixes nitrogen to raindrops and down they come to fertilize our tomatoes and corn. That's why lawns become greener after a good, rollicking thunderstorm. I love 'em. I sit on the front porch and applaud the performance. Jupiter was believed by the Romans to be the god in charge of the sky and the weather. It's a pure pleasure to watch his trainees flexing their thunder muscles.

The following map shows where the sky fertilizes the lawns and the gardens.

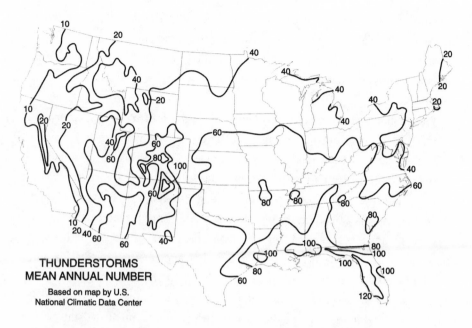

**THUNDERSTORMS
MEAN ANNUAL NUMBER**

Based on map by U.S.
National Climatic Data Center

Too Much Water Too Fast

The top news story of 1993 was the Great Flood that battered the Midwest—approximately 10 million acres of lakes where there had been homes, roads, towns, and farmland. The floods of 1889, 1937, and 1973 killed 2,100, 250, and 23 respectively. The 1993 flood killed *only* 26 people because of abundant warnings, evacuation plans, lack of flash floods, and a massive levee and dam system. Thousands of people had to leave their homes and many had no homes to return to—many buildings were beyond repair and were broken up and carried to a landfill. Some people rebuilt, some to new building codes that require elevated residences. Government estimates rose in one week from $500 million to $8 billion in damage.

In February 1996, Oregon's Willamette River drove tens of thousands from their homes and flooded some Portland homes to the roofs. Flooding in Oregon's extreme northwestern corner swept away homes, vehicles, and livestock.

All this in spite of billions of (taxpayer) dollars spent by the Corps of Engineers constructing an elaborate flood-control network, including 7,000 miles of levees. Are we or are we not the arrogant species? Perhaps one day even bureaucrats will concede that nature is in charge.

All waterways are subject to flooding; generally, the larger the watershed, the greater the possibility. Our little stream floods about twice each year. Its watershed, over 2,800 acres, is heavily wooded, so most water slowly soaks into the ground to recharge the several springs which provide steady year-round flow.

Occasionally we get a sustained heavy rain—say four inches in twenty-four hours—the ground stops absorbing, and the creek rises within a few hours to raging river status. At our road crossing, the stream has expanded from its usual 15-foot width and 12-inch depth to over 100 feet wide and 4 feet in depth. And the water moves *fast*. The house is nicely sited, about 200 feet back and about 15 feet higher than the stream at normal flow, so there is no danger. But the several days the stream takes to normalize is inconvenient unless we are both on the house side with our usual full stock of supplies and no rush orders for autographed books. Chris and I remember well the night she returned from a rainy day in the city and found the crossing flooded. We shouted our frustrations to each other over the roar of the torrent before she went off to stay with a neighbor.

A natural condition, a human challenge. I envision a dam with a very large underflow capability, a road on top of it, a trout pond behind it. In the meantime, I have built a log bridge, which has now survived its fourth year.

Too Little Water Too Long

Some climatological bureaucrat decreed that no rain for up to two weeks is a dry spell; anything longer is a drought. In that case there's a whole lot of droughting going on. Really serious droughts seem to occur at twenty- to twenty-two-year intervals in the western U.S. Our most famous drought area, the so-called Dust Bowl, covers an area of about 150,000 square miles, including the Oklahoma and Texas panhandles and adjacent parts of Colorado, New Mexico, and Kansas, an area of light soil, annual rainfall of about fifteen inches, and high winds. The dust condition is exacerbated by tilling for crops and the resultant destruction of grasses and other root systems that anchored the soil. The Dust Bowl does not qualify as an area for ideal home places.

Too Much Air Too Fast

Sounds like the description of a political campaign. Midwesterners think Californians are in imminent danger of falling into the ocean from earthquakes, whereas Californians envision Midwesterners being demolished by tornadoes. And everyone but those living there is convinced that Floridians and others living on the Gulf and east coasts will all eventually be blown away by hurricanes. They may be right; the 1995 Atlantic hurricane season was the most active since that of the 1930s. And before that, there was 1992.

"Although sophisticated warning systems have limited the loss of life, economic damage has been unprecedented because of burgeoning coastal development. South Florida's vulnerability was demonstrated on August 24, 1992, when Hurricane Andrew came ashore with sustained winds of 235 kilometers per hour [146 miles per hour]—the third most powerful hurricane to make landfall in the United States in the twentieth century. Andrew virtually flattened 430 square kilometers [166 square miles] of Dade County in Florida, destroying 85,000 homes and leaving almost 300,000 people homeless. Total losses were estimated at $30 billion—equivalent to the combined losses of the three most costly previous U.S. storms" (*State of the World 1996*).

The occurrence of mega-storms such as Andrew has frightened the insurance industry to the point that industry executives have contracted with Greenpeace to help get a handle on global warming, now understood to affect weather. When the ultraconservative insurance guys and the left-wing Greenies get together, you have to know it's serious business. Sort of like Goliath and David getting together on the stone thing. "Listen up, big guy. I've got something here that'll do you in, but I'm not discussing it with you if you don't show me some respect." And then it takes a stone against the head to make the point. Or an Andrew against the cash reserves.

Tornadoes, also known as twisters or cyclones, are often associated with severe thunderstorms. They typically leave a path of destruction less than 200 feet wide and average 5 to 15 miles in length. Most occur in spring and early summer in the central southern U.S., later across more northerly regions. Of the nation's yearly total of about 1,000 tornadoes, most occur in Texas, Oklahoma, and Kansas. But it's not the number, it's the severity. On February 23, 1998, surprise multiple tornadoes in central Florida killed thirty-nine, injured hundreds, and destroyed hundreds of homes.

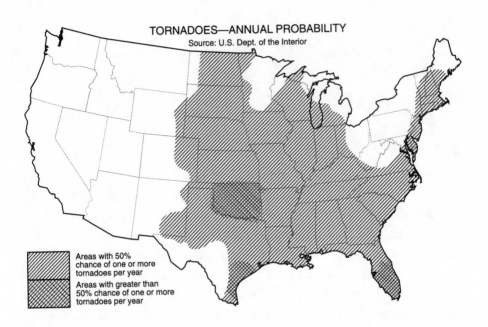

TORNADOES—ANNUAL PROBABILITY
Source: U.S. Dept. of the Interior

Areas with 50%
chance of one or more
tornadoes per year
Areas with greater than
50% chance of one or more
tornadoes per year

Contrary to the belief of Californians, we in tornado country do not run for our basements at every thunderstorm. Weather forecasts in twister country dependably include tornado alerts, and since tornadoes occur most frequently during mid-to-late afternoon they are rarely a surprise. Harold Brooks, a meteorologist with the National Severe Storms Laboratory, points out that, while the Tri-State Tornado of 1925 killed 689 people, a similar 1989 twister killed no one. The tornado warning system works—but we have to pay attention to it: a May 6, 1995, tornado in southern Oklahoma and northern Texas killed twenty-three who were inadequately protected. Californians take note: *the earthquake warning system does not work at all.*

"Shake, rattle, and roll"

"Nature bats last."

—BUMPER STICKER

Philosopher-historian Will Durant said that civilization exists by geological consent and is subject to change without notice. Those who have lived through strong earthquakes are most likely to concur.

Earthquakes are not part of climate but, as natural phenomena and acts of God, they fit here best. I have survived earthquakes in Japan and in both northern and southern California, including the magnitude 6.8 L.A. quake of January 17, 1994, which rousted me out of bed at 4:31 A.M. I have visited L.A. at better times. Durant's admonition rang loud and clear. That quake killed sixty-one and created the most expensive natural disaster in the history of the U.S. Some people will never be the same. I met a lady who survived the total destruction of her house in Santa Monica from the quake at a book signing in Tampa. Earthquake paranoia is real and painful.

Thirty-seven states have a significant danger from earthquakes, including the Northwest, New England, and the Midwest. The New Madrid fault is potentially the most damaging. Roughly 200 miles long and 40 miles wide, it is a crack within the tectonic plate that makes up North America. It lies two miles below parts of Arkansas, western Tennessee and Kentucky, southeastern Missouri, and southern Illinois. The New Madrid quake, 100 years ago, made the Mississippi River temporarily run north. That's a lot of muscle.

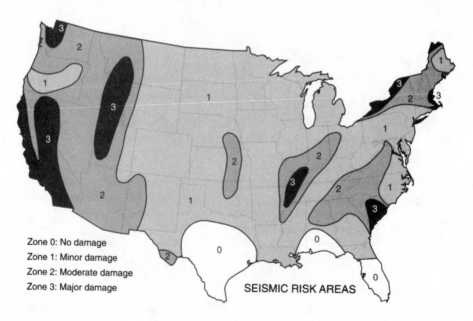

Zone 0: No damage
Zone 1: Minor damage
Zone 2: Moderate damage
Zone 3: Major damage

SEISMIC RISK AREAS

The danger from earthquakes exists primarily in and close to cities; in sparsely populated rural areas earthquakes are of less danger because of the nature, or absence, of structures. In the L.A. quake the greatest loss was from fire, damage to freeway overpasses, large concrete parking structures, masonry facades, multiple-story buildings (one three-story building collapsed down to two stories, killing sixteen), and homes built on the edges of cliffs or sides of unstable hills. Worldwide, earthquake damage includes landslides and dam collapses.

Single-story homes are usually damaged to a dangerous degree only when they are near the quake's epicenter. Nevertheless, the prudent person will not choose to live in an area of high seismic risk. As we have the entire country to choose from, there is no need to consider such a location.

The Bottom Lines

> *"The way I see it, if you want the rainbow, you gotta put up with the rain."*
>
> —DOLLY PARTON

Climate is a major factor contributing to quality of life. It regulates our activities and brain waves. It affects our moods. It also makes decisions that we must live with. You can fight city hall far more easily than the weather. Outside activities are often dictated by weather conditions. But inside our houses, with today's technology we can live in any climate in reasonable-cost comfort while remaining true to environmental sanity. Pick a climate that will allow you to enjoy your preferred activities, grow the food and ornamental plants you wish, provide health, interest, and vigor, and give you the sights you like to see. Now make notes about your climatic preferences on your criteria worksheet.

Resources

Climatic data for the U.S., each state, and 274 cities, in publications and maps, is available from the National Climatic Data Center. The NCDC data are derived from 275 primary and approximately 5,000 cooperative weather stations world-wide. Publications are available for each location at very low cost. To order, write:

National Climatic Data Center
151 Patton Avenue, Room 120
Asheville, NC 28801-5001
Phone: 704-271-4800; fax: 704-271-4876; e-mail: orders@ncdc.noaa.gov

Seismicity maps are available for nearly all states, for $4.00 each.
Earthquake Maps, U.S. Geological Survey
Box 25046, Federal Center, MS 967
Denver, CO 80225
Phone: 303-273-8477; fax: 303-273-8404

The World Almanac and Book of Facts provides various climatological data, including monthly normal temperatures and precipitation, based on the thirty-year period 1961–1990.

The U.S. Government Printing Office has weather-related publications. See Appendix A for complete inquiry and ordering information for these and the more than 12,000 other books, periodicals, posters, pamphlets, and subscription services.

— 10 —

Land Characteristics: Topography, Soil, and Vegetation

"The hills are alive with the sound of music . . ."

—Oscar Hammerstein II (and Richard Rodgers)

"The hills are alive—and it's pretty frightening."

—Barbra Streisand, *A Happening in Central Park*

The topography, soil, and vegetation of a place have a major influence on lifestyle. In our area, socializing is notably affected by distance—of roads, not straight-line. The roads of hills-and-hollows terrain cause forty-five-minute drives to visit friends only three miles away as the crow flies. In nice weather the alternative is to walk—up and down wooded hills, fording streams, occasionally using old logging roads. It is pleasant going during the daytime but even with flashlights, walking home in the dark through face-slapping branches is less wonderful. After heavy rains, bridges in narrow valleys sometimes become impassable, necessitating even longer drives.

There may be a psychic connection between people and place. Others and I have marveled at the high incidence of us Capricorns here in the Ozarks. We speculate that the heavily vegetated, rugged hill country is simply natural terrain for goats, who delight in climbing and will seemingly eat anything. We try to have annual Capricorn parties, although January road conditions are often the most challenging of the year.

The ideal country home place has at minimum enough good soil for a garden, orchard, woodlot, and sufficient vegetation to prevent erosion of sloping land and to provide a pleasing view. All these items are factors of topography.

Americans can choose to live in terrain that is mountainous, hilly, flat, coastal, desert, plains. Choices continue with ridgetops, valleys, hollows, bottomland, upland. Then we have forests, grasses, cropland, mixed vegetation, even swamps. Each of these land characteristics has advantages and disadvantages. Each has its own character and each shapes the character of the characters who live there. This influence of topography on humans is illustrated by the words that define those who live in certain places: swamp rat, desert rat, hillbilly, flat-lander, mountaineer, woodsman, and so on.

Topography 101

As the outside of the earth cooled down, cracks developed which created the giant plates that comprise the present mantle, the solid stuff we walk on and that underlies the seas. The swirling gasses settled down to a pattern, separated into layers, an atmosphere developed, water fell, hit the rock, and began wearing on it. The plates, floating on the hot inner magma, slowly moved. Where they pushed into each other, edges lifted and became mountains. A few billion years of plate bumping, rain falling, frost cracking and heaving, rivers forming, and Earth began to look like the neat place we see today. (We know all this because Cecil B. deMille was there to film it.) Up to this point we are talking about geology, which is sort of the underlayment of topography, which is on top, which is why—ahem—it is called top-ography.

The action of rain, wind, and freezing plus the action of the glaciers created soil from rock. Depending on the rock it came from, soil is composed of percentages of various minerals. In addition, when plants and animals die and decay they become humus, which becomes food for the next generation of plants. Depending on the incidence of type of soil, temperature, moisture, wind, sun angle, and some other things such as birds depositing seeds, unique plants grow in different places.

A Quick Topographic Trip from Sea to Shining Sea

Areas that have similar physiography often have similar geology, hydrology, and climate. The following map shows the physiographic regions and provinces of the contiguous states. A brief explanation of each numbered region follows:

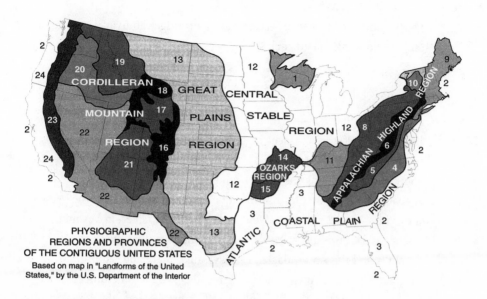

PHYSIOGRAPHIC
REGIONS AND PROVINCES
OF THE CONTIGUOUS UNITED STATES
Based on map in "Landforms of the United
States," by the U.S. Department of the Interior

1. Superior Upland—Hilly area of erosional topography on ancient crystalline rocks.

2. Continental Shelf—Shallow, sloping, submarine plain of sedimentation.

3. Coastal Plain—Low, hilly to nearly flat terraced plains on soft sediments. The east coast is like the edge of a broken jigsaw puzzle, with continuous inlets, bays, and sounds. The coastal plain extends from Long Island south to and around Florida, including the Gulf coast to Mexico. With an average width of about 150 miles this is approximately 10 percent of the land.

4. Piedmont Province—Gentle to rough, hilly terrain on belted crystalline rocks becoming more hilly toward mountains. Three hundred to 1,000 feet in elevation, a transition to the Appalachian Mountains. The east edge of the Piedmont is the "fall line," an escarpment down which rivers tumble in falls to the plain.

5. Blue Ridge Province—Mountains of crystalline rock 3,000 to 6,000 feet high, mostly rounded summits. Mount Mitchell, in the Black Mountains of western North Carolina, at 6,684 feet, is the highest point east of the Rocky Mountains.

6. Valley and Ridge Province—Long mountain ridges and valleys eroded on strong and weak folded rock strata.

7. St. Lawrence Valley (look in upper New York)—Rolling lowland with local rock hills.

8. Appalachian Plateaus—Generally steep-sided plateaus on sandstone bedrock, 3,000 to 5,000 feet high on the east side, declining gradually to the west. The Appalachians, a system of mountains, run northeast to southwest, paralleling the coast from above Maine all the way to Alabama. (Note: The East has mountains in more states than the West: the White Mountains are in New Hampshire, the Green in Vermont, Maine, and Connecticut; New York is pushed up twice, with the Catskills and the Adirondacks; Pennsylvania, Maryland, and the Virginias share the Alleghenies; Virginia also has the Blue Ridge, which lifts the west end of North Carolina and enters Georgia; the Great Smoky Mountains are in southeastern Tennessee; the Cumberland Plateau starts in northern Alabama and goes across Tennessee, up into Kentucky.)

9. New England Province—Rolling, hilly, erosional topography on crystalline rocks in the southeastern part to high mountainous country in the central and northern parts.

10. Adirondack Province—Subdued mountains on ancient crystalline rocks rising to over 5,000 feet.

11. Interior Low Plateaus—Low plateaus on stratified rocks. Includes diverse Kentucky, with mountain coal in the east (Appalachian Plateau), flat to rolling farming country in the middle, the Bluegrass region along the Ohio River, a rolling coal and farming area in the north bulge.

12. Central Lowland—Mostly low, rolling landscape and nearly level plains. Most of the area is covered by a veneer of glacial deposits, including ancient lake beds and hilly lake-dotted moraines. Includes the Lower Peninsula of Michigan, with 11,000 natural lakes shaped by glaciers; Minnesota, where glaciers ground out 15,291 lakes, one for every eighteen citizens; and dairyland Wisconsin (14,000 lakes), a mix of glacial hills and rolling hayfields, the better soil southeast, hills south-

west, woods and cranberry bogs north in the Superior Upland. Northwest Missouri is a plains region, the northeast nearly flat. The glaciers stopped at the Missouri River. Northern Missouri, Iowa, and Illinois are the land of megafarms. In some places the topsoil is many feet deep.

13. Great Plains—Broad river plains and low plateaus on weak stratified sedimentary rocks. Rises toward the Rocky Mountains, at some places to elevations over 6,000 feet. From North Dakota the Great Plains sweep southward, interrupted by the Badlands and Black Hills of southern and southwestern South Dakota. The plains—grassland, buffalo land— extend down through Nebraska and Kansas and through the panhandle of Oklahoma to Texas. Texas has high plains in the northwest extending down through vast prairie and plains with some hills to the Gulf coast in the Atlantic Coastal Plain Region.

14. Ozarks Plateau—High, hilly landscape on stratified rocks. The Ozarks Plateau is the oldest exposed land in America and the only major high- land between the Appalachians and the Rockies. Makes up southern Missouri and northwest Arkansas. Hills and hollows covered with oaks, hickories, short-leafed pine, cedar, dogwood, redbud. Rocky. Springs, streams, reservoirs. The best soil is in the bottoms.

15. Ouachita Province—Ridges and valleys eroded on upturned folded strata.

16. Southern Rocky Mountains—Complex mountains rising to over 14,000 feet. Includes Colorado, with the highest average elevation in the U.S.— 1,000 peaks higher than 10,000 feet. Eastern Colorado is Great Plains, western is Colorado Plateau—the Rockies go down the middle.

17. Wyoming Basin—Elevated plains and plateaus on sedimentary strata.

18. Middle Rocky Mountains—Complex mountains with many intermountain basins and plains.

19. Northern Rocky Mountains—Rugged mountains with narrow intermountain basins. Includes most of Idaho, the rugged Bitterroot Range in the north and the wide, arid Snake River valley across the south, the eastern part of the Columbia Plateau.

20. Columbia Plateau—High rolling plateaus underlain by extensive lava flows; trenched by canyons.

21. Colorado Plateau—High plateaus on stratified rocks cut by deep canyons.

22. Basin and Range Province—Mostly isolated ranges separated by wide desert plains. Many lakes, ancient lake beds, and alluvial fans. The Wasatch Range splits Utah, with Plateau land east, and west the Great Basin, third largest interior drainage region in the world—continues to the alpine Sierra Nevadas of western Nevada and eastern California.

23. Cascade–Sierra Nevada Mountains—Sierras in the southern part are high mountains eroded from crystalline rocks; Cascades in the northern part are high volcanic mountains.

24. Pacific Border Province—Mostly very young steep mountains; includes extensive river plains in the California portion. In the northwest the Cascade Range starts in northern California, defines western Oregon and divides wet, western Washington, lush with Douglas fir, hemlock, cedar, and spruce, from the dry, sagebrush east of the Columbia Plateau. The Coast Range dominates far western Oregon, more hilly than mountainous along the ocean. Between the Coast Range and the Cascades is the fertile Willamette River valley, up to fifty miles wide. The leading lumber state, Oregon contains vast forests of ponderosa pine, Sitka spruce, and hemlock. Western Oregon is wet; the southeast is semiarid high plain.

Soil Quality

> *"So long as one feeds on food from*
> *unhealthy soil, the spirit will lack the stamina*
> *to free itself from the prison of the body."*
>
> —RUDOLF STEINER

Soil serves as an anchorage for plants and as their nutrient reservoir. Soil quality is highly important if you want to garden or live among growing things like trees, bushes, grasses. Unlike the climate and politicians, soil can be improved. Gardens can be built from scratch. Soil can be imported or created from organic materials but it's a lot of work. Even rocky soil can be fertile and grow great trees, but digging holes for new fruit, nut, and shade trees might be a job for a backhoe. Unless you intend to farm, you only need really good soil for a garden, perhaps a quarter acre. Charles Long says in *Life After the City*: "Don't look for good garden soil on an agricultural map. Gardens are little pockets of soil that will take some special treatment regardless of what the rest of the country is like."

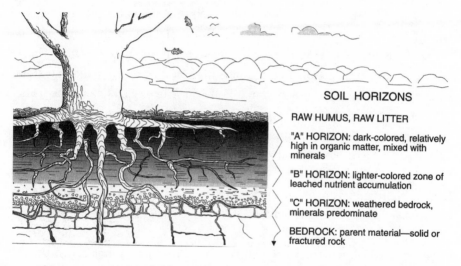

SOIL HORIZONS

RAW HUMUS, RAW LITTER

"A" HORIZON: dark-colored, relatively high in organic matter, mixed with minerals

"B" HORIZON: lighter-colored zone of leached nutrient accumulation

"C" HORIZON: weathered bedrock, minerals predominate

BEDROCK: parent material—solid or fractured rock

If you want to grow field crops or have a small farm operation get plenty of qualified local advice on the soil you are considering. The Natural Resource Conservation Service of the USDA has the mandate to test and map soils in all counties. Many counties have been completed. Check with the people at the local extension office or soil conservation department.

Soil is a complex natural material formed from disintegrated rock, which includes decomposed minerals. Other than minerals, plants get nutrients from decaying organic matter acted upon by soil microorganisms. Dark soil is generally more fertile than light-colored soil, the darkness deriving from humus, decomposing vegetal matter. Soils are classified according to the percentages they contain of clay, sand, silt, and humus. Loams, which have about equal percentages of sand, silt, and clay, have ideal texture and are typically the most fertile.

In the moist southeastern U.S., soil is often thick clay. The predominant red color is caused by the presence of iron particles. Similar soil is found along the northwest coast. In drier areas of the country, where weathering has been less intense, surface soil contains little clay. In moist mountainous regions such as the Appalachians or Ozarks, most hillsides are covered with colluvium—loose, weathered rock debris. The Rockies are similar but drier, so loose deposits are thinner.

The northern part of the country contains areas of glacial deposits. Glacial action extended down to Long Island, northern Pennsylvania, the Ohio and Missouri rivers, and Puget Sound lowland. In hilly New England, deposits are stony. In the central region, glacial deposits are overlain with windblown silt—loess. These areas contain some of the best agricultural land in the world but the fine soil is highly subject to wind and water erosion. It runs deep, so farmers have wasted much of it to erosion. In other areas the best soil is often found in bottom lands where flooding and runoff from hillsides have deposited fine soil particles.

The acidity or alkalinity of soil determines to a large extent what can be grown in it. A pH scale is used to express both acidity and alkalinity in soil; pH values range from 0 to 14, with 7 being neutral. Less than 7 indicates acidity, more than 7 shows alkalinity. Most common garden crops do well in the mid-range, from 6.5 to 7.5. A soil that is too acid can be corrected by adding lime. Alkalinity may be reduced with sulfur, but highly alkaline soil is useless. Soil that is highly alkaline often has a white, crusty look and supports little or no vegetation. A high percentage of organic matter, the goal of organic gardeners, seems to broaden the pH range in which a given plant will thrive.

Before soil tests, farmers judged the pH level of soil by tasting it. Considering the things farmers have been putting into and onto soil in the last few decades, I recommend against tasting soil. A soil test is most accurate, but you can estimate the acidity of soil by observing plants that thrive there. Acidic but usable soil is indicated by ferns, azaleas, rhododendrons, blueberries, strawberries, dande-lions, and plantain—the low plant in lawns with broad, strong-veined leaves that my grandmother used to make a poultice to draw infection after I cut my five-year-old foot on a piece of glass. A knowledgeable herbalist friend used the same treatment on my fifty-year-old toe where a pygmy rattlesnake nailed me. It still works. (The plantain—and the toe—but not the rattlesnake.) Never call it a weed again.

Hydrangeas are tolerant of a wide range of soil acidity or alkalinity but have the quality of reacting like litmus paper, the flowers being red in alkaline soil and blue in acidic soil. The reason is that the trace element aluminum, which makes them blue, is not available to the roots in alkaline conditions.

Tall, lush growth of a wide variety of plants generally indicates that soil structure, fertility, and pH level are appropriate for gardening.

You can test soil for texture by moistening some and rubbing it between your fingers. Clay feels and looks slippery. A gritty feeling indicates high sand content. Silt almost feels greasy but has less of the sticky, plastic feel of clay.

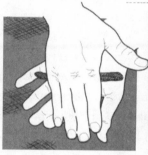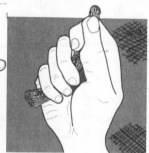

Soil texture can also be examined by the procedure shown here. First squeeze a moist handful. It should form a lump, what is called a cast. Roll the cast between your hands to form a soil rope. Lastly, work the end of the rope under your thumb, trying to make it thin, thinner than the dough strips on top of Grandma's apple pie. Too much sand and the rope will crumble. Too much clay and the strip will shape easily. Something in between with a good mixture of sand, silt, and clay is loam, the preferred soil texture for gardening and farming.

Soil Problems

Inadequate Drainage

Good drainage is necessary for plant health, roadways, building foundations, human bladders, basement drains, and septic tank leach fields. Land that retains large puddles for days after a rain breeds mosquitoes. Plant indicators of soil that is generally too wet for most fruit trees and vegetables include curly dock, horsetail, cattails, rushes, wire grass, and willows. Unless drainage problems can be easily corrected, such property should not be considered as a growing site.

Erosion

Despite forty years of conservation education, only about one quarter of U.S. agricultural land is managed according to sustainable soil-management practices. One thousand acres of new Louisiana delta land is created each year, formed from eroded Midwest topsoil carried there by the Mississippi.

Both erosion and loss of organic matter are serious threats to continued productivity. Minor erosion can often be reversed by seeding and regular mowing. Mow across the slope. I have halted erosion on the five or so sloping acres around our house by frequent summer mowing, which has thickened the grass stand, raised the humus level, and stopped runoff in all but the heaviest rains. A certain indicator that more rainfall is being absorbed is the increased flow from a small spring below "the backyard," a field of about two acres.

Severe erosion can be stopped, even reversed, but the process can be costly and time-consuming. If the land price is very good it may be worth considering. Consult with the local extension agent and conservation office on area soils prone to erode and what it will take to correct the condition.

After you move to your land, to avoid creating erosion channels on dirt roadways, get into the habit of always driving slightly to one side of previous wheel tracks. Encourage visitors to do the same.

Chemical Contamination

Land that has been farmed may be contaminated with herbicides, pesticides, and the salts and residues of chemical fertilizers. Potatoes, tomatoes, corn, beans, carrots, and other crops commonly receive chemical fertilizers and pesticides. If you are unable to obtain reliable crop and soil treatment history by talking to the owner and neighbors, soil tests will reveal the condition of the soil. It is safest to consider farmland guilty until proven innocent.

Vegetation

Plants respond to moisture, sunlight, soil type, and growing season. The primary visual difference between the arid West and the moist East and Northwest is the quality and quantity of vegetation. Much of the Southwest is cactus or chaparral. Western mountainous areas typically have trees on the west side, where most of the limited rain falls. Valleys often have the best soil and the best vegetation. The plains area was once famous for lush grass but farmers have destroyed most native grasses to plant grain crops. From eastern Oklahoma to the Atlantic, most states have substantial forests, although in farming country only scattered woodlots remain. Each state map at the end of this book shows wooded percentages. There are 490 million acres of timberland in the U.S. but less than 5 percent of the virgin forests remains.

I would rather have land with an overabundance of vegetation than a small amount. Land can be cleared if necessary but trees take decades to mature, and trees, shrubs, and grasses all contribute to soil fertility and water absorption. In addition to contributing to the scenery you look at each day, the vegetation on your land may contribute many valuable products.

Building materials and fuel

In a poll of 1,000 people, 29 percent said their ideal home was a log home in the woods. There are many areas with more than adequate trees with which to build a home. States with enough trees suitable for logs that log home companies thrive there include Washington, Oregon, California, Montana, Minnesota, Wisconsin, Michigan, Missouri, Arkansas, Tennessee, North Carolina, Pennsylvania, New York, Vermont, and Maine. I'm sure I've missed some and I do apologize.

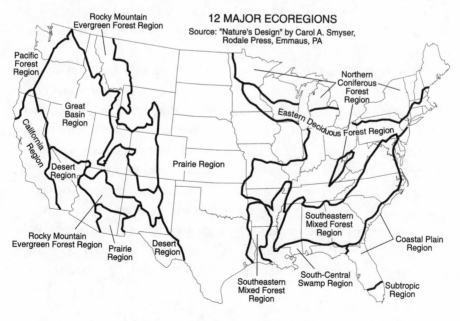

Altogether, some 500 log house companies offer homes made of local trees. (See Chapter 20 for information on log home companies.)

In addition to the great Northwest forests, large forested tracts still exist in most of the eastern half of the United States. If a log house is not your thing, local sawmills will convert logs into rough-sawn or milled lumber to your specifications, often at very reasonable rates. And there are several designs for home sawmills available with which homesteaders can make lumber themselves.

The best trees for firewood are the hardwoods—and in my opinion the best of the best is oak, three cords of which I cut and split each year. Hardwood trees are found throughout the northeast quarter of the country and south to northern Mississippi, Alabama, and Georgia. The ecoregion map shows major forest types and areas.

Food from Woods and Fields

Just about any area that has trees grows some kind of nut tree. The South is justly famous for its pecans. The Midwest and northern areas have black walnuts. On our place, although we have some fine old black walnut trees, the favorite for eating is the meat of the butternut, a smaller tree which grows along the stream. The natives call it white walnut. The shell is more elliptical and the meat is sweeter than a black walnut. The light brown wood is softer than black walnut and carves nicely.

Maple trees are beautiful in all seasons, glorious in autumn, make great furniture, and provide sap for syrup and sugar. I have no personal experience with sugaring but if you settle in the Northeast you will most likely have neighbors who can teach you how to tap trees and cook the sap down.

Natural fruit in our part of the Ozarks includes berries, grapes, persimmons, and pawpaws, sort of a wild banana. Our favorite is mulberries from a big old tree behind the house. Besides its fruit it gives us entertainment—we enjoy watching red squirrels use hanging tricks to reach the ripest berries out at the ends of limbs, while crows angrily protest from the top of the tree. Wild mushrooms, gathered with the knowledge to choose the correct ones, are a special treat. Morels, chanterelles, and coral mushrooms are all popular in our area. One of our spring treats here at Heartwood is fresh morel and asparagus omelets. We are also blessed with watercress in the stream and at the little spring below the backyard. Fresh watercress is superb, far superior to the limp impostor lying dead in supermarket produce bins.

Other areas have wild huckleberries, blueberries, dewberries, Juneberries, pecans, piñon nuts, and local favorites such as lotus and cattails. A good source of information on wild edibles is *Nature's Design: A Practical Guide to Natural Landscaping*, by Carol A. Smyser, published by Rodale Press.

House Sites

Think carefully about whether you wish to build a home. An existing house will often be sitting on the best building site on the property, creating the dilemma of whether to keep it as is, remodel, tear it down, or move it.

Land without a house will need to have at least one good building site unless you intend to live in a cave. Then the land will need a good cave—or a good cave site where you can build a cave. The ideal building site has enough fairly level land for not only a house, but garden, orchard, and outbuildings such as garage, workshop, henhouse, barn.

Perfectly flat land is actually a negative, as it inhibits drainage. This may create a wet basement or unstable foundation condition. Unless you use a composting toilet, which I recommend, you will probably need a septic tank, which uses a leach field system to drain wastewater. Sloping land is much more likely to drain well. Land that slopes more than slightly should be inspected for stability, as certain conditions create creep, or slide areas, often too unstable for houses without expensive foundations.

The best house site faces south to receive sun for light, gardening, and solar heating. A slight slope to the southeast is ideal, as it warms quickly in the morning. North-facing slopes are cool in summer but cold and possibly wet in winter, and a garden might have to be quite far from the house to be out in the sunlight. In a place where cooling degree days exceed heating degree days, a house on a north-facing slope might make energy sense. West-facing homes cook in the hot afternoon sun unless substantial shading is provided.

Access Roads

Access challenges occur with roads on north-facing slopes that ice up in the winter, then don't get enough sun to thaw; ill-drained roadways that develop deep muddy ruts; and stream crossings that flood. Any of these conditions warrant buying a four-wheel-drive vehicle—your life will be ever so much easier. In hilly areas with serious winters, unless you have a four-wheel-drive vehicle with a winch on the front and unlimited time and energy to fight your way up a steep, ice-covered road, you will want to give consideration to the cost of building and maintaining a good, year-round access road to your dream property.

The price we pay for our secluded valley setting is a north-slope road that drops over 300 feet in four tenths of a mile, then crosses a stream that sometimes floods. The worst condition occurs when snow melts during the day, freezes that night, then new snow falls on top of the ice, insulating it from daytime warmth. One Christmas season we were isolated for over a week while this condition persisted. Then we got an ice storm. The road was so slippery it could not be walked on at all. Visiting friends were directed into a neighbor's flat field up at the top, then we all carried their luggage (and gift case of wine) down through crusty snow in hillside woods to the point where our four-wheel-drive truck had been able to ascend. We had a great visit; it was one of those memorable occasions appreciated all the more for the outrageous conditions. The wine only helped.

You too may find a place that is your ideal in every way but access conditions. If you need not get out to a job, then the only major consideration is what to do in case of a medical emergency. In our case, though it would be slow, there is an old logging road on a south-facing slope that leads to the top of the north ridge, with negotiable woods between it and an old ridge road, which eventually leads to a county road. In case of extreme emergency, there is a helicopter at a hospital twenty-five miles away but only minutes by air.

One advantage of our difficult access road is protection from unannounced visits. Because of the slow, steep descent and the landform, we can hear gravel crunching under tires for about ten minutes before the vehicle comes into view across the stream—plenty of time to become prepared for "Surprise!" visitors.

Scenic Beauty

One of the biggest bonuses of country life is being surrounded by natural beauty—for many of us a primary motivation for living here. Someone has even coined a term—terrain therapy—as a name for the healing that occurs when we look at natural scenes. Being in a place of scenic beauty helps to overcome depression and improve various aspects of our health. It is now believed that the immune system is strengthened by the positive emotions produced by looking at the natural world.

Climate and scenery typically go together—dry and warm to hot usually dictates desert, mild often means southern coastal, and so on. The climate you embrace may prescribe the scenery you enjoy. The exception is four diverse seasons with cold winters—at Christmastime you could find yourself skiing white powder in the West, ice-sailing the frozen blue topping of a Northeast lake, or deciphering the puzzle of bird and animal tracks in a fresh Midwest woodland snow.

Now, on your criteria worksheet, write your landform, soil, and vegetation preferences.

Resources

Soil information and land classification maps are available from state conservation offices, local university extension services (sometimes called agricultural extension service, or just "extension office"), county land conservation offices, or from:

USDA Soil Conservation Service
Room 5105, South Bldg.
Washington, DC 20250
202-720-4525

The United States Geological Survey produces thousands of new and revised topographic maps and materials about mineral, land, and water resources. This earth science information is available in a variety of books, maps, and other formats, and many states have one or more Earth Science Information Centers. Call: 800-USA-MAPS.

If you have a CD-ROM drive, the latest U.S. Atlas disk contains maps of tectonic plates and other physiographic data, and is available anywhere computer software is sold. Many libraries have atlases such as *The National Atlas of the United States of America*, which contains 765 maps and charts.

Essential Country Skill #3: pumping water
Instructions: Grasp the pump handle as shown. Raise the handle. Push the handle down. Repeat until bucket is full. If the bucket does not fill, see Essential Country Skill #53: repairing wooden buckets.

-11-
The Cost of Living

"It's a great country, but you can't live in it for nothing."

—Will Rogers

The common goal of living large while spending small is most attainable in a rural place. Land and housing costs may be only one quarter of urban prices. Should you choose to produce much of your food and fuel, your rural overhead may be less than half your previous urban budget.

Professor and author Jack Lessinger portrays a certain group of modern Americans in *Penturbia*: "Caring Conservers have found a way to deal with over-consumption by the most astonishing feat of social alchemy. . . . [They] *change their sense of values*—by consensus. Faced with the necessity of buying less of what they prefer, people change what they prefer. . . . Caring Conservers don't turn grudgingly to their substitutes. *They adore them.*"

That reminds me of Faith Popcorn's concept of "Small Indulgences," in *The Popcorn Report.* We Americans are adjusting to the growing inequity of income and status between the upper and lower classes in creative and sensible ways, which is part of the reason that city-to-country migration is accelerating.

"Voluntary simplicity" is a phrase back in vogue. (Richard Gregg coined it in a 1936 article and it was the title of a 1981 book by Duane Elgin.) Gerald Celente, Director of Trends Research Institute, says, "Voluntary simplicity doesn't mean deprivation. It means buying things you really need, rather than things you simply want. It means reducing debt and dumping household clutter.

"It means spending time with family, gardening, canning and preserving foods, buying used items, bartering and bargaining. It means staying physically, spiritually and mentally fit" (*The Ithaca Journal*, 10-28-95).

Catherine Roberts Leach writes, "Voluntary simplicity is a viable, responsible choice. Many of us are ready for big changes and another chance. We're in it for the long haul. Intuitively we know that finding the work we value, the place we feel at home, the contribution we wish to make, will depend on our discovering pride and pleasure in the way the world works. And in the way we can participate. Simply" (*Country Connections*, March/April 1996).

Farmers and other rural people have been living simply for generations but few have done so as a matter of conscience. Voluntary simplicity is nothing special to country folks; it is often simply the natural way of life. Traditional ruralites work to live, not to accumulate.

Planning your move to the country is an excellent time to consider a cost-of-living adjustment. The reasons for moving to the country speak to values, how we relate to the condition of our self and our family, and to social, economic, political, and ecological conditions. In the next chapter we explore options for making a living. Lowering one's cost of living makes earning a living simpler. It may also allow us to pursue interests long repressed. This is a good time to weigh the pros and cons of working at home. One of the cons is uncertainty of income, a condition tolerated more easily from a position of modest needs.

Country Usually Costs Less . . .

Real Estate

For the price of a city lot you can buy many country acres if you avoid chic addresses and hot spots. The range of rural land prices is about $200 to $3,000 per acre, depending on distance from cities, size of parcel, soil quality, water quantity and quality, access, vegetation, and improvements. New homes cost about the same to build, with lower rural labor rates offset by higher costs of materials due to shipping expenses. Using local materials lowers the outlay. Older homes' prices typically reflect the economic condition of the area. Some old farms are priced according to the number of acres, with very little value given to the old buildings. You can save money if you are willing and able to take on a sound but outdated older house and bring it up to modern standards. Property taxes are less in the country, as are the services they pay for.

Food

Gardening is one of the great country living experiences (see Chapter 13). Growing a substantial part of your food will save you money, make you healthier, and likely give you a lot of satisfaction. If you plan to buy all your food be aware that grocery prices are often higher and selection and quality lower in remote areas, where delivery trucks travel more miles.

Clothing

The farther the city, the simpler the cloth. Power ties and designer suits create amusement where everyone else is in blue jeans and casual tops. Working at home will especially save on wardrobe costs. A pair of boots or sports shoes costs less than several pairs of high heels. An exception may exist if you plan to work in a bank. Bank employees in our area seem to have succumbed to city fashion fears.

Vehicle Purchase and Maintenance

This item can go either way. If you work at home you won't need a late model car. If you commute or operate a home business that requires substantial travel, your needs will be greater. If you have high-school-age children, expect to put on plenty of miles taking them to school functions.

The best single vehicle for the country is a pickup truck. If you need four-wheel drive, expect to pay a premium. How often you need to buy a new vehicle depends on miles driven, the condition of the roads driven on, and your maintenance mode. Country values contribute to the tendency to drive a vehicle longer, which saves on purchase costs but adds maintenance costs. Gravel and dirt roads are hard on tires and suspension systems. Air filters, oil, and oil filters need to be changed more often because of dust. Scrupulous maintenance saves money. Changing oil and oil filters every 3,000 miles is far less expensive than changing vehicles every three or four years.

Vehicle Insurance

Car insurance is substantially less than in the city, where the high rate of thefts and repair costs drive premiums up. Pickup truck insurance may be even less than for a passenger car if you buy property in an agricultural state; such states often have special insurance rules for farm vehicles used within a certain mileage radius of your "farm."

Utilities

Private water systems are safer and less costly than buying water from a municipal system. Some city people we know spend $100 per month on bottled water. It will cost far less than that to pump from your own well, stream, or cistern for household needs and garden irrigation.

There is generally no trash pickup in the country and that's a blessing. Rather than sending it "away" to a landfill we can compost all vegetable garbage, sort for recycling most paper, metal, plastic, and glass, and return batteries, appliances, and other dead items to where they may be recycled. In some areas the volunteer fire departments bolster their operating budgets through the sale of recyclable materials and are happy to accept appropriate items. As demand for old newsprint and other recyclables has risen, many new recycling centers have opened.

If you heat with wood cut from your own woodlot you can save hundreds of dollars on your yearly heating costs. But the biggest factor here is your choice of climate.

Furniture

Country homes are typically furnished more casually than city homes. In many areas, craftspeople make furniture from local woods. Buying directly cuts out the cost of all the wholesale and marketing middlepeople. In many rural areas there are auctions throughout the summer where furniture may be purchased at modest prices.

Contract Labor

Rural wages are lower than in the city. Plumbers, electricians, carpenters, painters, and others may charge half or less of city wages. This is a regional factor and also depends on how far out you are from the city. The flip side of the coin is that if you hire yourself out you also receive less.

Recreation/Entertainment

Rather than spectator activities, country recreation tends toward personal activities: hunting, fishing and other water sports, hiking, picnicking, sightseeing. Cable TV is often unavailable but satellite antennas are good buys. Entertainment costs will be higher if you make frequent visits to the city, for gas, meals, tickets, overnight lodging.

In our neck of the woods summer socializing runs heavily to community potlucks and volleyball or other sports, then making music. Wintertime get-togethers feature dinner and just plain talkin' and occasional parties, often benefits.

Mostly we prefer to stay home. Some of our finest summer evenings are spent sitting in the porch swing, counting trees and watching the grass grow. What with the state of the world, a body needs to dissipate tension.

... But Sometimes Country Costs More

Real Estate

Beware: trendy rural places are fast becoming expensive, both in real estate prices and living costs. In addition to the entertainment figures mentioned earlier, California migrants with more impatience and equity money than common sense have caused prices to quickly climb in Washington, Oregon, Montana, Wyoming, Idaho, Nevada, Arizona, New Mexico, and Colorado. One relocation service advises Californians to change vehicle license plates before visiting—locals hate Californians that much. Real estate agents love 'em. Price is but one of the many reasons to avoid hot spots.

Utilities

Your monthly rural telephone bill may be larger. Until you become established in your new community most of your calls are likely to be long distance. Get your city friends on e-mail and save bucks and interruptions. Yeah, I know, it's not the same.

Regarding service: rural electric and phone service are both subject to greater interruption from weather conditions. Private-line phone service taken for granted in the city may be temporarily unavailable in some areas and very expensive in others. This is an especially important factor if you plan to run a home business or use a fax or modem.

Electric costs may be somewhat higher in sparsely populated areas where it takes more poles and wire to serve fewer customers. Electric air-conditioning costs are therefore higher. Electric heating is inefficient and the most expensive of all heating systems, to be avoided if possible. Our electric company is a user-owned co-op and our rates are very low, have not been raised since 1985.

Residential photovoltaic systems have become cost-effective for many applications. Properties beyond power lines are good candidates for a home power generation system. The *Sunelco Planning Guide and Product Catalog* (see Appendix A, "Resources") uses one-third mile of utility line extension as the rule-of-thumb guideline for cost-effectiveness. Weigh the cost of bringing in a power line with the cost of your own system, including a gas/diesel/propane generator to back up the PV system when the sun shines not.

Bottom Lines

It generally costs less money to live in the country than in the city. How much less depends on how much you pay for your property, which tax/service concept you buy into (see Chapter 19), whether you subscribe to voluntary simplicity, and how independent you become. Gardening and cutting firewood can be first steps to lowering personal and environmental costs. Investing in solar heating, photovoltaic, or wind electric generation equipment, and especially energy-efficiency upgrades to your house can further lower monthly costs dramatically while also helping to heal the planet. Transportation costs are typically next highest; the lifestyle you choose will dictate what you drive. Or ride.

The true cost of living includes the economic, health, and cleanup costs to our environment and our communities. We can express and implement our values not only by how we spend our money but how we avoid the necessity for money and how we conduct ourselves in our homes, on our land, in our community. Buying locally will help keep our community economy healthy.

We have been urged to "think globally, act locally." In *Sex, Economy, Freedom and Community* Wendell Berry offers this perspective: "If we could think locally, we would take far better care of things than we do now. The right local questions and answers will be the right global ones. The Amish question 'What will this do to our community?' tends toward the right answer for the world. . . . In order to make ecological good sense for the planet, you must make ecological good sense locally. You can't act locally by thinking globally. No one can make ecological good sense for the planet. Everyone can make ecological good sense locally, if the affection, the scale, the knowledge, the tools, and the skills are right."

Resources

The Statistical Abstract of the United States is published annually by the U.S. Bureau of the Census. It includes a cost-of-living index. It is available from:

Superintendent of Documents

> P.O. Box 371954
> Pittsburgh, PA 15250-7954
> Or call: Census Customer Services Dept.: 301-457-4100, or fax: 301-457-3842

For a free "Subject Bibliography" of government publications on the cost of living, write to:

> Superintendent of Documents
> U.S. Government Printing Office
> Washington, DC 20402
> Phone: 202-512-1800, fax: 202-512-2250
> Fax-on-demand program, twenty-four hours a day:
> U.S. Fax Watch: 202-512-1716

Point your browser at http://www2.homefair.com/calc/salcalc.html and quickly learn what a given salary in your present location will mean in your desired destination. The site is called The Salary Calculator.

> *"Got no check books, got no banks.*
> *Still I'd like to express my thanks—*
> *I got the sun in the mornin' and the moon at night."*
>
> —IRVING BERLIN

— 12 —

Making a Living

"I would live all my life in nonchalance and insouciance,
Were it not for making a living, which is
rather a nouciance."

—OGDEN NASH

"Don't go around saying the world owes you a living;
the world owes you nothing; it was here first."

—MARK TWAIN

We proud Americans, in the land of the free and the home of the brave, descendants of men and women who paid for our freedom with their lives, lemming-like allow our employers to dictate where we will live. The modern American, designating money as the overriding consideration, willingly uproots children from school and family from community to go where the company dictates that one must go to do its work. Until the layoff. The good of the company becomes the downfall of the family and the community. Social scientists now believe that the high incidence of mental illness in the U.S. is tied to the loss of that sense of belonging to a community that results from following jobs.

"Money often costs too much."

—RALPH WALDO EMERSON

A most fulfilling life comes with living and working in one's ideal place. A vocation is sane and fulfilling if it is performed in one's community, is useful to the community, uses local resources at a level that can be sustained without hurting ecosystem or people. As with most human activities, if it is good for the community it is good for the nation and ultimately good for the world.

Wendell Berry has considered the ramifications of how and where modern Americans work. In *The Unsettling of America* he exhorts: "What is new is the *guise* of the evil: a limitless technology, dependent upon a limitless morality, which is to say upon no morality at all. How did such a possibility become thinkable? It seems to me that it is implicit in the modern separation of life and work. It is implicit in the assumption that we can live entirely apart from our way of making a living. . . . If human values are removed from production, how can they be preserved in consumption? How can we value our lives if we devalue them in making a living? If we do not live where we work, and when we work, we are wasting our lives, and our work too."

Your ideal country home place may not immediately seem to allow an opportunity for you to make a living. Best-priced property is often located in economically depressed areas where jobs are few, wages are low, prices paid for locally produced products are modest. Intentionally reducing one's level of consumption may be an unnerving process, especially for those who have always lived in cities and have no memory of the quality of a simpler life, but a reduction of expenditures can be a great contribution to personal growth by allowing greater latitude in one's vocation.

Talking to a variety of people living in an area may reveal work or business opportunities not readily apparent. If you have several skills or are adaptable, talk to people who would like to do business with you if you settle there. Bankers, insurance people, shopkeepers, and chambers of commerce personnel often know of possibilities. Living the ideal life includes working at something you enjoy. Use this time to consider and find your ideal work.

If finding immediate employment is a criterion, your ideal place may be near a known job market. If your skill is vital, like nursing or automotive repair, you should have little trouble finding work almost anywhere. If your skill is in reasonable demand you may wish to concentrate your search in rural areas outside edge cities, where employment opportunities and wages are better than in the country.

Rural work options today are truly unlimited. Indeed, only 10 percent of the U.S. rural workforce is in farming or mining. Now may be the time to teach yourself a new business or a new skill. Learn or expand computer skills—computers operate just as well in a log cabin as in a skyscraper. Being highly computer proficient is arguably today's greatest job security. IBM has cut 180,000 workers since 1987 but had trouble finding the 10,000 people it needed to hire to run its computer services department.

American Demographics, March 1996, reported: "Many of the fastest-growing occupations are small and specialized, while the greatest numbers of jobs will be added in lower-level occupations. But there are 8 that are on both top 30 lists for fastest- and greatest-growing: personal and home care aides, home health aides, systems analysts, computer engineers, special education teachers, correction officers, guards, and teacher aides. If you're looking for a new career, these are the safest bets."

Take an existing business to the country, or buy one once you get there. Again, this is a good time to consider what gives you the most satisfaction and to possibly make a major career improvement. That said, we will devote most of this chapter to identifying existing work opportunities.

Where Are the Jobs?

"He worked like hell in the country
so he could live in the city, where he worked like hell
so he could live in the country."

—DON MARQUIS

Most employment opportunities have previously been in metropolitan areas. Modern industry follows tax incentives, local inducements, low land costs, low wages, minimal regulations. There has been a substantial shift of manufacturing to rural and small-town areas. About 700 of our 2,304 nonmetropolitan counties now power their economies with manufacturing. Company headquarters and production facilities have also moved beyond the suburbs, into real country or within easy commuting distance to country. And commuting to a town or small city is quite different from commuting to New York or Los Angeles.

In *Rural and Small Town America*, Fuguitt, Brown, and Beale relate population movement to jobs: "Much of the recent transition in rural and nonmetropolitan America is intertwined with changes in industry." The trend of big business to move to rural areas is well established and shows no sign of reversing. All this is good news for the would-be country dweller.

Industry chases low wages predominantly, but other factors weigh in. States with right-to-work laws are pulling jobs from unionized areas because of union manning requirements, job classifications, advancement procedures, and task definitions. And there appears to be a backlash by professionals against steel, concrete, and glass surrounded by blaring traffic. Many high-tech firms are moving to rural areas because of the preference by managers and engineers and their spouses for attractive living areas. CEOs and board chairmen have decided to take their businesses where people want to live—and where they and their families want to live. The result of all this is that "since 1988, job growth in non-metropolitan areas has outpaced that in metro areas" ("The Boonies Are Booming," *Business Week*, 10-9-95).

Government tabulations as early as the late 1960s showed that manufacturing employment was growing more rapidly in the countryside than in metropolitan areas. City bureaucrats noticed also, took action to recapture those new tax bases, and petitioned the government to allow them to expand their areas. This is one reason why today's so-called metropolitan areas include large areas not even remotely metropolitan in nature. As examples, Kansas City and St. Louis metropolitan areas include ten and eleven counties respectively, many of which are decidedly rural.

In *The New Corporate Frontier: The Big Move to Small Town, USA*, CEO/author David A. Heenan says: "What we are seeing unfold is the selective preference for penturbia, particularly for those medium- and small-sized communities capable of providing the career opportunities and social amenities normally associated with big cities and suburbs. The most favored frontier towns are often linked to a major university, a state capital, a research park, or a similar institution that tends to provide the diversity and cultural spark sought by young professionals."

The primary place of American jobs has become edge cities, those places defined by Joel Garreau as out by the suburbs, where developers have created shopping malls and office parks. Garreau says there are more than 200 new edge cities, already holding two thirds of all American office facilities. Eighty percent of these new centers have emerged in the last twenty years. One of Garreau's qualifying criteria for edge cities is that they have more jobs than bedrooms. The expected pattern was for city dwellers to commute out to the jobs. Instead, city slickers have become clod kickers and commute in to the jobs from country homes.

In years past, corporations left the towns where they started and moved to big cities. After World War II, they started moving to the cleaner air, lower costs, and golf courses of the suburbs. These days, states Heenan, they're headed back to the hinterland. He feels that the U.S. could emerge as "the first postindustrial country without important cities." He feels that the perceived need for a big-city environment was always exaggerated anyway.

New York City, often referred to as the barometer of the nation, exemplifies the move outward. In 1960, 27 percent of the Fortune 500 industrial companies were located there; in 1970, 23 percent; in 1980, 16 percent; and in 1990, only 9 percent. Other large U.S. cities reflect a similar trend. Almost half of the Chicago area's forty-four Fortune 500 companies are outside of the city.

Big-business advisor Peter Drucker predicts that the city of the future will be occupied by headquarters of major companies with much of the clerical, accounting, and administration staff located in the suburbs or even thousands of miles away from major urban centers.

Examples of Companies Located in or Near Rural Areas

The following examples of companies in low-population-density areas are presented here to give you specific places where jobs may be available. If one of these towns is in your area of interest you may wish to write the company human resources department to determine employment potential.

L.L. Bean, the $600 million mail order empire, is run from Freeport, Maine, population 6,905. Wal-Mart is headquartered in Bentonville, Arkansas (11,257). With a name like Smuckers, you might know that the jam and jelly king is in the country—Orrville, Ohio, where 7,700 people think the name is beautiful. Corning, New York (12,000), is home to Corning Glass Works. Silk-screening is the business of Bacova Guild, Ltd., located in Bacova, Virginia. It does almost $17 million a year in this town of—fifty! Gerber Products is in Fremont, Michigan (3,875). Ben & Jerry's dandy dessert is swirled in Waterbury, Vermont (1,702).

Maytag, the $3 billion appliance maker, is headquartered in Newton, Iowa (14,800). The fastest growing supermarket in the country is Food Lion, based in Salisbury, North Carolina (25,000). Springdale, Arkansas (29,945), is home to Tyson Foods, the nation's largest chicken processor. The Andersen Window Company people call Bayport, Minnesota, home (3,205). Weaver Popcorn Company ($70-plus million sales) is in Van Buren, Indiana (935).

Johns-Manville located its international headquarters twenty miles outside of Denver; Kodak and IBM built new plants ten miles farther out. Dow Chemical's headquarters is in Midland, Michigan (38,053). Phillips Petroleum is in Bartlesville, Oklahoma (34,256). Toolmaker Adamus Carbide Corporation left its Kenilworth, New Jersey, home for the open space, reasonable wages, and hardworking people of Oak Ridge, Tennessee (27,310). Motorola put its new computer chip plant in Harvard, Illinois (5,975).

The big automotive story of 1985 was GM's announcement that it would build its $3 billion Saturn plant in Spring Hill, Tennessee (1,275). Disappointing locals, GM imported most of the workers, but the payroll created an array of new jobs in the community.

In "California in the Rearview Mirror," *Newsweek* (7-19-93) reported that in five years Coeur d'Alene, Idaho, and surrounding Kootenai County have nabbed 2,000 California jobs in fields as diverse as swimwear and computer software.

In 1995, Home Depot opened in Columbia, Missouri, and Waterloo, Iowa, a new type of store called Crossroads, featuring tools and materials for ruralites. Sears, Roebuck & Company, which in 1993 closed its catalogue operations, plans to have 800 new rural stores open by 1999.

Not only American companies create jobs outside cities. History professor Jon C. Teaford, in *Cities of the Heartland*, reports that Japanese automakers invested in America's heartland during the 1980s, but they studiously avoided locating their facilities in major urban areas. Instead, they chose to build their factories in cornfields outside Marysville, Ohio, Lafayette, Indiana, and Bloomington, Illinois. The Japanese clearly preferred areas where labor unions were weak, where the population was rock-rib Republican, and where the workers would be overwhelmingly white. This they found in the rural Midwest.

States Bidding for Payrolls—Smokestack Chasing

*"Industrial plants and other nonfarm businesses do not bring utopia
to the countryside any more than they have
to the cities. If they lack competition for labor force, they may
be exploitative—offering low wages and benefits."*

—CALVIN BEALE

Payrolls have become auction items for states wooing big companies to their nonurban areas. In 1991, Toyota decided to build an assembly plant in Georgetown, Kentucky—after the state had contributed $300 million. In 1992, South Carolina tossed out $130 million to snare a BMW plant.

Intel, the computer chip giant, announced in April 1993 that it was building a $1 billion, 1,000-employee plant in New Mexico, despite an ardent courtship by California. Rio Rancho used a $114 million tax-incentive package to get the deal. The Albuquerque suburb is a classic example of the new edge cities—in 1970 Rio Rancho's population was 2,000; by 1992 it was 38,000.

The Wall Street Journal (11-24-93) reported that Alabama promised over $300 million in various incentives to outbid North Carolina and become the site of the first U.S. Mercedes-Benz car plant. Somehow I doubt that M-B will follow Henry Ford's philosophy and pay employees enough to purchase the product they make. Besides the state package, I'm betting they moved there primarily for low wages.

Beware of Boom Towns

In *Places Rated Almanac*, Richard Boyer and David Savageau point out that in a boom town there are "rising personal incomes, which ensure real estate appreciation; expanding personal employment opportunities; improved infrastructures; somewhat lower violent crime; increasing amenities; and high-quality health care and education. On the other hand, the disadvantages of living in a boom town include rising costs of living; increased property crime rates;

environmental pollution; and, maybe worst of all, noticeable loss of personal discretionary time."

By the way, *Places Rated Almanac* provides an excellent example of the peril of making and depending on economic predictions. The book, published in 1989, predicted that the Los Angeles–Long Beach area would create the greatest number of new jobs in the country, 407,770. Then the Cold War ended, defense cutbacks were announced, and southern California entered its most difficult economic time in memory. By November 1993, southern California's 9.5 percent unemployment rate was the nation's worst.

Boom towns can even more quickly become bust towns, especially if most jobs are dependent on one or two commodities or companies. Wyoming's oil and coal industries yo-yo the state economy. The West Virginia coal area boomed during the 1974 oil shortage and headed back down as soon as it ended. Oil-influenced Texas has more empty bank-owned houses than any other state.

Any area that is dependent upon infinite supplies of a finite material is on thin economic ice. The mining and logging towns of the West are almost a cliché in this regard. The states in the Rockies notably have boomed from mining operations, and busted when the ore ran out. Jim Robbins notes in *The Last Refuge*: "If a town loses a sawmill or mine with one hundred workers, and it is the largest employer, the shutdown can be devastating. On the other hand, if there are ten small businesses, each with ten employees, the economy is more resilient and the power of any one company is reduced."

Our world is changing quickly. Don't trust your economic future to one company. The shoe factory or television assembly plant that you depend on for wages to buy groceries may move to Mexico or Bangladesh. Already, much shoe and clothing production has moved to Asia.

One-horse towns are fine (and superior to no-horse towns), but be skeptical of one-industry towns. The ideal home is in an area with a diversified economy.

Home Workers and Home Businesses

> *"Linked by telephones, fax machines, Federal Express, and computers, a new breed of information worker is reorganizing the landscape of America. Free to live almost anywhere, more and more*

*individuals are deciding to live in small cities
and towns and rural areas."*

—JOHN NAISBITT AND PATRICIA ABURDENE, *Megatrends 2000*

Citing savings on office costs and increased efficiency, many companies are embracing the concept of workers working at home. In mid-1991, John Niles, president of Global Telematics, said that 5.5 million people telecommuted and the number would double by 1995. *American Demographics* (8-93) reported Bureau of Labor Statistics data showing that 20 million people worked at home full- or part-time in 1991. The bureau does not count telecommuters. LINK Resources, a New York City–based research and consulting firm, reported that more than 39 million were working at home full- or part-time in 1993, including about eight million telecommuters. By 1995, LINK reported, the number of telecommuters rose to 11 million. John Niles's prediction was right on.

With computers, fax modems, and overnight mail delivery, many workers can now operate from their homes almost anywhere. Visionaries see fiber optics connecting head offices and home offices. The virtual workplace already exists— VeriFone, the company that makes those little terminals that merchants use to verify credit card purchases, is based in Redwood City, California. All 1,500 workers have personal computers hooked up to the Internet. Not only do the staff members perform their duties at home, the chief information officer works from his home in New Mexico. E-mail communication is nearly instantaneous and work documents can be sent via fax modem in less than a minute.

Technotribalism is a word coined by Gerald Celente in *Trends 2000* to describe near-future rural communities centered around computer technology. Celente predicts that televideophony will sweep the nation and largely replace the need for personal business meetings.

Lynie Arden writes in *The Work-at-Home Sourcebook* that as many as 500 large corporations offer some kind of work-at-home option to employees. She includes in her book over 1,000 smaller companies which have work-at-home arrangements available. Corporations cite an average 20 percent increase in productivity by home workers. Blue Cross/Blue Shield of South Carolina reported productivity gains of 50 percent. Other advantages for companies include very low turnover and near-zero absenteeism. Companies typically have savings in rent, utilities, maintenance, recruitment, training, and insurance.

Fort Collins, Colorado, is the first city to institute routine telecommuting. Several hundred city workers work at home with computer systems supplied by the city. Just about everybody is eligible to participate except fire fighters and police.

Cottage industry is growing. Many companies now employ home workers to craft marketable products. Chris and I for years bought casual cotton clothing from Deva, a rural company that uses home workers to cut and sew the patterns.

Village of the Smoky Hills, in Osage, Minnesota, was created by a group of mothers to market their crafts in a unique way. In only five months The Founding Mothers, Inc. wrote a business plan, found land, got a zoning variance, obtained a loan, built buildings, hired and trained employees. Over 100,000 customers showed up the first year. About 350 local artisans now bring their products from home to be sold at the Village. Customers pay for the privilege of watching artisans demonstrate their skills. A direct mail catalogue is planned.

Over 10 million self-employed Americans operate their businesses from their homes. The number is growing. In *Age Wave*, Ken Dychtwald states that "It is predicted that by the year 2000, over 20 percent of the work force will go to work without leaving home."

If you are one of us who think of a J-O-B as a Journey of the Broke, perhaps you will use this time as a transition to self-employment. If you start your own business, you enter the realm of entrepreneurs, we who have maximum control over our working conditions and hours. Many of us daily exhibit our belief in the inalienable right to work twelve to sixteen hours per day. But they are our hours, doing what we want, for our benefit. The vital factors for success are your level of knowledge, your focus, and your persistence. Most entrepreneurs who succeed have a passion for what they do and they obtain and keep a very high level of knowledge about their field.

If you anticipate working with computers, do not take rural electric or telephone service for granted. Electrical outages from storms are fairly common in areas with long, hard-to-maintain rights-of-way. Telephone line static, which affects modem and fax transmission, is more common in the country. If the fault is old, frayed lines the company may be willing to replace them. Our phone company replaced nearly half a mile of phone lines for us. An uninterruptible power source is a sound investment for computer users.

Working at home with computers spawned a new term: electronic cottage (Alvin Toffler, *The Third Wave*), and now the acronym ACW—Another Computer in the Woods. Having both a computer and an outhouse is an anomaly certain to impress your city friends and relatives, especially your parents. Perhaps one day the ultimate country chic will be to have a computer *in* the outhouse—a laptop, of course. Well, that may be, ahem, carrying it too far. Then again, some of the world's greatest thoughts were conceived during morning "sits."

If you plan on taking a business to the country, check out the competition and consider local conditions. Our nearest neighbor had experience on drill rigs so he bought a drilling outfit and set up a well-drilling business. Unfortunately for him there are two established drillers in the area who are well known and respected, one full-time and the other a farmer who drills part-time. Both know the local geology and usually hit water. After about a year of too few clients and too many dry holes my neighbor pulled up for the last time and sold out.

Instead of finding a job, consider buying one. *Rural Property Bulletin* nationally and bankers and chambers of commerce locally are good sources for leads on businesses and business properties for sale. As soon as you find your ideal area, contact all three for business opportunities. Subscribe to local newspapers and consider placing ads describing what you want.

If you can't find a job or buy one, then make one. Observe trends that create new needs. Invent something. Take my idea of generating electricity at fitness centers and make a living and save oil at the same time. Invent a more efficient solar distiller to make fresh water from salt water, so coastal cities can stop stealing other people's water. Create a job barter system for everyone in your bioregion. Design a kitchen stove that operates with the flue heat of a wood furnace. Figure out uses for the mountains of old tires. Design a homemade paper maker that will use local plant fibers. Perfect a process for recycling plastics and molding roofing shingles from the multicolored result.

Some of our friends' successful home businesses include campground, canoe rental, medicinal herbs, exotic animals, wreaths and dried flower creations, paintings, specialty seeds, sculpture, wooden jewelry, and emergency management consultation. This book was originally homemade and home marketed—a homely book indeed. Here are some other ideas for country home businesses:

appliance repair, auto repair, bed & breakfast, chainsaw repair, child care, chimney cleaning, cider making, desktop publishing, editing, firewood, fish farming, food cooperative, furniture making and repair, homeschooling, horse-shoeing, log home company distributor, mail order sales, market gardening, nursery/florist supply, photography, pottery, recycling, secretarial services, silk screening, sign painting, split-rail fencing, taxidermy, tire repair and sales, transcription, tree farming, weaving, welding, wild berry winemaking, woodcarving, wreathing.

Urbanites still earn more than ruralites but rural income is rising. "In 15 states, rural counties rank highest in per-capita income." And "In 1992, the non-metro unemployment rate was lower than urban unemployment for the first time since before 1980, and it has stayed that way since" (*Business Week*, 10-9-95).

Living the ideal life includes working at something you enjoy—at home or in your community. Stop thinking of yourself as a worker or an employee. Instead, start seeing yourself as the CEO of your livelihood and your life. Use this time of transition to consider what you really want to do. Use the lower cost of country living to give you the slack to develop your ideal work. On your criteria worksheet, write the work conditions you want, unless you are considering farming or market gardening as your work. In that case, read the next chapter before listing your work criteria.

> *"By working faithfully eight hours a day, you may*
> *eventually get to be a boss and work twelve hours a day."*
>
> —ROBERT FROST

Resources and Recommended Reading

Many of the place-rating books listed in the bibliography include employment considerations. Retirement books acknowledge and respond to the fact that most retired folks need to supplement Social Security and pensions.

Rural Property Bulletin
P.O. Box 608
Valentine, NE 69201

Phone: 402-376-2617; e-mail: rural@valentine-ne.com
Web site: http://www.cnweb.com/rural

Books

Arden, Lynie. *The Work-at-Home Sourcebook*. Sixth edition. Boulder, CO: Live Oak Publications, 1996.

Brabec, Barbara. *Homemade Money: The Definitive Guide to Success in a Homebased Business*. Third edition. White Hall, VA: Betterway Publications, 1989. Includes a substantial resource directory.

Germer, Jerry. *Country Careers: Successful Ways to Live and Work in the Country*. New York: John Wiley & Sons, 1993.

Naisbitt, John, and Patricia Aburdene. *Megatrends 2000: Ten New Directions for the 1990's*. New York: William Morrow, 1990.

Ross, Tom, and Marilyn Ross. *Country Bound!* Buena Vista, CO: Communication Creativity, 1992.

G. Scott Thomas. *Where to Make Money: A Rating Guide to Opportunities in America's Metro Areas*. Buffalo, NY: Prometheus Books, 1993. Rates seventy-three metro areas, many of which are accessible from rural areas with a half-hour commute.

"Explore, and explore. . . . Make yourself necessary to the world, and mankind will give you bread."

—Ralph Waldo Emerson

"What's money? A man is a success if he gets up in the morning and goes to bed at night and in between does what he wants to do."

—Bob Dylan

— 13 —

Farming and Market Gardening

"Those who labor in the earth are the chosen people of God,
if He ever had a chosen people, whose breasts He has made His peculiar
deposit for substantial and genuine virtue. It is the focus in which
He keeps alive that sacred fire, which otherwise might escape
from the face of the earth."

—Thomas Jefferson

Good family farmers are among the most admirable of people. Few other lifestyles are so honest with nature's laws—few other lifestyles are so full. The family's needs are met first; surplus is sold in the market for money to buy what the farm does not produce. True family farming is synonymous with subsistence farming. To choose subsistence farming is to commit to hard work and challenging conditions; to do it well requires an abundance of man's most admirable qualities. It is an ideal condition for raising children.

Or so it was until politicians, bureaucrats, and college professors collusively decided they knew best. Jefferson was prescient but incomplete with his warning: "Were we directed from Washington when to sow, and when to reap, we should soon want bread." While most of today's so-called bread is barely worth eating, what the direction from Washington has cost us is hundreds of thousands of our family farms, arguably the foundation of our society.

"Farmers are now members of a capital-intensive industry that values
good bookwork more than backwork. So several times a year
almost every farmer must seek operating credit from the college fellow
in the white shirt and tie—in effect, asking financial
permission to work hard on his own land."

—Andrew H. Malcolm

As an ex-farmer's son who has read the wrenching stories of farm fore-closures, suicides, and killings resulting largely and directly from oppressive governmental interference in farmers' lives, I caution you against farming if what you envision requires you to borrow money, use large machinery, compete with agribusiness, or be involved in any government program. Subsidy programs are seductive and counterproductive. A farmer's acceptance of such programs almost inevitably leads to dependence, loss of freedom, loss of pride and dignity. That cost is too high.

Let us hope that the media coverage of broke and broken farm families has provided adequate warning to those who contemplate farming. I am reminded of the story of the old farmer who had just won $10 million in the state lottery. A reporter asked him what he was going to do now that he was rich. The farmer replied that he guessed he'd "just keep on farming till I go broke."

Contrariwise, as an organic gardener and advocate who sees a swelling demand for chemical-free food, I am optimistic that small-scale producers of food and specialty products can make a decent living and enjoy high-quality lives with their families. If they follow a sound plan, produce multiple high-demand products for nearby markets, and stay clear of government subsidy programs there is good reason to believe that they can do well. Verlyn Klinkenborg's "A Farming Revolution" in the December 1995 *National Geographic* tells the stories of growers across the country who are producing food organically and profitably.

Midsized farms have become an endangered species. (Too bad they are not as protected as, say, the spotted owl.) Today's farmer can either be a small-farm operator or compete with the big boys: agribusiness, industrial agriculture, corporate food production. The odds are strongly against a midsized farmer with modest financial resources. James Bovard, writing in *Government Waste Watch*, reports that "the average full-time farmer—after subtracting liabilities and debts from assets—is a millionaire with a net worth of $1,044,396." Operating on a level above small-scale farming requires substantial dollars—few midsized farms produce sufficient earnings to bridge the years of weather or market disaster. In most cases, investment capital receives a higher return from a simple savings account than from farming. College agriculture professors, machinery sellers, chemical salespeople, bankers, and politicians are prone to give lengthy encouraging advice to midsized farm operators, but such farming is a much tougher life to live than talk to give. (It is not my intent to offend—if I have omitted any qualifying group, I do apologize.)

There are 3,098 counties in the United States. Of our 2,304 nonmetropolitan counties, about 700 are primarily agricultural. In 1995 there were 2,060,810 farm households earning an average of $44,392, with 89 percent of that income coming from off-farm sources. Farming operations range from immense agribusiness operations to very small herb, vegetable, floriculture, and specialty enterprises. To define this range in modern farms, rural sociologists have created a new term—two-tier farming—which relates to scale. It is as important to consider farming from the perspective of personal time commitment.

Full-time Versus Part-time Farming

Full-time farming on a large scale requires a huge financial investment in land and equipment. It means hard work for long hours, often seven days per week. It requires knowledge of soil, crops, farm skills, planning, marketing, and financial management. It means dealing with high land costs, high equipment costs, volatile interest rates, too little rain, too much rain, late freezes, early freezes, government programs and market conditions manipulated by bureaucrats, commodities brokers, and five agribusiness corporations. The margin between survival and failure is narrow. The margin between farm product prices and supermarket prices is wide.

Part-time, small-scale farming is, well, a growing trend. The Census Bureau reported in 1992 that there were 554,207 farms of less than fifty acres. Part-time farmers typically work at primary jobs in nearby areas and tend their crops and livestock evenings and weekends. The rewards are often seen as quality of life rather than just dollars—meaningful work, healthful exercise, high-quality food, and an opportunity to instill traditional values in children.

Agribusiness

> *"Corporate food giants seem determined to turn what used to be the temples of our bodies into way stations for chemical residue."*

—DOUG CAMPBELL, Letters, *Time* (1-29-96)

Do not buy property near an agribusiness operation. Modern food production has an industrialized, corporate structure. Agribusiness is owned by investors who see land as something to be mined for dividends, ignoring all consequential results, expecting and planning for the day when the land will be mined out, and using taxpayers, through government programs, to ensure their continued profits. In spite of efficiency claims made for huge acreages farmed with monster machinery, such farming is not only wasteful but threatens the food supply of future generations. The Land Institute's Wes Jackson is one of those who point out that agribusiness consumes more calories in fossil fuels than it produces in food. We taxpayers underwrite agribusiness owners' profits not only by subsidizing oil prices, but by paying for price support programs, footing the health costs of food tainted by pesticide residue, and dealing with air, soil, and water polluted by farm chemicals. And agribusiness owners are the prime beneficiaries of land grant college research.

In the insane hunger for profit at any cost, veal, pork, poultry, eggs, and milk are now produced in animal factories—intensive, close-confinement operations. The results are literally breathtaking for those who live downwind. In northwest Missouri, six spills of hog wastes killed an estimated 267,000 fish in tributaries to the Grand and Chariton rivers in August and September 1995 (*News-Leader*, Springfield, Missouri, 11-12-95). In North Carolina, the nation's second-largest hog producing state, "The worst hog-waste spill in state history sent 25 million gallons of waste gushing into the New River this week, killing fish and taking the battle over the hog industry to a new level" (*The New York Times*, 6-25-95). Hog feces and urine covered roads and tobacco and soybean fields.

The largest intensive hog operation in the world is being built about 190 miles southwest of Salt Lake City. More than 2.5 million hogs per year will be raised in barns that hold 120,000 at a time. The resulting waste will be greater than that produced by the City of Los Angeles (*USA Today*, 12-30-97).

Five agribusiness mega-corporations control the American food supply. Cargill, the biggest corporate agribusiness, is in sixty countries; ConAgra is in twenty-three. One third of our nation's food is produced by the largest 1 percent of agribusiness operations. Buying supermarket food means supporting agribusiness. Agribusiness runs on fossil fuel. Buying supermarket food means contributing to expenditures of up to twelve calories of fossil fuel for every calorie of corn used in breakfast cereal. Using such wasteful quantities of fossil fuel creates huge health and cleanup costs due to air, water, and soil poisoning, not to mention the enormous diplomatic and military costs of maintaining the oil flow. Even more oil is consumed, more pollution is created, and lower-quality food derives from long-distance shipping of produce. (Yes, Virginia—we slaughtered Iraqis to ensure our access to Kuwaiti oil.)

Agribusiness is insidious. Orville Redenbacher's obituary included the fact that Orville and friend, Charles Bowman, in 1976 sold their popcorn operation to Hunt Wesson Inc., which is now owned by ConAgra (*The Denver Post*, 9-25-95). It's hard to know where your food comes from anymore.

This quote will be a wake-up call for anyone who still thinks the present food production situation should continue (the very careful wording was done to avoid a potential lawsuit): "The alleged philosophy for the agribusiness giant Archer Daniels Midland, uttered on tape by the chairman's son, was supposedly, 'The competitor is our friend, and the customer is our enemy'" (*Time* 10-2-95, "Too Big or Not Too Big?," by Howard Chua-Eoan).

Family Farming

Family farming once was a self-sufficient lifestyle of feeding one's family and providing surplus to nearby communities. Today's "successful" so-called family farm is a specialized business, highly capital- and energy-intensive. It concentrates on the production of one or two market crops, uses machinery to the fullest extent on large fields, and depends on borrowed money for the purchase of equipment, seeds, chemical fertilizer, and pesticides to maximize yields on expensive land. Increasingly, the family that owns the farm lives in a nearby town to save the wife commuting time to her job. Two thirds of U.S. farmers live in cities or towns.

Successful family farmers typically grew up on their farms, love the land they inherited, and continue farming in spite of the many adversities and modest income. A typical Midwestern farmer might have a capital investment in land and equipment of $1.5 million, and sell crops worth $300,000. Net income—depending on production costs, weather, market demand, and other factors—might be $30,000 or less. That's a 2 percent return on capital investment. It has to be a labor of love—they sure aren't getting paid well.

The definition of a farm is a place from which $1,000 or more of farm products were sold in the prior twelve months or would normally be sold. About one half of all U.S. farm families now derive more income from nonfarm sources than from the sale of farm products. The USDA Economic Research Service reports that 89 percent of the average farm operator's 1995 household income of $44,392 came from off-farm sources.

Market Gardening

In *At Nature's Pace*, Gene Logsdon suggests that "gardens are the incubators of the new farm ecology. In Berkeley, California, a city 'farm' of one-third acre grosses more than $300,000 in salad vegetables for Konaki Farms."

Subscription farming, membership garden farming, community gardening, community-supported agriculture—a sensible method of food production that delivers dependable, high-quality food to nearby consumers. In Japan, it's called co-partnership farming. A natural extension of pick-your-own operations, the best method is where a grower contracts with a group of consumers to grow the produce they desire. Types of produce, quantities, and prices are agreed upon before the growing season. The grower knows he has a market and an income. The consumers know they have a source of high-quality, organically produced food at a predetermined cost. If Momma Nature cooperates. Products are harvested at peak flavor and nutrition time, often by the consumer/subscribers. It's a win-win deal, even better than farmers' markets because grower and consumer have a strong relationship.

Small-scale farming, easily confused with part-time farming, can be a viable full-time occupation. Organic fruits and vegetables, sheep and goats, chickens and eggs, flowers, ornamental shrubs, medicinal plants, and exotic animals are suitable for modest-sized operations. A retired professor from Tuskegee Institute has developed a plan for farming on 10 to 200 acres. In his book, *Booker T. Whatley's Handbook on How to Make $100,000 Farming 25 Acres*, Whatley gives complete instructions. Key issues: buy land close to a city so that subscribers to your Clientele Membership Club will drive to your farm to pick their own produce; grow or raise multiple high-value crops or animals that clients demand; bypass all middlemen; and adhere to a sound, year-round plan. Whatley warns that his plan is not for everyone: "You've got to be a good manager to operate one of these farms. You've got to be a good planner and you've got to think for yourself."

Informed consumers are demanding and paying for organically grown produce and animal products. Wendell Berry notes: "There is a rapidly increasing number of consumers who wish to buy food that is nutritionally whole and uncontaminated by pesticides and other toxic chemical residues. And these people would prefer not to pay the exorbitant food prices required by long-distance transportation, processing, packaging, and advertising, all of which result from 'agribusiness' control of food."

The Food Marketing Institute agrees—the people there found that three fourths of all shoppers have a major concern about chemical residues in food. This has created a great demand for food grown the old-fashioned way. Reminds me of visiting a farmer's market in Little Rock in the late 1980s. Admiring some exceptionally fine leaf lettuce, I asked the lady behind the counter if her produce was organically grown. She looked at me as if I were speaking a foreign language. "Honey," she replied, "we jus' digs up the backyard and plants the seeds and pulls the weeds. I don't know nuthin' 'bout what you talkin' about." If we had more food producers like that, the disease care industry would lose a lot of business.

The incessant push for bigger profits is creating some bizarre and scary situations in the beef and dairy fields. A huge controversy between milk producers (back when I was pulling, uh, teats, we were called dairy farmers) and consumers concerns the use of bovine somatotropin (BST), a synthetic hormone fed to cows that causes them to produce more milk. Until, that is, they collapse from what is called "falling-down cow syndrome." It seems their bones become robbed of calcium and their legs just can't hold them up. And they get mastitis, which then requires feeding them antibiotics. Antibiotic residue is then found in the milk. Now people are becoming immune to antibiotics. Consumers' understandable fears of various adverse health reactions to the suspect substance create yet more opportunity for organic producers.

"In December 1994 the European Union (EU) agriculture minister extended the current moratorium on use of genetically engineered recombinant Bovine Growth Hormone (rBGH) until the year 2000. It is not yet clear how this will affect imports from the U.S. and other countries where the artificial hormone is in use. Monsanto, manufacturer of rBGH, had previously warned the EU that a ban on U.S. products produced using the drug may be an illegal 'restraint on trade' under the new GATT regulations. In a letter to the FDA, the vice president of the EU Agriculture Committee said, 'Consumers in the European Union and their representatives in the European Parliament are apparently much more concerned about the unresolved human health issues related to recombinant bovine somatotropin than your agency when it authorized the product' " (*Our Toxic Times*, April 1995).

I first heard about this next item while listening to Howard Lyman, a fourth-generation Montana cattle rancher and feedlot operator who is the executive director of Voice for a Viable Future and who now eats "zero meat." Profit-hungry meat producers now feed cattle "bypass protein," a ground-up food supplement made from slaughterhouse waste products: carcasses, feathers, trimmings, and animals that have died from various causes and are not accepted at slaughterhouses. Lyman explained that cows have been designed through evolution to eat grasses and other plants, but not meat. When they are fed meat with disease organisms in it, their digestive systems fail to detect a problem and therefore absorb the organisms along with the meat. Cattle that eat diseased meat products can get "mad cow disease" (bovine spongiform encephalopathy, or BSE), which causes the brain of the animal and eventually the brains of those who eat its meat to become riddled with holes, resulting in dementia and eventually death. BSE was first confirmed in cattle in Great Britain in 1986. The *Times* of London reported in December 1995 that scientists there had stopped eating beef.

To agribusiness, profits come first, second, and third. Health is not even a consideration.

Genetically altered food is here. An article titled "Biotech on the Table," *Modern Maturity*, May/June 1995, reported on the creation of the Flavr Savr tomato, "the first genetically modified whole food." Supermarket tomatoes are picked green so they can be washed, sorted, and packed without bruising. Just before shipping, packers use ethylene gas to induce ripening and red skin. You've eaten the result—a hard, tasteless joke. The intelligent answer, of course, is to buy tomatoes picked ripe locally, even if greenhouse-grown in the winter. Agribusiness does not concur. Calgene, a Davis, California, biotech firm—whose shareholders are elated—created a genetically engineered bacterium to neutralize the production of polygalacturonase, the stuff that makes tomatoes soften naturally. Flavr Savr can be left on the vine to ripen with softening. Not everyone is thrilled. Even some supermarkets are reluctant to carry the creation. *Newsweek* wondered, "Will the new gene set off a chemical chain reaction that proves toxic or prompts unexpected changes in the environment?" Turns out that part of Calgene's process uses a "marker gene" to show if the bacterium is present and that the marker gene is resistant to an antibiotic used in health care. Responding to the various concerns of consumers, Calgene senior scientist Virginia Ursin says, "The magnitude of the risk is the same as with anything else in the supermarket food aisle." Yeah, that's what we're afraid of.

If you intend to grow food crops or raise animals organically, buy land that is not poisoned with the residue of chemical fertilizers, herbicides, and pesticides. Some constituents of these products may persist in the soil decades after their application. Organic certification programs require soil tests to prove that the land is free of chemicals.

If you choose this route, educate yourself well. Visit successful pick-your-own operations. Check out local farmers' markets and food co-ops. County extension agents in progressive areas are a good source of information. The Cooperative Extension Service of the U.S. Department of Agriculture was established in 1914 to apply the results of agricultural research done at U.S. land grant colleges. Operating through state and county extension agents, it helps U.S. farmers to learn and use new techniques. They are becoming more responsive to small farmers. Home-demonstration agents supply information and advice on food-preserving and cooking techniques and on farm economics. The 4-H programs train young people in agricultural, food-processing, and management techniques.

Alas, Big Brother has gotten into the organic act. BB involvement started with the National Organic Foods Production Act of 1990. In 1991 the USDA appointed a National Organic Standards Board charged with defining what is and isn't organic. Now we even have a new farmer: the Transitional Farmer, who is not yet certifiable but is presumably headed in that direction. Inasmuch as it is the close collaboration of our federal government, agribusiness lobbyists, and land grant colleges that has created our present poisonous food situation, consumers should be skeptical about claims of organic compliance. I suspect that federal standards will be more lax than state and local standards already developed. Should you choose to become a certified organic food producer, I recommend that you contact the local organic growers' association in the area in which you will farm. Its members will know what is happening on the federal level and how it relates to local conditions.

Regenerative Farming

Good regenerative farmers, practicing what is also called sustainable agriculture, share much with organic gardeners. In fact, the term—regenerative farming—was coined by Robert Rodale of *Organic Gardening and Farming* magazine. Regenerative farmers care about the quality of their products. They love their land and work to improve it. Regenerative farming is practiced by farmers who take responsibility for their actions, who are sensitive to the environment, who know that land is a national treasure. They rotate crops, use chemical fertilizers sparingly or not at all, protect against erosion, strive always to improve fertility. They are becoming more appreciated by society as a whole, which is becoming educated to the value of food grown without chemicals.

Sustainability is defined as actions that meet the needs of the present generation without compromising the needs of future generations. Soil erosion epitomizes the need for sustainability.

"Globally, crop lands damaged between 1950 and 1990 by moderate to extreme soil erosion total an area equal to China and India combined. Yet to feed the world's projected population, output must triple in the next 50 years, according to the U.N. Development Program" (Robin Wright, "Learning to Give as Much as We Take from Earth," *Los Angeles Times*, 1-18-94). Wright's article reports that while population is growing, the supply of food and good water is diminishing.

Farmland Prices

Farmland includes cropland, pasture, orchard, and woodland. Cropland prices are typically higher than prices for woodland. Demand for farmland for nonagricultural uses is highest in coastal regions. Urban sprawl in the form of housing developments and shopping centers is converting former farmland near cities, driving up prices.

According to the USDA, the average value of U.S. farmland and buildings on January 1, 1995, was $832 an acre, a record high, although adjustment for inflation ranks 1981 the highest. Rhode Island has the top average farmland prices in the country ($6,947 per acre), and Wyoming has the lowest ($192 per acre). Average area prices, in order, were Northeast ($2,414), Southeast ($1,533),

Corn Belt ($1,448), Appalachia ($1,436), Pacific ($1,190), Lake States ($1,048), Delta States ($972), Southern Plains ($550), Northern Plains ($458), and Mountain ($346).

Perhaps the USDA does not consider growing grapes to be an agricultural use. California's Napa Valley vineyard land will set you back $40,000—per acre.

Keeping the Right to Farm

All fifty states have right-to-farm laws to protect farmers from being sued by neighbors for smells and sounds. Those laws are in jeopardy with the Supreme Court's refusal to review an Iowa decision that struck down Iowa's right-to-farm law (*USA Today*, 2-22-99).

If you are considering producing food as your work, then note appropriate needs on your criteria worksheet in the areas of climate, soil quality, acreage, farming choices, water quantity, and market demographics.

Resources and Recommended Reading

ATTRA (Appropriate Technology Transfer for Rural Areas)
P.O. Box 3657
Fayetteville, AR 72702
800-346-9140

Its technical staff will record your needs, research your question, and send you a report within two to four weeks.

USDA/CSREES
Office for Small-Scale Agriculture
Ag Box 2244
Washington, DC 20250-2244
Phone: 202-720-5425; fax: 202-205-2448

Provides information on growing crops and raising animals.

Alternative Farming Systems Information Center
National Agricultural Library, Room 304
10301 Baltimore Avenue
Beltsville, MD 20705-2351

Phone: 301-504-6559; fax: 301-504-6409

Web site: http://www.nal.usda.gov/afsic

The Information Center is a source for scientific or popular literature on all types of alternative farming practices.

Books

Berry, Wendell. *The Unsettling of America: Culture and Agriculture.* San Francisco: Sierra Club Books, 1977.

Davidson, Osha Gray. *Broken Heartland: The Rise of America's Rural Ghetto.* New York: The Free Press, 1990.

Lee, Andrew W. *Backyard Market Gardening.* Burlington, VT: Good Earth Publications, 1993.

Logsdon, Gene. *At Nature's Pace: Farming and the American Dream.* New York: Pantheon, 1994.

————. *The Contrary Farmer.* Post Mills, VT: Chelsea Green Publishing Company, 1993.

McCaig, Donald. *An American Homeplace.* New York: Crown, 1992.

Whatley, Booker T. *Booker T. Whatley's Handbook on How to Make $100,000 Farming 25 Acres.* Emmaus, PA: Regenerative Agriculture Association, 1987.

> *"There are thousands, perhaps millions of people in urban situations who are unhappy because they belong in farming and do not know it. They have the true farmer's spirit in them—that blend of creative artistry, independence, manual skill, and love of nurturing that marks the true farmer. If some of these people had been exposed to intelligent and craftsmanlike farming, perhaps they might be living on and working their own little farms. And with these hundreds of thousands of carefully kept little garden farms dotting the landscape, all of society would profit."*
>
> —GENE LOGSDON, *At Nature's Pace*

~14~

Air

"*She* [mother] *took us out in the yard one day and asked us
if we knew the price of eggs, of apples, of bananas. Then she asked
us to put a price on clean air, the sunshine, the song of
birds—and we were stunned.*"

—Ralph Nader

Air is the most essential element for life. Once dependably clean, alas, unpolluted air can no longer be taken for granted. Many of our homes and offices have unhealthful air caused by improper ventilation, outgassing from carpet and furniture, emissions from equipment. Numerous modern buildings have what has become known as "sick building syndrome." Fungi and bacteria in ventilation ducts and gases produced by man-made materials in tight buildings with inadequate fresh air intake may only cause headaches, sore throats, and shortness of breath. If the fresh air intake of a sealed building is close to the cooling tower of another, the fine mist, called drift, may cause bacterial infections as serious as Legionnaires' disease.

A study by the Harvard School of Public Health showed that living in a city with even moderately sooty air may shorten life spans of residents by a year, possibly longer (*Energy Times*, 11-12-95).

In certain natural areas the air can actually improve health and alertness. Tony Hiss reports in *The Experience of Place* that experiments have shown that "unscented air, if it contains a certain quantity of small-air ions—clusters of molecules with a negative electrical charge—can also have the effect of a drug, lowering the amount of serotonin in the midbrain; high levels of serotonin are associated with sleepiness. . . . Mountains, forests, and streams . . . naturally have an abundance of small-air ions."

Forests are clean air factories. Natural areas produce carbon dioxide from decaying vegetation. Living trees utilize carbon dioxide and sunlight through the miracle of photosynthesis to create growth and oxygen. Fortunate are those who live in a forest.

Best-quality air is immediately downwind from where natural conditions cleanse air and create oxygen. Landforms may create exceptions to that. The west coast receives prevailing winds coming in off the ocean, fairly clean air. But because of the hills surrounding the Los Angeles basin, pollutants from factories and vehicles linger, creating very unhealthful air conditions. Mile-high Denver has a similar condition.

After wafting across the Pacific, west coast air is generally clean until it encounters industrial and vehicular pollution. Midwest air is a combination of winds down from Canada and up off the Gulf of Mexico in addition to the prevailing westerlies from the Great Plains, primarily agricultural land. Most of the wind path is sparsely populated and relatively clean except for drift from farm spraying. Much of the eastern states, especially downwind of industrial centers, have relatively poor air quality.

Some areas have such bad air that the American Lung Association is suing the Environmental Protection Agency for not enforcing standards of the Clean Air Act (National Public Radio, 4-29-94). The EPA sometimes seems more sensitive to commercial entities than common citizens. But do not depend on bureaucrats to ensure your clean air.

It is of prime importance to find a place with healthful air conditions. Study the wind and storm maps and become aware of pollution sources for your preferred areas. Then avoid considering areas downwind from air pollution producers. See Chapter 27, "Places and Conditions to Avoid." Also read Chapter 28, "Toxic Pollution."

Resources and Recommended Reading

EPA Emergency Planning and Community Right-to-Know Hotline: 800-535-0202. Reports on local pollution rates, in addition to contaminated landfills, toxic waste sites, and polluted lakes and beaches.

American Lung Association: 800-LUNG-USA.

Books

Hall, Bob, and Mary Lee Kerr. *1991–1992 Green Index: A State-by-State Guide to the Nation's Environmental Health.* Washington, DC: Island Press, 1991.

Hiss, Tony. *The Experience of Place.* New York: Alfred A. Knopf, 1990.

Essential Country Skill #1: working off stress

Instructions: Find a shade tree. Sit down and lean against the tree. Chew on a blade of grass. Briefly contemplate city life. Observe wildlife, count trees, watch grass grow. Dozing is optional.

— 15 —
Water

"The quality of the water, after all, is the quality of us."
—JOHN TODD

Earth's water system is a perfect design. No new water is being made—it is simply recycled. The water we drink today may have been drunk by Confucius 2,500 years ago. Too bad wisdom is not transmitted so easily.

When we open the tap and water comes out, we take it for granted. When it tastes good, we trust it. When it looks clear, we fear it not. All of these reactions are dangerous. The quantity and the quality of our water are no longer dependable—especially in and near cities.

Water Quantity

Water is the most valuable and indispensable resource of any land. Abundant healthful water is a prime ingredient of the ideal life. Each of us each day needs minimally about seventy-five gallons for drinking, cooking, bathing, and cleaning. Irrigation of garden and landscape can increase water requirements enormously. A stream, pond, or cistern is an excellent source of irrigation water, which need not be free of bacteria. Unless situated above point of use, such a system will require a pump and pressure tank. All piping must be separate from the household system to avoid cross contamination.

Almost 2 percent of the total area of the U.S. is covered with water. The country averages twenty-nine inches' annual precipitation (based on a seventy-seven-year record), but excepting the coastal area of the Pacific Northwest, the western half of the country is generally dry and the eastern half is generally wet. Many western states are using groundwater faster than it is being replenished and face serious regional water shortages. In 1980 five western states—California, Texas, Idaho, Kansas, and Nebraska—accounted for nearly 55 percent of the total volume of groundwater used in the U.S. In these and other western states the groundwater levels are sinking. *State of the World 1996* reports that net depletion of the Plains aquifer system totals some 325 billion cubic meters, roughly fifteen times the average annual flow of the Colorado River. Irrigated acreage dropped 26 percent between 1979 and 1989 in the Texas High Plains. In the central and eastern states, groundwater levels are still at about the same levels as they were in the early part of the century.

A modern insanity is that the largest consumer of energy in California is the system of pumps that move water. Thousands of miles of aqueducts traverse the state, requiring continual pumping. The California broccoli consumed in Cincinnati is a product of both water and oil.

The groundwater map shows major U.S. aquifers, defined as capable of yielding fifty gallons per minute or more to wells. Depths to water vary, of course. In addition to areas indicated, wells along river basins generally are recharged by the river water migrating outward. While drawing this map I consulted two different maps published by the U.S. Geological Survey—each showed the same general patterns but indicated substantially different specific boundaries. Therefore I suggest that you use this map only as an indicator of general groundwater distribution. Seek the advice of a local well driller regarding aquifers in your chosen area.

MAJOR GROUNDWATER AREAS

Based on maps in "Ground Water" and "Water Dowsing," U.S. Department of the Interior, U.S. Geological Survey

Rainfall and groundwater distribution do not always correlate, as can be seen by comparing the annual precipitation map in Chapter 9, "Choose Your Climate," with the groundwater map here. In fact, the rainiest part of the country, along the Oregon and Washington coastline, shows relatively little groundwater.

Living where naturally occurring water is inadequate for the population is living in direct conflict with the laws of nature. In truth there is no shortage of water—there are simply places with a surplus of people. As Henry Miller noted: "The world is not to be put in order, the world is order. It is for us to put ourselves in unison with this order."

Effective Precipitation and Effective Moisture

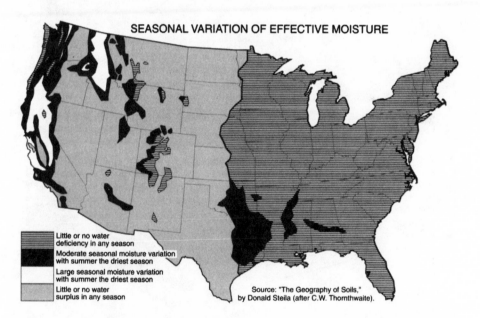

Total annual precipitation alone is an insufficient measure of moisture available at the Earth's surface, as it does not take into account the manner in which it is distributed throughout the year. In many areas agricultural activities are geared to precipitation patterns, any deviation from which may result in reduced or failed crops.

The significance of seasonal distribution relates to the concept of precipitation or moisture *effectiveness*. A considerable amount of moisture is returned to the atmosphere by evaporation and transpiration, as depicted in the drawing of the hydrologic cycle. These two factors are directly influenced by the temperature at which precipitation occurs. When precipitation occurs as snow, no moisture is available until spring melt, which may result in excessive runoff and loss of water.

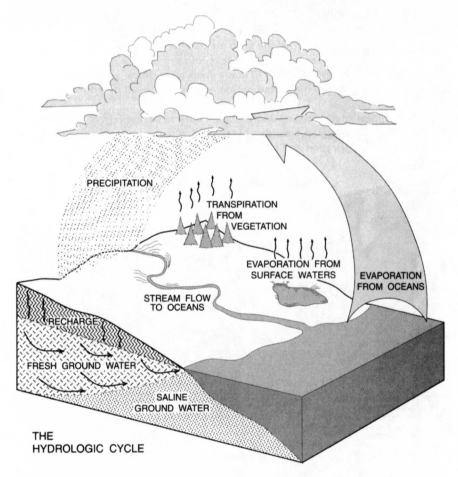

PRECIPITATION

TRANSPIRATION FROM VEGETATION

EVAPORATION FROM SURFACE WATERS

EVAPORATION FROM OCEANS

STREAM FLOW TO OCEANS

RECHARGE

FRESH GROUND WATER

SALINE GROUND WATER

THE HYDROLOGIC CYCLE

Effective moisture is that portion of total precipitation that becomes available for plant growth. Effective moisture is determined by calculating the *potential evapotranspiration*, the amount of water that could be evaporated and transpired under conditions of optimal soil moisture and the normal amount of heat energy sent down by the sun. Various formulas have been devised to calculate effective moisture. Fortunately, there are people who just love to measure and calculate such things so you and I can simply look at the map and say, aha!, there's the place to grow things—like vegetables and hay and trees and stuff—that won't require constant irrigation. Or, aha!, there's the place to be for summer fun without rain showers to wilt my hairdo. If having a bad hair day is a disaster for you, studying this map, the precipitation map, and the humidity map will help you find your best potential area and save you needless suffering.

By looking at the seasonal variation map we can see where adequate moisture is almost always available, where there are summer shortages, and where there is often inadequate moisture. One could quite easily predict from this map where the most and least amount of vegetation occurs. The moist eastern half of the country, for instance, is much more heavily wooded than the west, with the notable exception of parts of the Northwest, especially west of the Cascade Range.

As shown in the illustration, the hydrologic cycle is elegant: water primarily evaporates from the surface of the oceans, seas, and lakes, is lifted by warm air, is moved by winds, collides with cooler air, condenses out of the sky, and precipitates according to gravity. Whether precipitation is rain, snow, sleet, or hail depends on temperature and air movement. Some water soaks into the ground, some evaporates or transpires, and the rest flows to the ocean to repeat the cycle.

The ideal home place includes an abundant supply of naturally occurring healthful water. There are still areas where groundwater is pure and surface water allows swimming and fishing with no danger to health. While many places have insufficient natural water to maintain life, many other areas have a great excess, making them a superior choice for a home place. There are filter and treatment systems that allow you to purify polluted water, but except for a property that is outstanding in every way but water quality, they are an unnecessary expense and maintenance item.

Country home water is most often supplied by a well with electric pump and pressure tank system. Less frequently the source is a spring. In the most fortunate cases the spring is at a higher elevation than the house and water flows into the house by gravity. Such an idyllic system is most appreciated during electrical outages and when paying the electric bill. A stream with adequate flow and drop can power a ram pump, which uses no electricity and can lift water to a storage container on a hill. Voilà, a gravity system! Ram pumps are available from companies listed under Alternative Technology in Appendix A. If rainfall is adequate, consider the possibility of using a cistern. The money saved by not drilling a well will be many times what a purification system will cost.

Water Shortage Areas

> *"Man is a complex being: he makes*
> *deserts bloom—and lakes die."*
>
> —GIL STERN

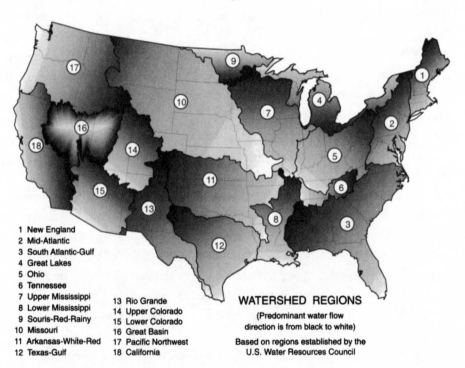

1 New England
2 Mid-Atlantic
3 South Atlantic-Gulf
4 Great Lakes
5 Ohio
6 Tennessee
7 Upper Mississippi
8 Lower Mississippi
9 Souris-Red-Rainy
10 Missouri
11 Arkansas-White-Red
12 Texas-Gulf
13 Rio Grande
14 Upper Colorado
15 Lower Colorado
16 Great Basin
17 Pacific Northwest
18 California

WATERSHED REGIONS
(Predominant water flow
direction is from black to white)
Based on regions established by the
U.S. Water Resources Council

Americans use one third of all the flowing water in the country every single day. The Mississippi is losing flow; the Colorado is being depleted yearly and no longer carries water the full length of its channel. One of Earth's miracles, the Ogallala aquifer, holds as much water as Lake Huron plus one fifth of Lake Ontario. The level of the Ogallala, the irrigation source for the huge grain belt from South Dakota to Texas, is sinking rapidly—the water that now creates life in 20 percent of all irrigated cropland in the country may run dry in as little as forty years. Some predict that the eight-state region it underlies will eventually have to make do with rain only. In a mere 100 years we will have emptied what was once the largest underground body of fresh water in the world. If you have flown over the area, those little green circles you see from 35,000 feet are eighty-acre crop plots with center-pivot irrigation systems pumping from the Ogallala. Circles of fortune, they're called.

California's most recent drought, which ended in 1993, lasted seven years. Prior documented droughts since the 1400s have lasted twenty, forty, and sixty years. Michael Hudlow, former director of the National Oceanic and Atmospheric Administration's office of hydrology, has predicted severe U.S. water shortages in the 1990s. University of Colorado professor of natural resource law Charles Wilkinson, author of *Crossing the Next Meridian*, believes there should be an extraction tax on water. Are you ready for that?

Some say that the water wars of the past are minor compared to the water wars of the future. The West is far overbuilt for its water resources. Major and fast-growing populations live in arid areas of California, Arizona, Colorado, and Nevada, all of which covet and use the water of the Colorado River. But its flow is a mere 2 percent of the Mississippi and only 5 percent of the Connecticut, Delaware, Hudson, and Susquehanna rivers combined, which drain an area about the same size as the Colorado. "With a deep snowpack in the Colorado Rockies and a spring of heavy rains, 1995 looked to be a year of abundant water in the Colorado River basin. Runoff during the months of April to July was 50 percent greater than normal. Still, the river that carved the Grand Canyon ended up suffering its usual fate: it ran dry before it reached the sea" (*State of the World 1996*).

Small-acreage landowners in low-rainfall areas are at risk as fast-growing cities go after their water. Las Vegas water officials filed water claims to an aquifer underlying twenty-six valleys in three rural counties north of the city. A public outcry forced them to reduce their claims. The stated moral defense was that they feared California was going to file claims first. Vegas may get temporary thirst-quenching from Utah, which is considering leasing some of its Colorado River water to the gambling oasis. The title of Dennis Cauchon's article in *USA Today*, 11-17-97, paints a dry picture: "By 2007, Las Vegas Will Be All Tapped Out." Still, enormous new casinos and hotels continue to be built. Still, the subdivisions spread across the desert. How will the insanity end?

In *The Last Refuge*, Jim Robbins shows how powerful cities take water rights from rural residents: "In 1992, large city utilities from Denver, Las Vegas, Phoenix and elsewhere formed a Western Urban Water Coalition to lobby for more water for cities and to 'oppose uneconomic and inefficient water uses.' Which means agriculture. . . . What is taking place, essentially, is a transfer of subsidies. The developers of the sprawling western cities are shouldering out the farmers and taking over the expensive, federally built dams in the West. And they have managed to convince Congress of the need for more subsidies. A $5 billion [that is not a typo—that's a b] concrete-lined ditch called the Central Arizona Project, which slices several hundred miles east from the Colorado River through the Sonoran Desert, is a good example. Originally intended for agriculture, the water will now be used by Phoenix and Tucson."

No part of America so dramatically illustrates the arrogance of our species and the insanity of building cities with insufficient water as the West. Phoenix receives about eight inches of rain annually but continues to grow like a blue-spotted cancer across the desert—the blue of thousands of swimming pools. The semiarid Los Angeles area has over 15 million people who depend on water pumped in from the Owens Valley, the Colorado River, and from northern California. That's right—L.A. area residents fill their swimming pools, water their golf courses, wash their cars with water from the northern Sierras.

Reservoirs

After World War II the U.S. Army Corps of Engineers needed work so it built dams for flood control, electricity generation, and irrigation. The dams created reservoirs of high-quality water. Today, while the original purposes are usually maintained, the Corps has yielded to political pressure and allows fishing, other water sports, and land development around the lakes. Many of these reservoirs are surrounded by beautiful scenery. The combination is irresistible and has created retirement and recreation-oriented communities.

Rapid growth has occurred along lakeshores, rivers, and smaller streams feeding into reservoirs. If you consider buying property adjoining a reservoir or feeder stream, find out what restrictions are enforced on permits and construction of homes and dock facilities. In some places no new permits for docks are being issued. Be aware that the Corps controls lake water levels, which causes

Water

friction with homeowners and sportsmen whose activities may be adversely affected. Private property lines begin at a federal "take line," above the high-water mark. Boaters, picnickers, campers, and nude sunbathers can use the federal property up to the take line, which means that these and others can party in the "front yard" of lakeside property owners if they choose.

Water Use Laws

Riparian rights are the law in those states with adequate rainfall—from Minnesota to Louisiana and east. In these states each landowner may use a reasonable amount of the water on or under owned land but may not appreciably diminish flow to those downstream.

Idaho, Montana, Wyoming, Nevada, Utah, Colorado, Arizona, and New Mexico use the Colorado Doctrine of prior appropriation—first in time is first in line. Early settlers were granted the right to extract a certain amount of water; downstream landowners may have no right to use any of the water that flows across their land. If you consider land in these states you must never assume that a spring, stream, or even a river flowing over or adjacent to the land ensures that water is no problem. It often is. Water rights are bought and sold like commodities. The city of Phoenix bought a ranch entitled to 14 percent of the underlying aquifer, now to be pumped to the city.

The remaining western states on both sides of the Colorado Doctrine group use the California Doctrine, a combination of riparian and prior application laws. California farmers with water rights, including rights to take water from the taxpayer-funded canal that moves northern California water to the L.A. area, are allowed by federal law to sell water to municipalities. In the arid and semiarid West, water always flows—to money.

Fire Protection

Unless carefully engineered, home water systems rarely have adequate pressure and flow to serve as dependable fire-fighting systems. The best country home fire protection system is careful construction of safe electrical and heating designs, constant vigilance, smoke detectors, a number of appropriate fire extinguishers placed in strategic locations, and a substantial cleared area around buildings.

137

Using Water Wisely

Few water systems are without cost to operate, maintain, and purify. Even if a water supply is unlimited and pure, it makes sense not to waste water because it takes energy to deliver it to the tap, and energy usually comes from fossil fuels, the burning of which contributes to the destruction of our environment. The only system I know which costs nearly nothing to operate is a gravity flow system, and, since gravity flow water usually means a high spring or water lifted by ram pump from a surface stream to a high point, most such systems require treatment to ensure safety.

The EPA estimates that 37 percent of household water is used to flush toilets. A good way to save water plus the cost, maintenance, and potential problems of a septic system is to use a composting toilet. There are many models presently available. See Alternative Technology in Appendix A.

Garden irrigation uses huge amounts of water. Water is conserved, weeds are diminished, and plants are fed by applying a thick layer of organic mulch around plants, shrubs, and trees.

Raise the cutting deck on your lawn mower. Lawns that are cut higher do not dry out so fast. Mowing at regular intervals thickens the grass stand, causing rainwater to be absorbed that might otherwise run downhill. Such a program also diminishes erosion and helps to maintain the water table.

Water Quantity Guidelines

- Water abundance usually corresponds with area rainfall and snowfall.
- Wells should be tested for quantity as well as quality. Minimum recharge rates can be tested by continuous pumping during dry periods.
- Small streams may not flow year-round. Talk to area residents about stream history. If stream flow is critical to your needs, observe it at the driest time of the year and talk to those who have lived there for many years.
- If a water source is on the land of another, determine that your property has a deeded easement or right-of-way for piping, canal, or other systems to deliver the water.
- Never buy a property lacking a reliable year-round supply of good-quality water.

Water Quality

When water seeps through overlying material to the water table, particles in suspension, including microorganisms, may be removed. How much is removed depends on the thickness and character of the overlying material. Clay, or "hardpan," provides the most effective natural filter for groundwater. Silt and sand also provide good filtration if fine enough and in thick enough layers. The bacterial quality of water improves during storage in an aquifer because conditions there are usually unfavorable for bacteria. Clarity alone does not guarantee that groundwater is safe to drink; this can only be determined by laboratory testing.

WASTEWATER TREATMENT RETURN FLOW
BY WATER-RESOURCES REGION—1990
(Return of treated water generally is to surface waters.)

The most prudent position is that all water sources are assumed to be contaminated until proven otherwise. As a general rule, all household water should be tested before use and again at regular intervals. If the plumbing in your home has been unused for a period, open all faucets and let the system thoroughly flush before using the water.

Good water is essential for high-quality life. It is necessary to become aware of the condition of water in the various areas you consider. The following unpleasant information is included to alert you to potential problems and areas to avoid. Should you wish more information, a resource list follows. The really ugly information has been limited to Chapter 28, "Toxic Pollution."

Almost all human activities threaten water purity. For decades, manufacturers and agribusiness operators have sent criminal amounts of poisons into our waters. In 1969 the heavy oil layer on the Cuyahoga River in Cleveland caught fire and blazed out of control, horrifying the nation. A federal report declared that the lower Cuyahoga had no visible life, not even lower forms such as leeches and sludge worms that usually thrive on waste.

Partly as a result of the public outcry following the Cuyahoga fire, Congress created the Clean Water Act in 1972. Yet, in 1991, according to EPA reports, industrial, municipal, and military facilities knowingly discharged over 243 million pounds of toxic substances into surface waters. An additional 411 million pounds of toxins were transferred to treatment plants, which in turn transferred partially treated sewage to surface waters. And then we and our children went swimming and fishing in those waters.

Twenty-one years after the Clean Water Act was passed, the EPA listed 18,770 impaired water sites, only 529 polluted primarily by toxic point sources; most of the rest are polluted by runoff (Michael Parfit, "Troubled Waters Run Deep," *National Geographic Special Edition: Water 1993*). Forty-four of the states report groundwater contamination caused by farm and ranch runoff containing sediments, pesticides, herbicides, and fecal matter.

The Washington-based Environmental Working Group reported that traces of herbicides used to control weeds on corn and soybeans have been found in tap water in the Midwest, the Chesapeake Bay region, and Louisiana. Fourteen million people, including 65,000 infants, drink the tainted water (*U.S. News & World Report*, 10-31-94).

In 1993, runoff from livestock areas carried a parasite called Cryptosporidium to the Milwaukee, Wisconsin, municipal water system. A hundred who suffered immune-system deficiency were killed and thousands more became ill.

Municipal water supplies often arrive from far away, affected by conditions foreign to users. A 233-mile-long aqueduct from Owens Valley helps slake L.A.'s huge thirst. New Yorkers have been advised that people with low salt tolerances shouldn't drink too much city water—the rock salt used in the Catskill Mountains to keep roads ice-free is filling city reservoirs in the area. The average

American city dweller drinks water that has been filtered, chemically treated to kill bacteria, then delivered to the tap through a vast network of old pipes constructed of various materials. The EPA reported that of the nation's 660 large public water systems, 130—which provide drinking water for 32 million people—exceeded the "action level" for lead content.

In *The Truth About Where You Live*, Benjamin A. Goldman writes of pesticide waste dumps, municipal landfills, toxic waste pits, injection wells, pesticide applications, mining and oil exploration sites, and septic tanks that pollute groundwater—the water that cities, small communities, and rural homeowners tap with their wells. Private rural water supplies are usually wells. In areas of high agricultural chemical use they are vulnerable to contamination. Public supplies are even more vulnerable. The EPA's National Pesticide Survey Project Summary of 1990 found that community water systems were two and a half times more likely to register pesticides above minimum reporting limits than were private rural wells.

It's enough to make you sick. Avoid considering property near these facilities and conditions. Even private septic tanks can now be avoided by using one of the many commercially available composting toilets. John Todd, co-founder of New Alchemy Institute, is doing great things with biological waste treatment facilities. The biotreatment consists simply of running wastes through channels in which various plants grow. In areas of cold winters, the channels are protected by green-houses. After enough different plants absorb nutrients, the endpoint water is cleaner and safer than the output of most municipal treatment plants—without using an ounce of chlorine. Todd says: "Since the Clean Water Act in 1972, we've spent billions of dollars and haven't really improved water quality. We use 70,000 different chemicals routinely in commerce and then dump them into the water. Those chemicals are ungluing the natural world."

Agricultural Water Pollution

Beware of potential well contamination from agribusiness operations. U.S. farmers apply nearly 400,000 tons of pesticides per year. Over thirty years after biologist Rachel Carson explained the danger in *Silent Spring*, we continue to poison our bodies and our children's bodies. In *Broken Heartland* Osha Gray Davidson reports that a 1986 EPA study found seventeen different pesticides in the groundwater of twenty-three states. In the food basket of the nation, fifty-eight pesticides were found in 3,000 California wells. In *Toxic Nation* Fred Setterberg and Lonny Shavelson state that two thirds of California's wells are contaminated. In "The Mississippi River Under Siege" (*Water, National Geographic*), William S. Ellis wrote that DDT continues to be found in the Mississippi although it has been banned in the U.S. for more than twenty years. In *Born in the Country: A History of Rural America*, David B. Danbom writes that "In 1986, one-third of Iowa's wells contained pesticides, and half of Nebraska's municipal water systems were similarly contaminated. Because many of these compounds do not break down naturally, they are likely to be with us for a long time. . . . In many parts of the corn belt, water supplies carry such high concentrations of nitrogen—which has been linked to birth defects and some cancers—that people are advised to drink bottled water."

The Department of Agriculture estimates that areas of greatest potential pesticide contamination are California's San Joaquin Valley, western Texas and Oklahoma, Kansas and eastern Nebraska, the upper Midwest, western Pennsylvania, and the entire southeastern coastal plain from southern New Jersey to Florida.

Mining Pollution

Avoid areas downhill or downstream from current or old mining operations. Almost every place where minerals have been extracted is now polluted. Decades of coal mining have poisoned much of Appalachia's water. Still, there are nonpolluted places. In *An American Homeplace*, Donald McCaig writes of his farm in Highland County, Virginia: "There are several reasons our farm has clean water. . . . Though the Chamber of Commerce and other forward-thinking citizens here have begged industry to come and set up shop, provide employment and paychecks, so far industry has declined this offer, preferring to ruin the water of communities with better roads. And there's never been much in Highland County worth stealing. We lack coal and other minerals, there's no oil. The best timber was taken off in the early twenties."

Wells

In rural America, approximately 97 percent of us depend on underground water sources. The average depth of all domestic U.S. wells is less than fifty feet. Shallow wells are more subject to local pollution sources but even deep wells may be affected by distant pollution sources.

Wells are subject to contamination from both surface and belowground contaminants. Pesticides, herbicides, chemical fertilizers, and industrial wastes are common sources of pollution.

The EPA has stated that there is some toxic substance in all U.S. groundwater. In light of this, it is imperative to test all household water and if necessary to consider point-of-use water purification devices.

Most wells were created by well drillers who kept a detailed log of the drilling history, the depth, the quality, and the amount of flow developed. Consult with well drillers about a well's capacity to meet your needs. County health officials or extension agents may be able to refer you to a local laboratory that tests water.

New wells are expensive. Again, local well drillers are the best source of information. Nobody can guarantee to find water but local drillers stay in business by being successful a high percentage of the time.

Springs

Some people still believe that a spring emits pure water because it has miraculously been filtered by the ground. Not usually so. Michael Parfit, a writer in *National Geographic*'s *Water*, gets his water from a spring at a mountain in Montana. He always figured his water was safe, because it was "at the beginning of the flow." Then he had the water tested. The lab reported: "Too numerous to count—background bacteria."

In 1982, I had the opportunity to join a college field trip to hydrologist Tom Aley's place in southern Missouri. Tom first walked us around the surface of his land, teaching the difference between general recharge and discrete recharge, the two ways that rainwater moves down into the ground. One of the discrete recharge areas was a sinkhole caused by the collapse of a cavern ceiling, now a stagnant, scum-filled pond, with living and dead plants and various animal remains. We later climbed down into his Tumbling Creek Cave, which Tom calls Ozarks Underground Laboratory. We were shown the gush of water falling from a crevice in the cave's ceiling, the beginning of the stream; water gathered from recharge areas above, including the sinkhole. Tumbling Creek meanders along the cave floor (we admired blind cave salamanders and avoided disturbing the bat colony) and exits a mile away at the base of a bluff, what anyone would call a spring. Almost zero filtering takes place between the recharge area and the outlet, the "spring." And we all know what accumulates under bat colonies.

Aley has performed many dye tracings, proving the recharge sources of springs to be numerous, distant, and dangerous, including abandoned dump sites full of old batteries, paint cans, and chemical containers. He explains that the greater the spring flow, the greater the probability that the collection area is large and diverse and includes such toxic recharge areas.

The point is that springs are simply outlets for underground water flows, not far from the surface, and little filtered. Rain falls on the land, finds cracks in the surface, gathers with water from other sources, and makes its way into an underground stream. When it appears as a spring, it may or may not have been filtered. Until tests prove otherwise, always assume that a spring is polluted. And if you use it, have it tested annually, as conditions in the recharge system may change.

Surface Water

Water for household needs is vital, but why settle for survival? Springs, streams, rivers, waterfalls, ponds, and lakes enhance not only the water supply but are pleasurable additions to any property. Some of our favorite times are spent sitting on our porch, listening to the unceasing sounds of our little stream tumbling over rocks, a reassuring, happy background of natural song.

Suface water attracts wildlife. Most mornings a great blue heron comes for a breakfast of minnows. Often we are visited by a pair of wood ducks. Once a bald eagle came and sat for an hour in a sycamore overlooking the wide part of the water. Deer, turkeys, and kingfishers make regular appearances. Beavers have established themselves upstream.

The quality of any surface water is directly caused by the nature of its watershed. A stream receiving runoff from an agricultural area may have bacteria from animal wastes and chemical residues from fertilizers and pesticides. A creek below a clear-cut hillside will be full of silt. After full vegetation returns the same stream may run clear.

The advantages of property adjoining or crossed by a waterway are many—the downside, less obvious, is that water is a magnet to others. Depending on the size of your waterway you may be bothered by boaters, fishermen, and floaters, the traffic that water brings.

Check the history of flooding with neighbors. Also determine laws regarding usage, damming, and diversion. And check with local officials for new laws being considered.

Coliform bacteria and *Giardia lamblia* are two of the most common disease-causing organisms. Coliform is the standard indicator of harmful organisms in water. All surface water should be considered to have a high coliform bacteria count, which is caused by the animals that live in, on, and around it. If surface water is to be used for household purposes it should be filtered and treated.

Small streams are preferable to rivers because they are closer to the source, are generally clearer and less polluted, and attract fewer tourists.

If There Is No Well or Surface Water

If you consider buying property with no existing well and there is no available surface water, you must ensure that a successful well can be installed. Check with neighbors to find how deep their wells are, if they ever run dry, and if they know who drilled them. Your best information source will be well drillers with substantial local experience. They can tell you the odds and the cost of creating a good well.

Heart Disease, Cancer, and Water

We once thought that hard water decreased heart disease. Some now believe that it is magnesium, not calcium, in our water which reduces heart disease. Above-average magnesium content in water occurs in North and South Dakota, Oklahoma, Nebraska, Kansas, most of New Mexico, eastern Montana, eastern Colorado, western Arkansas, western Missouri, all of Texas but the southeast corner, and northwest Utah. Many of these same areas also have had the longest-lived persons in the U.S.

Rapid City, South Dakota, drinking water contains a high concentration of selenium, a mineral believed to help prevent cancer and heart disease. The rate of cancer in Rapid City is far below the national average. Of course, moving to a place to get selenium would be rather extreme, since selenium is available as a supplement. It is one of a group called antioxidants.

From Bad Water to Good

Physical contamination can result from surface runoff during periods of heavy rainfall, carrying various substances into the water source. Physical contamination includes oils, salts, dirt, and bad taste and smell from the growth of algae.

Chemical contamination occurs from mine drainage, landfill leakage, storage tank leaks, spills, fertilizer, and pesticide runoff.

Biological contamination comes from municipal, industrial, agricultural, and household wastewater systems. It occurs naturally in surface water, the result of animal life. Bacteria and viruses come from animals: wild, domestic, and human. Septic tank leaks can contaminate wells.

Any water can be made safe to drink. Polluted water can be used safely if it is appropriately filtered and treated at the point of use. If a property embodies all other characteristics you want in outstanding proportion, then the expense of water treatment may make sense. Make a thorough investigation to determine the source and extent of pollution and to determine if it will improve or if it is likely to worsen. Other considerations include cost of equipment, cost of operation, maintenance, and degree of safety. Get the advice of experts.

Water Quality Guidelines

- The ideal home place is far from pollution sources.
- Rural areas generally have cleaner water than cities.
- Deep wells are usually safer than shallow wells.
- Springs, creeks, and rivers are typically cleaner near their source and more polluted farther downstream.
- All water sources should be considered unsafe until tested. Check with county officials and well drillers for a testing source.
- All rivers should be considered polluted.
- Major polluters include agricultural, industrial, municipal, and military facilities.

- Avoid buying property downwind or downwater from farms that may use chemical fertilizers, herbicides, and pesticides.
- Heavily developed lakeside areas often have pollution from excessive numbers of septic tanks.
- Upstream logging operations create high amounts of sediment.
- Oceanside waterways and wells may be affected by saltwater intrusion at high tide.

On your criteria worksheet circle the water features your ideal place will have and show your preferences on water and waste systems.

Resources and Recommended Reading

Acid rain is discussed in Chapter 28, "Toxic Pollution"

Water Information

A free booklet, *Ground Water and the Rural Homeowner*, is available from:

U.S. Geological Survey, Lakewood ESIC
Box 25046, Bldg. 810
Denver Federal Center, MS-504
Denver, CO 80225
Phone: 303-202-4210, fax: 303-202-4695

The USGS also has a brochure simply titled *Ground Water* which has a good map showing major groundwater areas in the United States.

U.S. Environmental Protection Agency safe drinking water hotline:
800-426-4791

Soil and Water Conservation Society: 800-THE-SOIL
For a free conservation packet and other information.

American Groundwater Trust: 800-423-7748

Water Environment Federation
601 Wythe Street
Alexandria, VA 22314-1994
Phone: 800-666-0206; fax: 703-684-2492

Presents materials on water quality issues.

Water Tests

County and state health departments may help in selecting tests and locating testing laboratories. If you can't find someone local, you can have water tested by Watercheck National Testing Laboratories. Call them at 800-458-3330.

Water Tests, Purification Devices, and Composting Toilets

Solar Living Sourcebook is a combination catalogue and compilation of useful articles. Sort of a *Whole Earth Catalog* of energy-efficiency and alternative energy systems. Offerings include water testing and treatment systems. Includes a selection of water filtering and purification devices and composting toilets.

Real Goods Corporation
555 Leslie Street
Ukiah, CA 95482-5507
Phone: 800-762-7325; fax: 707-468-9486
E-mail: realgood@realgoods.com
Web site: http://www.well.com/www/realgood/

Books

Brown, Lester R., ed. *State of the World 1996*. New York: W.W. Norton, 1996.

Ford, Norman. *The 50 Healthiest Places to Live and Retire in the United States*. Bedford, MA: Mills & Sanderson, 1991.

Goldman, Benjamin A. *The Truth About Where You Live: An Atlas for Action on Toxins and Mortality*. New York: Times Books, 1991. Eye-opening text and maps are the result of use of the Freedom of Information laws.

Graves, William, editor. *National Geographic Special Edition: Water: The Power, Promise, and Turmoil of North America's Fresh Water*. Washington, DC: The National Geographic Society, 1993.

Mitchell, John G. "Widespread as Rain and Deadly as Poison: Our Polluted Runoff." *National Geographic*, February 1996.

Robbins, Jim. *The Last Refuge: The Environmental Showdown in Yellowstone and the American West*. New York: William Morrow, 1993.

Setterberg, Fred, and Lonny Shavelson. *Toxic Nation: The Fight to Save Our Communities from Chemical Contamination*. New York: John Wiley & Sons, 1993.

—16—
Health 101

"Like any other activity, the practice of health involves one or more choices.
We choose to live quietly and simply, to exercise in the open air, to keep
sensible hours and not overdo physically. We choose to exercise our bodies not in
gymnasiums or on golf courses or tennis courts but doing useful outdoor
physical work. We choose to live in the country rather than the city,
with its polluted air, noise and stress. We prefer clean fresh air, sunshine,
clear running water. We choose to cut our own fuel in our own woods rather than
pay the oil barons. We design and construct our own buildings. We grow and
prepare our own food, rather than shop in the supermarkets."

—HELEN AND SCOTT NEARING, *Continuing The Good Life*

Scott Nearing was 100 when he decided to die. He split firewood until he was ninety-eight. Helen was more active than most women half her age until her accidental death in 1995 at age ninety-one.

Nutritious food and positive mind-set are arguably the best medicine, but it is clear that the place in which we live affects our physical and psychological health. This chapter provides health information for you to consider as you develop criteria for your ideal place. It will help you to find a place that is conducive to your best health. It will help you to avoid places that are bad for your health. These are different things.

Most rural environments are more healthful places to live than most urban environments. For starters, there is more space between knuckles and noses and the tree-to-auto-tailpipe ratio is superior. There are fewer industries per square mile spewing death into water and air; the conversations of urban refugees change from how awful the smog to how pretty the sky. Country folks appear to walk more slowly but apparently take longer strides—they get where they're going as fast but are less stressed upon arrival. Men who live in rural areas are less likely to develop bladder cancer than urban men. We are told it is because they drink more liquids and urinate more often. Is it ruralites' greater physical activity? Or is it that urban water tastes so awful, or that urban men suffer from lack of trees, bushes, wide-open spaces? Or is it all of the above?

"Living in a large city shortens life expectancy."
—Norman Shealy, M.D., PhD.,
Director of Shealy Institute for Comprehensive Care and
Pain Management, Springfield, Missouri

Environmental factors contributing to good physical health are clean air, pure water, healthy soil. Health destroyers include water and air poisoned by industrial and vehicular emissions, pesticides, other agricultural residue. Less widespread but potentially worse are retired and active toxic waste dumps which somehow manage to poison nearby residents. Chemical industry defenders deny the connection.

If you have a medical condition that requires treatment, then your criteria for an ideal country home will include ready access to medical staff and facilities. If you are presently healthy and determined to stay that way, then you should locate in an area that contributes to good health. Evidence suggests that the most healthful places are where doctors are scarce.

Better Health Equals Fewer Doctors

Most people equate rural health quality with the ratio of doctors per capita. This does not seem to be an accurate guideline, as "counties with the best mortality rates from all diseases have half as many doctors per capita as the national average, and those with the worst mortality have 8 percent more doctors per capita than the country as a whole" (Benjamin A. Goldman, *The Truth About Where You Live*). One must conclude that, rather than diminishing the incidence of disease, doctors locate their practices where demand for treatment exists. It's just good business—in the biggest business.

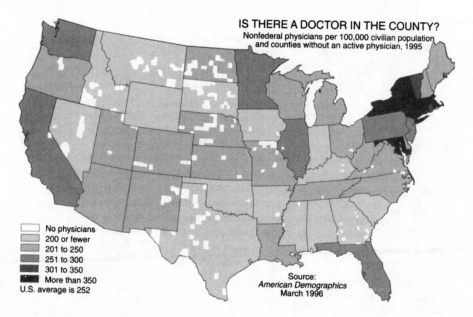

IS THERE A DOCTOR IN THE COUNTY?
Nonfederal physicians per 100,000 civilian population
and counties without an active physician, 1995

No physicians
200 or fewer
201 to 250
251 to 300
301 to 350
More than 350
U.S. average is 252

Source:
American Demographics
March 1996

Health Care Services

The greatest reductions in mortality during the past two centuries are not due to better medical treatment. The leading killers at the beginning of this century were infectious diseases. These were largely eradicated with environmental improvements: sewage systems, purified public water supplies, and better nutrition—long before the discovery of antibiotics and other medical cures.

In certain diseases, medical technology is simply inadequate. Even though billions of dollars and decades of research have been invested, cancer is devastating America. Cancer is expected to surpass heart disease as the number one cause of death in the U.S. by the year 2000 (Patricia Braus, "Why Does Cancer Cluster?," *American Demographics*, March 1996). AIDS, with 61,301 new cases and 44,052 deaths in 1994, is another health disaster in search of a solution. For all disease, prevention seems to me easier, more logical, less expensive than cure. The Atlanta-based Centers for Disease Control found that for every dollar a company spends in preventive health care and exercise programs for employees, the company saves seven dollars in future health costs.

Some feel that a health care crisis exists in rural America. According to the American Hospital Association, 280 rural hospitals closed between 1980 and 1990. In 1988 the National Rural Health Association prepared an estimate for

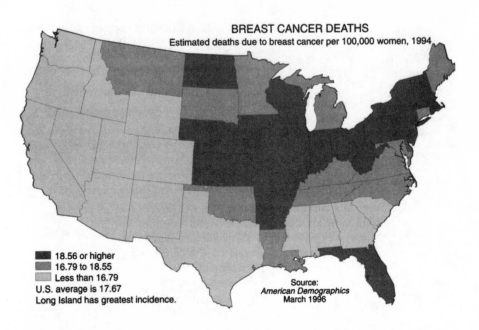

BREAST CANCER DEATHS
Estimated deaths due to breast cancer per 100,000 women, 1994

■ 18.56 or higher
■ 16.79 to 18.55
□ Less than 16.79
U.S. average is 17.67
Long Island has greatest incidence.

Source:
American Demographics
March 1996

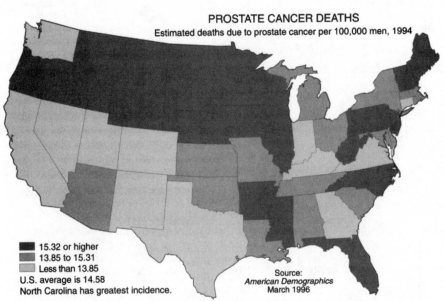

PROSTATE CANCER DEATHS
Estimated deaths due to prostate cancer per 100,000 men, 1994

■ 15.32 or higher
■ 13.85 to 15.31
□ Less than 13.85
U.S. average is 14.58
North Carolina has greatest incidence.

Source:
American Demographics
March 1996

Congress that showed 1,280 rural counties were "health-professional-shortage areas," with fewer than one doctor for every 3,500 residents. The problem is most acute in the South and in sparsely populated western states, but every state has at least two such areas. While the number of physicians in the U.S. has grown from 260,500 in 1960 to 670,300 in 1993, according to the American Medical Association there are 149 counties with no physicians at all. (See map: "Is There a Doctor in the County?")

There are notable exceptions to the above. Many small towns actively recruit ("seduce" comes to mind) young doctors. Many medical schools encourage physicians to do at least part of their training in rural areas. The National Health Service Corps is a federal agency that offers scholarships and loan repayment plans to medical students who agree to practice in a doctor shortage area (*American Demographics*, March 1996). Small towns typically give new doctors grand treatment. One example in the *American Demographics* article ended: "There's something to be said for the life here. The board passed an official resolution asking them [a husband-and-wife team] to stay. They really are heroes in this town. A lot of doctors don't get to feel that way anymore." Another plus is that the government has raised Medicare rates and will now pay rural hospitals equally with city hospitals.

Some doctors are joining the city-to-country movement. In *The New Heartland*, John Herbers notes that the ninety-seven-bed Baxter Hospital in Mountain Home, Arkansas, has a number of specialists who followed retirees to the area, often taking cuts in pay because they like the lifestyle of the region. (Nineteen ninety-nine update: there are now 197 beds, over seventy physicians; a 100,000-square-foot expansion is under way.)

The latest in rural health care is telemedicine. Doctors use interactive video to "see" patients in distant clinics. Doctors feel that diagnosis is just as accurate and patient monitoring is better than in person because both doctor and patient can see each other more often.

If easily accessed health care is one of your criteria, you should make a special investigative effort to satisfy yourself. After you choose an area of interest, when you write to chambers of commerce for general area information, request a report on health care availability.

On the subject of seducing doctors, an enjoyable movie is *Doc Hollywood*. Michael J. Fox as Dr. Ben Stone is a newly minted M.D. whose cruise toward the medical fast lane takes a small-southern-town detour when he swerves his Porsche to miss cows in the road and wipes out the judge's new picket fence— while the judge is still painting it. The town woos him with copious home cooking, a guaranteed salary, and the mayor's lusting daughter (well, that was her idea, and she mostly just wanted a ride to Hollywood). I give it two thumbs-up for entertainment and a chuckle for reality.

Stress and Place

Stress kills enjoyment of life, relationships, people. It promotes heavy drinking and cigarette smoking and causes irritability. It is a prime factor in ulcers, high blood pressure, heart disease. It leads to alcoholism, drug dependency, divorce, and dog-kicking. Get rid of it—the stress, not the dog.

The geography of healthfulness seems to be connected to a lack of stress. *Psychology Today's* study on low-stress "cities" found them all to be small towns. An area of Polish farms in Nebraska is perhaps the most healthful place to live in America. The active stress-free lifestyle is considered the primary reason that residents there, for many decades, have lived longer than people in any other place in America. The area has freezing winters and hot, humid summers. So much for the health benefits of a gentle climate.

Being in the wrong place combined with job pressures can create a lethal amount of stress. When I was a city real estate broker I became close friends with

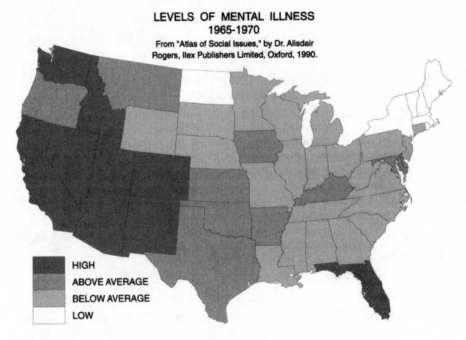

LEVELS OF MENTAL ILLNESS
1965-1970

From "Atlas of Social Issues," by Dr. Alisdair
Rogers, Ilex Publishers Limited, Oxford, 1990.

HIGH
ABOVE AVERAGE
BELOW AVERAGE
LOW

my chiropractor. It was inevitable—I saw him several times a week because of my almost-constant tension headaches. During the years I have both lived in the country and avoided the real estate business I have not once needed a chiropractor. Maybe it's because Heartwood is in a valley—I look up a lot, which seems to keep my cervical vertebrae happy, which tends to make my head happy. Which makes chiropractors' travel agents unhappy.

Mental Health

Those who study cause and effect of social problems suggest that mental illness is higher among those who change their home places often. Such a pattern, it is implied, creates a condition of being in limbo, a feeling of not belonging to a place, a loss of community, unsettledness.

Or is it that those who are unhappy are more prone to move, hoping the new place will magically cure the underlying problem—but do so impulsively and carelessly? The premise of this book is that a move can be a highly positive action—but only when the move is conducted after a thorough examination of self and potential places.

Where Death and Disease Are Caused by Environmental Factors

Benjamin Goldman performed a great public service by compiling *The Truth About Where You Live: An Atlas for Action on Toxins and Mortality*, a book representing the culmination of five years of work at Public Data Access, Inc., in New York. PDA exploited the Freedom of Information Act and used computer processing techniques to evaluate government information and appraise environmental and health conditions. Goldman writes: "Across the United States, an average of four industrial accidents a day spill toxic chemicals into the environment. Factory mishaps release 370 thousand tons of toxins into the air each year. Industrial plants routinely discharge another 7 million tons of toxic chemicals into the air and water, and dump another 500 million tons of hazardous wastes into the ground—in full compliance with existing government regulations. To complete the picture, add another 4 billion tons of wastes that farms and cities discharge annually into the nation's air, waterways, and land."

The Truth About Where You Live uses many maps to provide a comprehensive picture of counties that are suffering from disproportionate shares of environmental contamination and death. Deaths from cancer and other diseases follow the nation's rivers. Runoff from pesticides and other agricultural chemicals and industrial wastes has turned rivers into gutters of chemical soup. The counties bordering the Mississippi River have some of the worst mortality rates in the country. Below the Ohio River, 80 percent of the counties bordering the Mississippi have shamefully high levels of excess death.

Death rates are generally highest in the eastern part of the country. High mortality rates exist in the coastal plain states of the Southeast, including Georgia, South Carolina, and North Carolina, in the Appalachian regions of Kentucky, Virginia, and West Virginia, and in western Pennsylvania. As measured in 1992, the nine worst states for death from heart disease are New York, Arkansas, Oklahoma, Missouri, Kentucky, Louisiana, West Virginia, South Carolina, and Ohio. A factor that experts agree on is that blood pressure is significantly higher in the South. They disagree on why.

In general, avoid areas where corporate farming is conducted—big companies tend to be sensitive to profits and insensitive to human health. They use large amounts of herbicides, pesticides, and chemical fertilizers, many of which become airborne and many of which find their way into groundwater. Studies have shown a high rate of leukemia among Midwest farmers. Farmers who use certain pesticides are at greatest risk of cancer (*American Demographics*, March 1996). To avoid corporate agriculture, search for a place in areas where soil or topography make large-scale farming impossible.

Avoid petrochemical industrial areas like the plague that they are. Stay far upwind and upriver from nuclear reactors, active and closed military bases, old dumps, landfills, waste incinerators, mining and oil sites (including exploration sites), and industrial facilities.

Goldman's book, published in 1991, derives primarily from federal data collected in the 1980s. Since then, various acts and laws have been adopted and some Superfund sites have been declared safe for habitation. Be skeptical. Only you can be the final judge of what is a healthful place for you to live. I suggest you use the information from *The Truth About Where You Live* as a caution and a starting point, then carefully make your own current investigation.

Are there any healthful areas left to live? Yes. They are usually far from industrial and corporate farming areas. For your and your family's health, take the time to identify them. Make a thorough investigation of present, past, and planned land use around your potential home site before you commit to living there.

According to Northwest National Life Insurance Company, the states with the healthiest people are Utah, North Dakota, Idaho, Vermont, Nebraska, Colorado, Wyoming, and Montana. Utah may be rated so high because the predominantly Mormon population eschews smoking and riotous living.

In Praise of Homegrown Food

> *"One of the healthiest ways to gamble is with*
> *a spade and a package of garden seeds."*
>
> —DAN BENNETT

Supermarket tomatoes are picked green—homegrown tomatoes are picked at their height of sun-ripened goodness. Commercial fruit and vegetable varieties are chosen for fast growth, uniform ripening, transportability, presentation, profit. They are grown using chemical fertilizers, herbicides, and pesticides on soil typically deficient in tract minerals essential for good health. Picked green, gassed, sprayed with wax, handled, and bruised by machines and individuals and trucked long distances, most supermarket produce is deficient in vitamins, minerals, taste, satisfaction.

One cannot overestimate the health benefits of food grown from living, organically rich soil, unpoisoned by chemicals, the produce untouched by pesticides. Homegrown varieties may be chosen for vigor, suitability to local conditions, and flavor. And the nutritional value of produce minutes-fresh from the garden surpasses anything commercially available to even the wealthiest shopper. Home gardeners eat better than Bill Gates.

High-quality soil is alive with millions of earthworms and microorganisms converting organic matter into plant food. By contrast, most commercially produced food is grown in dead or dying soil devoid of essential minerals.

Chromium, essential for converting fat to energy by the mitochondria of our cells, has been mined out of soil by decades of wheat monoculture. The result: nine out of ten Americans are deficient in chromium, and many of us are obese. The fact that the U.S. ranks second worldwide in per capita pork consumption may also be a clue to our high incidence of obesity.

Doctor's Data, a Chicago trace mineral analysis lab, found that organically grown wheat has twice the calcium, five times more magnesium, six times more manganese, and fourteen times more selenium (an antioxidant that prevents cancer) than conventionally grown wheat. Compared to crops grown with pesticides, organically grown crops were found to contain significantly higher levels of twenty of the twenty-two beneficial trace elements measured in the study (David Steinman, "Internal Affairs," *LA Village View*, 10-14-94).

Chemical fertilizers, herbicides, and pesticides are killers of earthworms, microorganisms, humans. The growth of chemical agriculture has been paralleled by the growth of so-called health care (what is practiced should be called disease care), which in 1994 became the biggest business in the country—$700 billion per year. Purposefully applying poisons to our soil and our food crops is the result of ignorance, unconscionable greed, and criminal indifference to consumer health.

> *"It is one of the miracles of science and*
> *hygiene that the germs that used to be in our food have*
> *been replaced by poisons."*
>
> —WENDELL BERRY, *The Unsettling of America*

We can beat the grim legacy of chemical farming by growing much of our own food and by buying the rest from conscientious growers. Buy property with poison-free soil. Ideal garden soil has not been commercially farmed for decades. If you are unsure of soil quality, ask one of the many organic growers' associations that certify organic produce for sources where soil may be tested for poisonous residue. If it is free from poisons, you can build a good garden. The key to growing healthful food is building healthful soil. If you can't or won't garden, buy organically grown food. Organic food is still more expensive but, without health, what good is money?

Living Healthy and Living Long

If Dr. Roy Walford is correct with the title of his book, *The 120-Year Diet*, we're giving up on living more than forty years too soon. The cover story of *Life*, October 1992, "Can We Stop Aging?," quoted scientists using the 120-year figure as if it were an accepted fact.

Heart disease and cancer kill 75 percent of us. Information widely available today, read and acted upon, could virtually eliminate these two killers. If we live in a healthful place, engage in healthful work, eat healthful foods, and follow a few commonsense precepts, we can live far longer than insurance companies currently predict.

Health is one of my most rewarding hobbies and about it I am biased. My bias is that most of us can achieve and maintain excellent health without help from doctors. Don't get me wrong about doctors; I think they are essential assets. I just hate to see them driving better vehicles than teachers, farmers, writers. Seriously, each of us should be in charge of our own health—which means being responsible for our health. The benefits far outweigh the effort required.

As a no-extra-cost bonus in a book that you thought would limit itself to helping you to find the perfect place to park your heart, I offer my personal list for staying healthy and living long.

WARNING: I AM NOT A DOCTOR. THEREFORE YOU MUST TREAT ME AS IF I AM A HEALTH IGNORAMUS. IF YOU HAVE A MEDICAL CONDITION, CONSULT A DOCTOR BEFORE DOING ANYTHING YOU READ HERE.

Don't you just hate these stupid disclaimers made necessary because of lawsuits? Reminds me of a story: There was a terrible accident at a building site, and a construction worker rushed over to where a well-dressed woman was pinned beneath an iron girder. "Hang in there, lady," he said helpfully, "the ambulance will be here soon. Are you badly hurt?" "How should I know?" she snapped. "I'm a doctor, not a lawyer."

NONDOCTOR GERUE'S HOPEFULLY HELPFUL HEALTH HINTS:

- Move to a rural place that has healthful air, water, and soil.

- Eat a low-fat (20 percent or less) diet with minimal amounts of meat and dairy products but lots of fruit, vegetables, nuts, and grains. Grow food or buy organic. Eat only foods that are delicious.

- Use antioxidants—vitamins A (beta-carotene), C, and E, and selenium. Antioxidants are the best health news in decades—read all about them.

- Use best-quality vitamin and mineral supplements. Few diets provide optimal nutrient levels. Educate yourself.

- Exercise (brisk walking qualifies) at least three times a week for a minimum of thirty minutes each time. Country living automatically takes care of this. "The sovereign invigorator of the body is exercise, and of all the exercises walking is best" (Thomas Jefferson). When you visit the city, laugh at elevators and those who ride them. Have a little fun—ask people waiting for elevators for directions to the stairs. Don't be surprised if they don't know where the stairs are. Indulge in activities you enjoy. "A satisfying sex life is the single most effective protection against heart attacks" (Dr. Eugene Scheimann). Erma Bombeck relates to that: "The only reason I would take up jogging is so that I could hear heavy breathing again."

- Don't smoke. Don't breathe others' smoke. "Now that I'm gone, I tell you: don't smoke, whatever you do, don't smoke" (Yul Brynner, cancer victim, in a posthumous antismoking commercial).

- Avoid stress. When people are rude, smile—it'll totally confuse them. Live below your means. Maintain perspective. "One way to get high blood pressure is to go mountain climbing over molehills" (Earl Wilson).

- Work hard at something you feel good about.

- Get adequate rest. Ignore rules dictating how many hours "adequate" is—trust your body's messages. "The amount of sleep required by the average person is about five minutes more" (Max Kauffmann).

- Avoid unprotected sun exposure. Use sunscreen. Get a broad-brimmed hat that reminds you of one of your heroes. (According to NASA, in 1992 the ozone layer hole was three times the area of the forty-eight contiguous states.)

- Touch. Give and receive hugs and massage.

- Be happy—live where you prefer, do the work that impassions you, be with one you love. Married people seem to be happiest. "By all means marry; if you get a good wife, you'll become happy; if you get a bad one, you'll become a philosopher" (Socrates). When you feel unhappy, straighten your back, lift your chin, show your teeth, and act happy. Soon you will be.

• Stay mentally active—forever. Garden. Read. Think. Debate. Write, paint, sculpt, craft. Mow your lawn creatively. Study nature.

• Laugh a lot—especially at those who disagree with you and at all politicians. "Laughter is inner jogging" (Norman Cousins). "He who laughs, lasts" (Dr. Robert Anthony).

• Give of yourself to others. "When you cease to make a contribution, you begin to die" (Eleanor Roosevelt). "If you want to lift yourself up, lift up someone else" (Booker T. Washington). "You cannot do a kindness too soon, for you never know how soon it will be too late" (Emerson). "Long-range studies imply that doing something with other people, especially something for them, is the most powerful of all stimuli to longevity and health" (Jon Poppy).

• Install a full-length mirror in your bathroom. Make a list of all of your positive accomplishments. Tape the list to the mirror. If the naked truth in the mirror causes suicidal depression, read the list. Then follow the suggestions on this list.

• As Peter McWilliams observed: understand that life is not a struggle—it's a wiggle.

• Expect to live well past 100 years. Remember Eubie Blake's words: "If I had known I was going to live this long, I'd have taken better care of myself."

Resources and Recommended Reading

EPA Right-to-Know Hotline: 800-535-0202. An information specialist will direct you to a state agency that can give you information about toxic conditions in specific locations. The EPA's Web address is: http://www.epa.gov/gils

If you have trouble finding a source of whole grains, organically grown produce, and minimally processed foods near your place, consider joining or organizing a food co-op. For a free list of co-op stores for any state, send a note and a stamped, self-addressed envelope to Co-op Directory Services, 919 21st Avenue South, Minneapolis, MN 55404.

Food and Water Incorporated and the Environmental Research Foundation note that, "Recently Congress banned the sale of assault rifles. However, it is still perfectly legal to kill someone with a zucchini." For information on the pesticide problem and their grassroots campaign, call: 800-EAT-SAFE.

Books

Ford, Norman. *The 50 Healthiest Places to Live and Retire in the United States.* Bedford, MA; Mills & Sanderson, 1991.

Goldman, Benjamin A. *The Truth About Where You Live: An Atlas for Action on Toxins and Mortality.* New York: Times Books, 1991.

Herbers, John. *The New Heartland: America's Flight Beyond the Suburbs and How It Is Changing Our Future.* New York: Times Books, 1986.

Setterberg, Fred, and Lonny Shavelson. *Toxic Nation: The Fight to Save Our Communities from Chemical Contamination.* New York: John Wiley & Sons, 1993.

"To lengthen thy Life, lessen thy Meals."

—Benjamin Franklin

"Happiness is good health and a bad memory."

—Ingrid Bergman

"Never deny a diagnosis, but do deny the negative verdict that may go with it."

—Norman Cousins

~ 17 ~

Community Lost and Found

"There can be no vulnerability without risk; there can be no community without vulnerability; there can be no peace, and ultimately no life, without community."

—M. Scott Peck

❧

We commonly think of community as a group of people who live near each other, have common interests, and socialize. In truth, most think of community as simply a neighborhood or an area of political designation.

Community is much more. Community inherently includes the natural elements of its place, for those features shape all humans who live there. The features are climate, water, landform, trees and shrubs and grasses, animals domestic and wild, large and small, feathered, finned, furred. Features include the ground and those things within the ground, the soil, humus, minerals. Community includes all the parts of the place that comprise its economy, and in this all elements of a place contribute. Without all these parts community is incomplete, cannot thrive.

The qualities of the natural environment, a sense of place, common interests and values, and shared experiences create the condition we call community. A community is composed of people who belong to one another and to their place. Community exists to receive membership and to give service. The commonality of the features and conditions of a place causes membership. The health of the individual—mental, physical, economical—is inextricably tied to the health of the community. A community is most healthy when it is self-sustaining.

Natural community is similar to a bioregion, but bioregions exist independent and above political boundaries, while community must sometimes consider those boundaries in matters of law, taxes, representation. Community is more similar to an ecosystem, an interrelated system of parts that coexist in harmony.

*"In speaking of community, then, we are speaking of a complex
connection not only among human beings or between humans and their
homeland but also between the human economy and nature, between forest or prairie
and field or orchard, and between troublesome creatures and pleasant ones.
All neighbors are included."*

—WENDELL BERRY, *Sex, Economy, Freedom and Community*

When it exists freely, honestly, and fully, community occupies that essential place between the individual and the public sector of society. There are certain critical human conditions that effectively can only be dealt with by community.

Community provides a sense of belonging. There is good reason to believe that much modern unhappiness—even mental illness—is the result of moving too often and with too little thought. A change in venue can improve our mental condition if it is well thought out—indeed, that is one of the premises of this book—but the modern nomad moves carelessly, with insufficient thought or commitment.

*"It's hard to believe now, but for a long time
the loss of community was considered to be liberating."*

—AMITAI ETZIONI, *The Spirit of Community*

A fundamental reason why city life is chaotic is because community functions have been usurped by public entities. A bureaucracy can never understand and be sensitive to an individual in the way that a community can. A public entity's actions are often deadly to community, undermining its authority, stealing its purpose, destroying its soul. The current strong interest in renewing connection to community is the result of widespread recognition that urban areas have largely lost it. In poll after poll, a common reason given by urban refugees for moving to the country is a yearning for community.

"The longing for community is one of the
oldest themes in our nation's young history."

—OSHA GRAY DAVIDSON

Even those of us who cherish privacy, enjoy self-sufficiency, and have a high level of independence need to be responsible to other people and know that we have others' support. Ever since our ancient ancestors huddled in caves with others, community has been one of the strongest of human bonds. Lives have been lost defending it. Robert Wright explored the new field of "evolutionary psychology" in "The Evolution of Despair" (*Time*, 8-28-95). He noted that: "Because social cooperation improves the chances of survival, natural selection imbued our minds with an infrastructure for friendship, including affection, gratitude and trust."

Examples of Community

"Community life is by definition a life of cooperation and responsibility.
Private life and public life, without the disciplines of community interest, necessarily
gravitate toward competition and exploitation. As private life casts off all
community restraints in the interest of economic exploitation or ambition or
self-realization or whatever, the communal supports of public life also
and by the same stroke are undercut, and public life becomes simply the arena
of unrestrained private ambition and greed."

—WENDELL BERRY, *Sex, Economy, Freedom and Community*

While most urban places have lost community because public entities have taken over its function, most rural areas still have well-established communities. Community is more common in low-density population areas because people depend on themselves and each other more than they depend on public entities.

Indeed, the rugged independence of ruralites resists the intrusion of bureaucracy and its attendant high taxes.

Economic cooperation is evident where communities are healthy. In some places food growers interface with consumers to create local food systems. Organic growers' organizations, buyers' cooperatives, subscription gardening have resulted to the benefit of all. Indications of strong community also include viable volunteer fire departments, well-attended PTA meetings, strong voter turnout and rejection of tax-funded programs, low crime rates, thriving local economies. Community is evident by the attitude of people you meet on the street and in local stores. Common courtesies. Smiles and greetings to strangers. Genuine expressions. And service.

We lost our nearest neighbor recently. Mike was fifty-one, a wonderful man, an extraordinary neighbor—the eulogy was easy to write, hard to deliver. His wife was in California visiting her mother when Mike's heart stopped beating as he slept. By the time his wife flew back, the house had been cleaned, clothes and bedding washed. A financial difficulty became known. There were small cash gifts. Two men began making a wooden coffin. Community members shuttled relatives from the airport two hours distant. Food was prepared and delivered.

The funeral and grave site service were well attended. In the handmade coffin, Mike lay on a patchwork quilt, also handmade. A rose-colored concrete "stone" cast in the shape of a heart was another handmade contribution.

Since that terrible but community-revealing time, kindnesses to Mike's widow continue. Grocery and mail delivery. Firewood. Company. Hugs.

Little defines and exposes community so clearly as a perceived common threat. Rural Missourians rallied together to fight and defeat a misnamed Natural Streams Act which threatened to create unbearable police state conditions for those of us with flowing water on our land or living on a watershed—essentially all ruralites. Many of these people were residents of my county whom I had never before met. The threat to our freedom brought us together—it revealed and illuminated our larger community.

The Old and the New

In some areas community appears to be divided between old-timers and new-comers. Newcomers commonly focus on the challenge of learning how to live in

166

the new place. They would do well to remember that old-timers have lived and lasted in the place under all of man's and nature's conditions. It is wise to observe how they do things. With time, some from each group integrate the other.

Your strongest initial connection will be with those who have similar backgrounds, who share your values, who came to the place by a similar path. Finding, building, and preserving community is a vital part of our human condition but urbanites have largely lost the practice. Consider carefully your motivations to become absorbed into a strong existing community.

Fitting In

"Every community demands conformity to its laws,
expects the acceptance of its customs and folkways, and prefers
to have none but native sons at its firesides."

—HELEN AND SCOTT NEARING, *Living the Good Life*

Helen and Scott tried to persuade people in their adopted Vermont community to make some adjustments in their conduct. It didn't work out very well and it frustrated the estimable Nearings, who took community very seriously in those challenging, early homesteading days. The lesson is well made: existing communities are resistant to change.

Most rural communities are gracious and welcoming to new residents. It is wise to accept early invitations even though you may be busy getting settled. If you wait until you "have time" you may find that the invitations have stopped. There likely will be ample opportunities for service work. Volunteer fire departments, PTAs, 4-H clubs, recycling groups, food buyers' co-ops, churches, and service clubs are always looking for additional membership. This is an excellent way to show the community who you are and for you to understand it. Just don't push your personal agenda and you'll do fine. In *Little Town Blues*, Raye C. Ringholz writes of the different priorities of outsiders and locals in a small Utah town: "Not of the predominant Mormon faith, environmentalists and vegetarians as well, they still live comfortably and are accepted in the tight-knit community of ranchers because they don't attempt to force their ways on longtime residents."

Country folks are often poor but proud. Poor, that is, by urban definition. It will not do to push them or talk down to them. Restrain yourself from telling them how "we did it back in Metropolis." They get all they want of Metropolis on television. And you did leave Metropolis for good reasons. If you are very lucky, one of the natives will take a liking to you. Most old-timers are proud of what they know and will share hard-won knowledge with someone who really listens. Listen carefully and you may avoid painful and costly mistakes. Give respect and you will be respected.

As for advancing your well-researched, well-thought-out, perfectly logical, totally irrefutable solutions for saving the natural world from destruction by ignorant and greedy people, keep them to yourself—or write a book. Show what you believe by how you conduct yourself. If it makes sense to the natives, why, in twenty or thirty years some of them may begin to follow your example. You will be there in thirty years, won't you? They will.

> *"A community identifies itself by an understood mutuality of interests. But it lives and acts by the common virtues of trust, goodwill, forbearance, self-restraint, compassion, and forgiveness. If it hopes to continue long as a community, it will wish to—and will have to—encourage respect for all its members, human and natural. It will encourage respect for all stations and occupations. Such a community has the power—not invariably but as a rule—to enforce decency without litigation. It has the power, that is, to influence behavior. And it exercises this power not by coercion or violence but by teaching the young and by preserving stories and songs that tell (among other things) what works and what does not work in a given place."*
>
> —WENDELL BERRY, *Sex, Economy, Freedom and Community*

How to Use Community as a Criterion

Find out where like-minded people are going. Read the following chapter on demographics and Chapter 22 on states (political, not mental). If strong community is a very high priority, you may wish to consider an intentional community (see Chapter 26).

Once you have targeted a specific county, make contact with people there. Ideally you will visit. Purposely get lost. Go into a likely looking homestead and explain your situation. Keep doing this until you find someone who will take the time to talk to you and show you their place. A few hours spent this way will tell you much about local conditions and attitudes. And you may begin a friendship that will continue after your move.

Place a small ad in the local newspaper asking for contacts by people who have recently moved there. Phone calls to the newspaper editor, banker, insurance agent, county clerk, school superintendent, and chamber of commerce are additional ways to gain feelings and information about the community.

Recommended Reading

Berry, Wendell. *Fidelity: Five Stories*. New York: Pantheon, 1992.

———. *Sex, Economy, Freedom and Community*. New York: Pantheon, 1993.

Etzioni, Amitai. *The Spirit of Community: The Reinvention of American Society*. New York: Simon & Schuster, 1993.

Norwood, Ken, and Kathleen Smith. *Rebuilding Community in America: Housing for Ecological Living, Personal Empowerment, and the New Extended Family*. Berkeley, CA: Shared Living Resource Center, 1995.

> *"Now we are all poor folks down here, we live on fresh air and mountain scenery, and we have so many ways you've just got to like some of them."*
>
> —JOHN CONKLIN "UNCLE JOHNNY" HARLIN

~18~

Demographics and Social Conditions

"It is easy to travel the United States and be impressed both with the commonalities of existence that all its residents share and with the diversity that is still imposed by vastness, the wide range of climate and physiography, the residue of history, differences in resources and agriculture, and variations in ethnicity and culture."

—Calvin Beale

Go west, young man.

No, north! No, south! No, go back east!

The history of Americans has been to move. We moved west because of furs, minerals, free land, weather, and Horace Greeley's bombast. Since the West was settled we have moved to wherever economic conditions flourished. Our movement has been and continues to be much more prevalent than our stability. If current trends continue, the average American can expect to move 11.7 times during his lifetime (*The World Almanac and Book of Facts 1996*). How many people do you know who live in the same town, city, or county in which they were born?

For most of this century more people left rural areas than moved there. By the late 1960s, social and economic conditions began to slow this migration; in the 1970s there were more people moving to rural areas than away from them. That trend continues today.

For our purposes here, what is happening on a national scale is of less interest than what is happening in specific regions and counties. Some rural counties are in fact losing population, especially in the Great Plains from the Dakotas

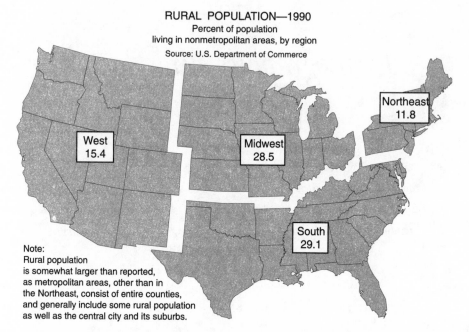

RURAL POPULATION—1990
Percent of population
living in nonmetropolitan areas, by region
Source: U.S. Department of Commerce

Northeast
11.8

West
15.4

Midwest
28.5

South
29.1

Note:
Rural population
is somewhat larger than reported,
as metropolitan areas, other than in
the Northeast, consist of entire counties,
and generally include some rural population
as well as the central city and its suburbs.

down into Texas, the Corn Belt, and the Mississippi River region. Areas where rural population gains are most prevalent include the Rocky Mountain states, the Northwest, the upper Great Lakes area, the Ozarks, parts of southern Ohio and Indiana, Tennessee, parts of Georgia, Florida, parts of the Carolinas, and a few counties in New England.

Peter Francese wrote "America at Mid-Decade" in the February 1995 issue of *American Demographics*. He noted: "Interstate migration to the South and West are old trends. What is new is heavier out-migration from the Northeast than the Midwest, and rapid growth in the Mountain States. . . . Every state in the Northeast saw net internal migration losses between 1990 and 1995. . . . More than 550,000 residents left New England alone."

Counties that are destinations for retirees continue to be fastest growing, and recreational counties are second fastest growing. Slower but continued growth is occurring in counties with an economic base in manufacturing or government. Farming and mining counties continue to lose population, except those mining counties that are now considered recreation areas, notably in the Rockies. In all cases, population gains are greatest in rural counties adjacent to metropolitan counties. Apparently we want our country homes and our shopping malls, too— or city jobs are still supporting new country dwellers.

I believe that a majority of Americans will move to rural areas once they realize that economic conditions now permit. This is supported by the conclusions of the Gallup polls cited earlier. The fact that retirees are moving in such great numbers to rural areas is further evidence. Modern industry has both followed people to the country and relocated, with workers following (see Chapter 12, "Making a Living"). The information age combined with computer technology has freed many workers to work in the country for city clients or employers. As retirees, telecommuters, and others have established themselves in the country, service industry owners and employees have followed. I think of all this as the Great Migration to the Boondocks.

Immigration, Ethnicity, Outmigration

> *"The United States is spending huge amounts trying*
> *to create a cultural presence in Latin America. But we are doing it*
> *an easier way. Little by little, with 30 million*
> *Latin Americans already here, we are taking over this country."*
>
> —GABRIEL GARCÍA MÁRQUEZ

The ethnic mixing of America is speeding up—33 percent of 1980–1990 U.S. population growth was from immigration. The Immigration Act of 1990 allows 700,000 legal immigrants per year but 4.6 million entered between 1990 and 1995, 56 percent to California, Texas, and Florida. Most immigrants settle in cities but, increasingly, many are going straight to the suburbs. Immigrants and minorities have higher birthrates than the majority population—the sum of immigration plus birthrate accounts for the fact that the ethnic minority population is growing more than seven times faster than the majority population. Minority population grew from one in five Americans in 1980 to about one in four in 1995.

The strongest influx of immigrants is in the Southeast and the Southwest. There is very strong Mexican immigration in California, Arizona, and Texas. It is predicted that the Hispanic vote will predominate in California by 2040. The dominant culture of Miami has become that of Cubans, who are also moving in large numbers to New York City and northeast New Jersey.

Asian populations are fast expanding in Seattle, San Francisco, Los Angeles, and San Diego and are settling as well on the east coast. *American Demographics* (10-93) reported that Atlanta's Asian-Americans are more visible than its Hispanics. Business signs written with Oriental characters have become common in Atlanta suburbs.

Even interior areas have experienced strong immigration—during the 1980s, 15,000 Hmong (pronounced "Mung") tribesmen from Laos settled in Minnesota. Sizable Hmong populations are also established in Wisconsin and Georgia.

The *Los Angeles Times* reported the most common last names of 1992 home buyers in L.A. County. The top ten, by ranking number of homes bought, were: Lee, Smith, Garcia, Kim, Lopez, Hernandez, Nguyen, Rodriguez, Johnson, and Gonzalez. Of the top fifty, seventeen were Latino, eleven were Asian.

University of Michigan demographer William H. Frey is concerned that a "Balkanizing" trend is occurring, with minority-dominated immigration and "white flight" leading to "sharply divergent racial and socioeconomic structure areas in broad regions and states." Several states with strong foreign immigration

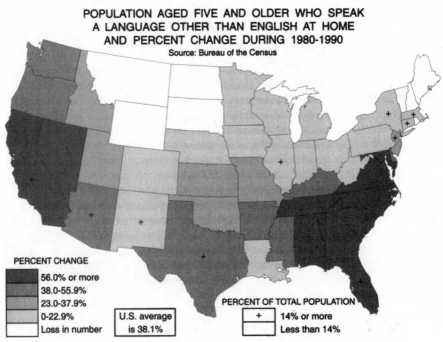

**POPULATION AGED FIVE AND OLDER WHO SPEAK
A LANGUAGE OTHER THAN ENGLISH AT HOME
AND PERCENT CHANGE DURING 1980-1990**
Source: Bureau of the Census

PERCENT CHANGE
56.0% or more
38.0-55.9%
23.0-37.9%
0-22.9%
Loss in number

U.S. average is 38.1%

PERCENT OF TOTAL POPULATION
+ 14% or more
Less than 14%

also have strong outmigration to other states. These states include Texas, Illinois, New York, and New Jersey. In *The New York Times Magazine*, 8-20-95, Frey writes: "For every immigrant who arrives, a white person leaves. Look collectively at the New York, Chicago, Los Angeles, Houston and Boston metropolitan areas—5 of the top 11 immigration destinations. In the last half of the 80's, for every 10 immigrants who arrived, 9 residents left for points elsewhere. And most of those leaving were non-Hispanic whites. . . . Blacks, like whites, are also leaving most of the high-immigration metropolitan areas, if not in the same numbers as whites, and their No. 1 destination is Atlanta. By contrast, the No. 1 destination for Hispanic-Americans is Miami, and the No. 1 destination for Asian-Americans is Los Angeles. . . . Consider California. It will be less than half white within a decade because of a massive influx of minority immigrants and a disproportionately white exodus, mostly to neighboring states, which are among the whitest in the nation."

In *American Demographics*, January 1996, Shannon Dortch writes about the Lone Star State, which in 1994 became the nation's second most populous state: "Within 15 years, Hispanics and other 'minorities' will be a majority of Texans."

Ethnic groupings are a historical American condition. British, French, Germans, Swedes, Irish came to the U.S. in waves of immigration, typically settling where others of the same origin had preceded them. Within each region of the U.S. there are places of vibrant ethnicity and pervasive local attitudes, although not just from those who have come here from another country. Place creates character. The attitude of a New England farmer is strange to a Louisiana Creole shrimp fisherman. Wyoming cattle ranchers have little understanding of Alabama cotton growers.

Beyond native American differences, newly arrived immigrants bring with them characteristics and traditions that sometimes clash with local customs and laws. Language and clothing styles are the most obvious differences but others are more dramatic. Those from cultures that commonly eat dogs, for instance, do not blend well in areas where valued pets run loose. In Asian nations fishing is done not for sport but for food and requires no license.

When I was in Minneapolis on a book promotion tour, my author escort, a young woman, told of taking a walk in the woods of southern Minnesota. "Suddenly, I was face-to-face with these small brown men with painted faces, minimal clothing, and weapons." She finally realized they were Hmongs on a group hunt. The only damage was to Eliza's composure.

If you would have a problem living in an all-white (possibly bigoted or racist) area, if you want your children to be exposed to a racial mix, or if your Norwegian parents insist that their grandchildren retain that cultural conditioning, you will need to do extra research. During consideration of any area, write or talk to local people to see who they are, who they favor, and what their biases are. The local newspaper is also revealing of local characteristics.

Prejudice and bias linger longer in the country, where tradition is strong and attitudes are less buffeted by the media. TV is not always a barrier breaker—I know people who would not allow their children to watch the *Cosby* show even though it was the number-one-rated family sitcom.

Beyond obeying laws, most of us treat our fellow humans with respect, as we wish to be treated. By no stretch does it follow that we should live in an ethnic atmosphere with which we are uncomfortable.

Where Is Everybody Going?

Nearly seven million Americans move from one state to another each year. The strongest migration is to retirement counties, which constitute one fifth of all nonmetropolitan counties. States of greatest retiree influx are, in order, Florida, Arizona, North Carolina, Nevada, and Oregon. Those with the heaviest losses are New York, Illinois, New Jersey, and California. Nonretiree urban refugees are largely shunning the Sunbelt and are instead moving to areas of lower prices, clean air, scenery, recreation, perceived safety. The strongest migration to rural counties is occurring in the following regions.

Rocky Mountain States
After life in the smog, former West Coasters find Rocky Mountain air exhilarating, the open spaces intoxicating, and the skiing superb. Seven of the nation's ten fastest-growing states during the 1993 to 1994 period were Rocky Mountain states. Beyond real estate agents and merchants, not all residents are happy about the invasion. As in Seattle and parts of Oregon, there is anger against California "equity refugees" who sell expensive Golden State homes and build or buy big homes in the mountains, driving up prices. Resistance to growth is growing, most strongly in Boulder and the area west of Denver. *The New York Times*, 11-5-95, ran a feature titled "Colorado Tries to Keep Lid on Population Boom": "The slow growth movement is taking hold as memories fade of the Rockies' bitter recession

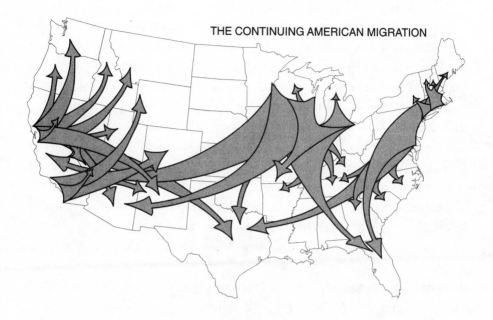

THE CONTINUING AMERICAN MIGRATION

of a decade ago, a bust triggered by falling oil and gas prices. With Colorado's economy increasingly diversified, many economists believe that the state may be breaking a century-long boom-and-bust cycle. . . . In Tucson, Arizona, sign-waving protesters confronted construction workers last month. From 1991 to 1994, Arizona and Colorado each experienced about 11 percent population growth, fastest after Nevada and Idaho."

And then there's the water shortage.

Time (9-6-93) featured an article with a paragraph title: "Sky's the limit, the Rocky Mountain home of cowboys and lumberjacks has become a magnet for lone-eagle telecommuters and Range Rover–driving yuppies. So far, it's been a booming good time." The emphasis was water. "For all its steam, the Rockies boom has its pitfalls and built-in limitations. For one thing, it cannot go on for-ever in the continued absence of a general economic recovery. . . . The region's scarcity of water poses as much of a challenge as it always has. The northern tier of Montana, Idaho, and Wyoming, with plentiful rivers and low population den-sity, expects no problem satisfying its pockets of growth. The semi-arid southern tier of Utah, Colorado, and New Mexico, however, has to give water high priority. *Denver is now judged to have only about 20 years' worth of identifiable water sources left*" (my emphasis).

William Kettredge is a short-story writer living in Missoula, Montana. In "The Last Safe Place," a follow-up in the same issue of *Time*, he says: "You hate seeing your paradise overrun by latecomers from some seaport. Many are coming to the Rockies to retire. Their children are long out of school. They're on fixed incomes and resist supporting education. But these good folks don't seem to give a damn about the welfare of our next generation. They want to buy into our functioning culture on the cheap. What's drawing these crowds? It's not so much, I think, the beauties of nature, or cheap land, as it is safety. Sanctuary. As we know, our old America fantasy—a New World and social justice all around—has gone seriously defunct. Millions of citizens in our cities quite justifiably count themselves disfranchised. Some are angry, armed, and dangerous."

From a different perspective, Steamboat Springs, Colorado, is actively recruiting "lone eagles" as part of its economic development strategy. The term describes professionals who work at home and are perceived as "clean industry" that brings prosperity to the community without any downside.

Midwestern States

"Since 1940, the United States has added at least 13,000 square miles
of inland waters (exclusive of Alaska), largely in the form of reservoirs created by
dams. Whatever the primary purpose of the dams, they have usually attracted
people for both recreation and permanent living. The effect has been particularly
great in those inland states that lacked natural lakes. For example, in Oklahoma,
Missouri, Arkansas, Kentucky, and Tennessee, there was a 133 percent
increase in inland water area from 1940 to 1970, compared with less than
25 percent in the rest of the United States. The great majority of counties with
major dam reservoirs in these states have had rapid population growth."

—CALVIN BEALE

With beautiful scenery, four distinct seasons but moderate winters, numerous large, clear reservoirs, and low prices, the Ozarks area has been attracting retirees and back-to-the-landers since the 1960s. Even after all the growth it is still pretty much just a sprinkling of retirement enclaves and small towns in huge areas of farms and wooded hills and hollows. Not all Midwesterners opt for gentler climes. Many are attracted to the beauty and recreational aspects of Wisconsin and Michigan, still close to major cultural and commercial centers.

Southern States

From Tennessee to the coast and southward through the Appalachians, urban

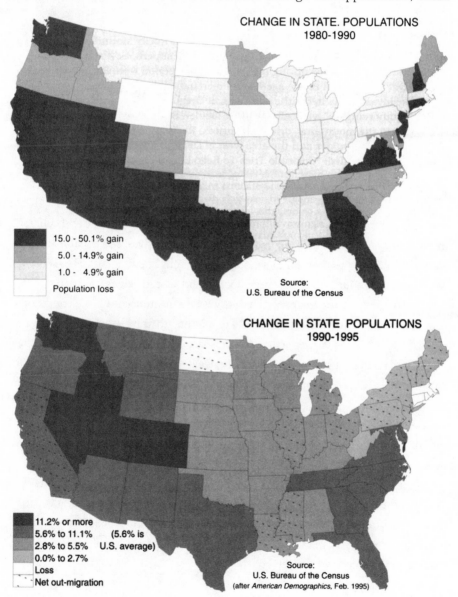

CHANGE IN STATE. POPULATIONS
1980-1990

15.0 - 50.1% gain
5.0 - 14.9% gain
1.0 - 4.9% gain
Population loss

Source:
U.S. Bureau of the Census

CHANGE IN STATE POPULATIONS
1990-1995

11.2% or more
5.6% to 11.1%   (5.6% is
2.8% to 5.5%   U.S. average)
0.0% to 2.7%
Loss
Net out-migration

Source:
U.S. Bureau of the Census
(after *American Demographics*, Feb. 1995)

refugees from east coast cities and Midwest industrial areas are following industry and staking claims to the rural dream. Georgia and North Carolina are growing at above-average rates. Florida continues to attract huge numbers of people in spite of rising prices, growing congestion, and crime. The Carolinas are siphoning off some people formerly headed farther south. Texas now ranks second in population.

Northeastern States

Some areas of Maine, Vermont, New Hampshire, and upstate New York have filled with second homes and permanent residences for refugees from the Boston to New York area who choose to stay in the region. In Vermont, the proportion of native-born residents has fallen from nearly 72 percent in 1960 to just 57 percent today. Most of the Northeast has net outmigration; only more births than deaths is causing the population to rise slightly.

Social Habits

Traditional rural social habits follow patterns established by work and religion. In most rural American areas today, as in yesteryear, natives' social habits revolve around home, work, community, school, and church. The tendency is to socialize with those individuals that one meets locally and whose values are shared.

City migrants bring their social habits with them, subject to place conditions. A common newcomer lament is how far one has to travel to socialize. In the country everybody is farther apart and the space condition definitely contributes to less socializing. In our area residents typically cherish visitors but are loath to leave home. The common end to conversations is "Come visit us—we'll be home."

Some rural areas have conversational distinctions—not making eye contact, avoiding a controversial issue, prolonged goodbyes—that you may find awkward or frustrating.

After the fast pace and congestion of city living some rural immigrants feel lonely and isolated. I know of more than one person who left our area because they could not adjust to living far beyond the sidewalks. If socializing is a prime requisite for you, you may wish to locate in or close to a town of some size. Put that on your criteria worksheet.

Culture

It is incorrect to assume that culture is lacking in the country. Founded in 1957, the Santa Fe (population 65,000) Opera has risen to become one of the top ten opera companies in America. John Naisbitt and Patricia Aburdene have a section in *Megatrends 2000* titled "From Broadway to the Boondocks": "One reason behind record-breaking audiences for opera, theater, and symphony is that people in small and medium-size cities and in rural areas can attend hometown productions in some very impressive places. . . . In remote Orono, Maine, private contributions built the stunning $7.5 million Maine Center for the Arts on the University of Maine campus. In 1986 the 1,628-seat concert hall opened with a gala bash featuring musicians Isaac Stern and Yo-Yo Ma. During intermission audiences can walk through the museum of pre-Columbian sculpture that encircles the hall. Best of all, locals can attend world-class performances in their own backyard instead of driving five hours to Boston."

City residents are acting out their country desires by decorating their homes country style, square dancing, line dancing, wearing cowboy hats and boots, and driving four-wheel-drive vehicles. Country music stars pack city amphitheaters. Even the stars are changing their habits. Nashville has long been the country music capital of the world, but with over thirty big-name performers now based in town, tiny Branson seems destined to inherit the title. In 1994 Branson hosted nearly six million visitors.

Most rural places do, however, offer far less "high culture" than metropolitan areas. Your lifestyle criteria should reflect whether you need to find a country home within reasonable driving distance of cultural events.

Crime

> *"Another innocent bystander shot in New York yesterday.*
> *You just stand around this town long enough and be innocent and*
> *somebody is going to shoot you. One day they shot four. That's the best shooting*
> *ever done in this town. Any time you can find four innocent people in*
> *New York in one day you are doing well even if you don't shoot 'em."*
>
> —WILL ROGERS

Crime is the number one concern of urban Americans with good reason. U.S. federal and state prison population in 1970 were 196,000. By 1996, 1,164,356 Americans lived in 1,560 federal and state prisons, with nearly four million on probation or parole and half a million in local jails (Bureau of Justice Statistics). Over 5.1 million American adults were in serious trouble with the law, more than the population of Wisconsin (*American Demographics*, February 1996). The December 1998 *Atlantic Monthly* puts the total behind bars at 1.8 billion. Even more graphically, by mid-1997, one in every 155 of us was behind bars (*American Demographics*, March 1998). The U.S. has the highest incarceration rate of any industrialized nation in the world. One in every 118 American men are in jail (Bureau of Justice Statistics, 6-22-97). In addition to the adult figures, nearly 600,000 juveniles were in some type of correctional program. The American Humane Association reports that since 1988, American teenage boys are more likely to die from gunshot wounds than from all natural causes combined. In 1995, California and Florida spent more money on prisons than on schools (Justice Policy Institute).

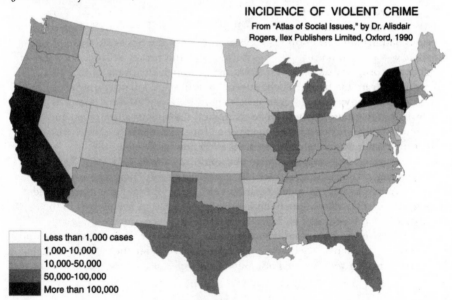

INCIDENCE OF VIOLENT CRIME
From "Atlas of Social Issues," by Dr. Alisdair Rogers, Ilex Publishers Limited, Oxford, 1990

Less than 1,000 cases
1,000-10,000
10,000-50,000
50,000-100,000
More than 100,000

Shame, shame on us.

It is most difficult to stay alive in Texas, California, and New York. In 1994, 4,096 murders were committed in California. In the past decade California has built and opened sixteen new prisons and several maximum-security camps.

Four more are under construction. State officials are asking for twenty-five new prisons. According to *The New York Times*, 1-28-96, New York City killed 1,182 of its own in 1995. In 1997, Texas executed thirty-seven convicts, more than all other states combined.

"Every year when it's Chinese New Year here in New York,
there are fireworks going off at all hours. New York mothers calm their
frightened children by telling them it's just gunfire."

—DAVID LETTERMAN

North Carolina is often held up as the new ideal form to which our society is evolving. North Carolina has estimable resources: a university with many satellite campuses, high rates of employment, a good highway system, a great diversity of homesite choices, including nearly every type of rural setting. Yet on National Public Radio (11-5-93) I heard a piece on a serious North Carolina crime problem. It seems that there is insufficient jail space to incarcerate new criminals, so inmate sentences are being shortened or curtailed. "Build more jails," the injured and fearful citizens implore. But there are inadequate state funds to build new prisons.

"The issue is the extent to which Americans are becoming a country of
separate communities walled off inside their fortresses. It's too bad we need
gates to protect ourselves from each other, but on the other hand, it's
really nice to know that you can go for a walk at night and not get hurt."

—JEFF BUTZLAFF, City Manager, Canyon Lake, California

"During the past two decades roughly a thousand new prisons and jails have been built in the United States" (*The Atlantic Monthly*, December 1998). The average cost to taxpayers for keeping each criminal in prison is nearly $15,000 per year.

Nina J. Easton and Ronald J. Ostrow wrote in "Ms. Reno Objects," *Los Angeles Times Magazine*, 10-31-93, that U.S. Attorney General Janet Reno "worries that tough, mandatory minimum sentences have filled limited jail space with two-bit crooks, enabling more dangerous criminals to get out early because of prison overcrowding."

Back in North Carolina, the governor's office reports that 60 percent of felony parolees are back in jail within three years, convicted of new felonies.

Crimes occur in rural areas but with less frequency than in cities. Family values and discipline, school discipline and community disapproval of hoodlumism are typically stronger in areas far from cities. Moreover, criminal activity is not as profitable in sparsely populated areas. The Bureau of Justice Statistics shows that there is four times as much violent crime per capita in the cities as in the rural communities of the U.S.

Writing this stuff depresses me. Let's take another humor break.

> *"Anybody can be good in the country;*
> *there are no temptations there."*
>
> —OSCAR WILDE

Potential Social and Community Challenges

Some old-timers resent newcomers who arrive with big money, fancy cars, city attitudes and seemingly try to "take over." Others are simply amused. It's amazing how place creates values—after a few years in their chosen home, old newcomers often share the same attitudes toward new newcomers as natives. You may, too.

Private property rights are often ignored in the country where large private holdings contribute to a public land image. Established patterns often conflict with changing needs. Our farm was owned for fifteen years by city people who used it only for summer vacations and occasional long weekends. The natives used the stream road, which passes about 150 feet in front of the house, to travel through the hollow and hunt for deer and turkey. For many years one neighboring property owner took city hunters through the property to a part of his land remote from his house. The first year we were here we allowed the activities to continue because we wanted to be good new neighbors. But the hunters' trucks driving through before daylight woke us up and the shooting destroyed our peace and quiet and caused us safety concerns, so the next year I stopped it. The deep resentment from that neighbor continues even now, many years later.

Determining the complete nature of communities is sometimes difficult without spending substantial time there. We have friends who bought a place on a North Carolina mountain, worked hard for two years building their homestead, and then, when they had time to socialize, discovered that the natives in their immediate area were not at all friendly—in fact, they were downright hostile to newcomers who showed intentions of staying. After enduring various insults and even threats of violence, they went looking elsewhere. After they identified their next area they ran the following ad in the local paper:

SITUATION WANTED

Mature, responsible couple experienced in rural living seeks small farm or country home to caretake for absentee owner. Maintenance and protection of your property in exchange for living quarters and garden space.

They received several offers, chose one, moved there, and lived rent-free for a year while they assured themselves that this time they had indeed found their ideal place. They and I recommend a lease agreement signed by all parties that spells out the terms of the caretaking agreement. This ensures that there will be no surprises, like being told to move out on short notice. Offering references should favorably impress the owners that you are good people and may eliminate the requirement of a security deposit.

During the seven years between finding my place and moving there I had two caretakers. They received free rent in return for minimal maintenance and improvements. The first was a family who had purchased an acreage nearby that lacked a house. After living at my place for three years they decided to sell their land and move closer to a city. The second caretaker, a single woman, later bought land nearby. In both cases, they and I profited by the experience.

Living in an area for a year, either caretaking or renting, provides time to develop income, experience the climate and the community and look at lots of properties, thereby becoming aware of values. If you will take the time, it is a low-cost way to verify that you have indeed found your ideal place.

Country people have a different focus than city people. They are more attuned to nature and natural rhythms. It is unlikely that you will be able to engage in conversation about the latest best-seller list in a neighborhood dominated by long-established subsistence farmers. If one of your treasures is a lifetime subscription to *The New Yorker* or if you find discussions about the weather incredibly boring you may be disenchanted with life in the country lane. Your criteria worksheet should reflect this.

That is not to say that country folk are less intelligent or even less well read. I think the fact that they were living and surviving in the country first says a lot for their smarts. It's just that city living tends to be faster, more tense, more focused on what's hot and what's not. Country living smoothes one out. Rural folks tend not to get very excited about fads. I suspect there were few sales of pet rocks in the Ozarks. On the other hand, if you know anyone who would like to buy some rocks real cheap, why, send them on by. For no extra charge we'll even give each rock a proper name.

If an area has been losing population or gaining very slowly, then the cultural makeup of the citizenry is likely to be that of the natives. But if the area has been growing rapidly you can expect to find a large number of people just like you who have moved there from the cities. Certain areas are so popular with urban refugees that the newcomers outnumber the old-timers. The resulting community culture is that of city people learning how to live in the country.

Independence

Country culture, attitudes, and habits are the result of people finding out what works. Land creates the human character—the harder it is to extract a living, the tougher and more independent are the residents. Country folk had to be independent to survive—a commonality between peoples of sparsely populated areas. Independence sometimes evolves into isolationism. Ozarks natives have a deserved reputation of low regard for "revenooers," a result of moonshiners and tax collectors not mixing well. A government agent was killed downhollow from our place in the 1950s because he got too close to the still in a cave up one of our side hollows. The farmers around Mechanicsville, Iowa, have exhibited similar qualities. In *Broken Heartland*, Osha Gray Davidson reveals: "In 1931, when the government began testing all dairy cows in Iowa for tuberculosis, scores of armed area farmers vowed to shoot the first son-of-a-bitch to touch a Cedar County cow."

The farmers thought the testing was a good idea—they just didn't like being told that they *had* to do it.

Politics

Rural citizens are usually conservative, especially regarding finances. When cash money comes hard, the tendency is to not part with it easily. With the city-to-country movement now in its fourth decade, some rural areas are showing the effects of increased numbers of liberal voters. In some counties, newcomers have become the majority. It saddens me that natives in those places are losing control.

City visitors are surprised to learn that the old-timers in our country, many living below the so-called poverty level, overwhelmingly vote Republican. They are astonished to learn of the poor couple who refused to sign up for an assistance program urged on them by university researchers. The scholars were disconcerted by the response: "Why, that would be like taking *charity*, wouldn't it?" Entitlement was not the issue. Values was.

Political leanings can quickly be uncovered by reading the local newspaper and talking to local people. Feed store operators, restaurant workers, the person

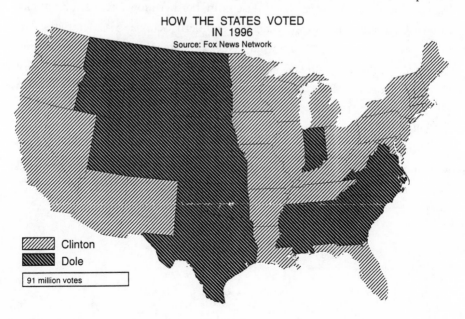

HOW THE STATES VOTED
IN 1996
Source: Fox News Network

Clinton

Dole

91 million votes

repairing your flat tire—one or two carefully worded questions may give you more information than you expected. Voting history can be found with the county clerk. When in the area, listen to talk radio. You are guaranteed to get at least one side of the political community.

Religion

> *"There is only one religion, though there*
> *are a hundred versions of it."*
>
> —GEORGE BERNARD SHAW

Rural churches are typically small and numerous, spaced according to horse-and-buggy days when trips were necessarily of short distance. Judging from the number of cars out front on Sundays, Ozarks congregations may be as few as four or five families. Denominations reflect those found in nearby towns and cities, which typically have larger facilities.

Nationally, the areas of strongest church affiliation are Utah, Texas, North Dakota, South Dakota, Minnesota, Wisconsin, northern Iowa, western Kentucky, eastern Louisiana, Mississippi, Alabama, southern Georgia, Massachusetts. The most godless areas are California, Nevada, Oregon, Washington, Idaho, Colorado, Arizona, southern Montana, Michigan, southern Indiana, West Virginia, Maine, Florida. (Based on a map in *American Demographics*, August 1995. Great map. The upward-bound are shown in heavenly blue, those headed for hell in fiery red.)

If finding a church of a particular denomination is a high priority for you, write it on your criteria list, next to demographics. You can learn of the churches in any area through the local newspaper or chamber of commerce.

> *"He charged nothing for his preaching,*
> *and it was worth it, too."*
>
> —MARK TWAIN

Alcohol

Years of sybaritic California living conditioned me to shopping habits that don't work in the Bible Belt. Shortly after moving to the Ozarks I inquired of a clerk in the local grocery store where I might find the beer. I may never forget the sight of that fine young man drawing himself to his full height and proudly declaring: "Sir, it is the policy of Town & Country Supermarket to not sell alcoholic beverages!" When pressed, his good manners prevailed and he did tell me where the town's only package store was located.

Some counties south of us in Arkansas are dry and most ban the sale of alcoholic beverages on Sunday. Some counties actually have laws prohibiting the transportation of more than a modest amount of beverage through their counties even though legally purchased in more liberal counties. Do not take such laws lightly—if stopped for a traffic violation your car may be searched. Rural law enforcement personnel tend to be very serious about their authority. It is not inconceivable that they will strike you as humorless.

Sex

Rural adults take role model responsibilities seriously. Traditional rural values include matter-of-fact but not "modern" attitudes toward sex. Children who regularly see animals breeding lack the curiosity of city kids. But attitudes toward talking about sex are conservative. If you are coming from one of the more liberal cities be aware that in many rural areas modern, open sexual conversations are considered totally unacceptable, especially within hearing distance of women or children.

There are sexual distinctions that may seem archaic. In our county it is a custom for drivers to acknowledge approaching cars with a wave. (I find it not only neighborly but nostalgic—reminds me of my early sports-car-driving days, when MGs, TRs, and Healeys were uncommon enough that we elite waved—only—at each other.) I quickly adopted the practice. But I noticed that female drivers rarely returned my wave. I finally deduced that it is inappropriate behavior—such provocative communication from a man to a woman one does not know and who is away from her spouse.

Homophobia is prevalent in the Bible Belt and what fairly are called redneck areas, both of which tend to be conservative and traditional. Homophobia exists so strongly in parts of our county that two prominent businesspeople finally left the area after continued, serious threats, rumors of deadly threats, and a partial boycott of their business.

Some rural areas have an imbalance of the sexes. Herman, Minnesota, population 485, has an excess of sixty-eight bachelors aged twenty to fifty over eligible women in the same age group. The town is especially interested in attracting a plumber, a lawyer, and an accountant. Check it out, ladies.

Some readers and talk show hosts have advised me to write more about sex. I should, they say, point out that sex is better in the country. They urge me to point out how clean air, increased privacy, fewer distractions, and romantic scenery all contribute to higher sexual energy and pleasure. I'm not sure Mom would approve of her son writing about sex. Besides, I figure my readers are way ahead of me on this subject. So I won't embarrass myself by pointing all this out.

Enclaves

Even today, in areas isolated by topography and poor roads, there are groups of people who are far out of the mainstream, are culturally unique, who live in the shadows of civilization. They may exhibit simplistic attitudes and behavior, may have intermarried, may be clans distrustful of others, as evidenced by the earlier story about our friends' experience in North Carolina.

While remoteness increases this likelihood, there is no way to know for certain whether such a condition exists without visiting the area and talking to shopkeepers, the sheriff, residents, and, ideally, local census takers, those duties have taken them into the most remote areas.

Radical Groups

Clans, cults, militants, other secretive groups and individuals like to headquarter in remote country where their unique ways will not attract attention. The local sheriff will be aware of such groups and their location. Ironically, such people are often considered decent neighbors by those who live near them; the primary anger of dissidents is usually with federal government agencies and laws. In our county, a group calling itself The Arm, the Sword, and the Covenant lived without incident while committing crimes in other states. Unabomber Theodore

Kaczynski was considered a decent, law-abiding neighbor in the Montana community where he lived while carrying out horrendous mail bombings. Oklahoma bombing conspirator Terry Nichols was a respected farm co-op manager in his Herington, Kansas, community. There are likely exceptions to all of these examples. Follow your instincts and make local inquiries to satisfy yourself of unusual individuals or groups in the area you are considering.

On Your Criteria Worksheet . . .

Of all criteria, the social nature of a place is the one most likely to be overlooked and the one that could most easily destroy your happiness in an otherwise ideal place. Consider well your needs and preferences and next to demographics write them down.

> *"Don't be fooled by what you see today.*
> *The present trickle will accumulate into a river, then a flood.*
> *Try to imagine the eventual transformation. In the*
> *next century, most middle-class Americans will be living in*
> *the penturbs. . . . Penturbs—the fifth region of*
> *opportunity—is the new frontier."*
>
> —JACK LESSINGER

— 19 —

Services and Taxes

*"It seems correct to say that we did not foresee the extent to which
the growing number of older people would include many people with*

(1) retirement incomes large enough to make them mobile,

(2) the option of retiring at a comparatively early age, and

(3) a desire to choose a rural or small-town setting

*for their retirement despite the poorer quality of medical and
community services that many such areas have."*

—CALVIN BEALE

It is a fact that many rural counties and communities provide minimal services. The reason is both cultural and economic. Country people are independent, often dollar tight, and loathe paying someone else to do things they can do for themselves. Many rural communities predictably reject ballot measures that would raise taxes to provide services perceived as not critical. "Critical" is often limited to law enforcement, schools, and roads.

Law Enforcement

Small towns often have a modest police force and a small jail. County areas are most often serviced by a sheriff and a minimal number of deputies. In low-population areas one local dispatcher may coordinate calls for the sheriff, town police, fire departments, and the ambulance service.

Our county of 9,500 has a sheriff and two minimally trained deputies who provide their own cars and guns. We provide the sheriff's car and we buy everybody's bullets. Bullets are not a big budget item. The sheriff is not as good-looking as Andy Griffith was in *The Andy Griffith Show*, but he smiles just as big, especially with the approach of election time. Our deputies are several notches above Barney Fife and we give them a whole box of bullets. Like the judge, our sheriff is elected by county voters. I can best explain the condition of our county jail by reporting that repeat offenders are only those with really bad memories. The dispatcher, the jail, and the sheriff's office are in the courthouse building in our county seat, which is also the main town in the county—its population is substantially less than a thousand and holding steady.

Schools

"A child's education should begin at
least one hundred years before he is born."

—OLIVER WENDELL HOLMES

Rural schools parallel city schools in that they are a reflection of the values of the residents. Community interest and support for student activities is often every bit as valuable as tax dollars. Don't expect as many frills as big-city or affluent suburban schools offer; Olympic pools and multiple tennis courts are unlikely. There are notable exceptions—visit schools to assure yourself of the facts.

Small-town schools often have big-time spirit. Among the schools represented in the 1994 Rose Parade was the award-winning high school marching band of Pipestone, Minnesota, town population 4,500. One third of the entire high school student body was in the band.

Sandy Banks wrote in "Finding the Best School Means Seeking a Culture of Success" (*Los Angeles Times*, 10-23-94): "Finding a school that will nurture a budding intellect, salve self-esteem and set your child on the road to the Ivy League has little to do with such mundane concerns [as large classes and low test scores]. . . . Instead, look at how the desks in the classroom are arranged, find out the teacher's hobbies, be a 'student' on the campus for a day." Other suggestions are: find a school where people can tell you why and not just what and how they are teaching as they are.

Living outside of town means students ride buses, as I did my last three years of high school. It was a novel experience—out of twenty-six riders, only two of us were boys, I the older. The girls schemed for the privilege of sitting with us. Two boys trying to be fair to twenty-four girls was an awesome—and rewarding—challenge.

Since 1978, the number of children being homeschooled has jumped from 12,500 to one million (*The New York Times Magazine*, 10-8-95). Laws affecting homeschooling vary widely from state to state and are changing, sometimes month to month, as more advocacy groups are successful. The nonprofit National Homeschool Association has volunteers throughout the country who are knowledgeable about specific state laws or have contacts who are. The NHA address and phone are listed at the end of this chapter. My contact advises me to tell you to be skeptical of "free" homeschool advice given by individuals or companies offering insurance or other services for a fee.

For those skeptical about the efficacy of homeschooling, know that both Thomas Edison and Albert Einstein were homeschooled—by single mothers.

Transportation and Roads

> *"Thanks to the interstate highway system, it is now*
> *possible to travel from coast to coast without seeing anything."*
>
> —Charles Kuralt

The interstate highway system is finished and the U.S. Department of Transportation, state transportation departments, and road engineers are now working on the National Highway System, which will connect the interstates and principal arteries. The new roads will be designed to serve commuter and commercial traffic and will connect cities, ports, airports, border crossings, public transportation facilities, and major travel destinations.

By city standards country roads range from adequate to deplorable. County roads are usually dirt or gravel while state roads traversing counties are usually paved. If you expect to commute to work you will want land near a good highway. If you will work at home and clients will not need to visit, you may wish to buy property far from highways, which will lower land costs, lessen traffic noise—which travels far in country quiet—and raise the level of privacy.

Some states help finance rural transportation systems for those who don't drive, typically older folks. Most do not. School buses serve nearly all areas sending children to public schools. Taxis are usually found only in cities—so if you take one to the country, don't lose it.

Fire Protection

Unless you live in town, you would do well to learn to depend on yourself. Rural areas may or may not have fire departments. If they do they are probably staffed by volunteers. In our county there are twelve member-supported volunteer fire stations spaced to provide minimum response time. Even so, most house fires result in loss of the structure, with the firefighters' work confined to preventing the fire from spreading. Some only respond to members' fires, which helps to keep annual dues paid on time. In many rural areas, the state conservation department and U.S. Forest Service maintain a fire-fighting capability primarily to protect forested areas but available for nonstructural emergency private use.

Utilities

Rural electric service is provided by a variety of business entities. Ours is a cooperative, owned and operated by members. Rural electric rates are affected by the ownership entity, the type of fuels used for generation, and whether the owners invested in nuclear generation—the shutdown and cleanup costs of nuclear facilities are substantial and will be passed on to customers through increased rates. The property you buy will either have electricity to the house, it can be brought in at a price, or it will be too far away to be affordable. The alternative to buying electricity is home generation by photovoltaics, water, or wind, plus a backup generator powered by gas, diesel, or propane. Photovoltaic costs have not become low enough to make this a viable option unless you build about a third of a mile or more beyond existing power lines.

Where there are electric power poles and lines there will usually be telephone lines. If you plan to use a modem, be aware that some old rural phone lines may have line noise that will affect fax modem transmissions.

Radio and TV reception is weaker in the country and worst of all down in a hollow or valley. If TV is important to you, a satellite dish receiver may be in your future. New models are about the size of a giant pizza and give excellent service. The flavor and nutrition of what they bring in varies.

Waste Disposal

Even small towns usually offer trash pickup service. Most areas have some sort of recycling operation, either administered by a town or county government or by a local group. In some places the area landfill management will provide dumpsters to individuals or businesses who then share the service with others for a fee.

In many rural areas there is no trash pickup. This is an opportunity. In truth, there is very little that needs to be sent to a landfill. We sort for recycling, compost all food trimmings and leftovers, and burn paper products that we can't recycle. We buy in bulk to minimize containers. It's amazing how quickly you can find ways to cut down on so-called waste material. It's a good feeling to evolve from being an Earth kicker to being an Earth kisser.

Sewage Disposal

Rural sewage disposal systems are usually private. They may be as simple as an outhouse, as modern as an indoor composting toilet, as elegant as a greenhouse/water hyacinth system, or as common as a septic tank and leach field. Whichever system you encounter or build, you will be responsible for maintenance. Outhouses and composting toilets need periodic emptying, hyacinths are cut and added to the compost pile, and septic tanks need to have sludge pumped out periodically. A leaking septic tank can pollute a well.

Health Care

This subject is covered in Chapter 16, "Health 101."

Libraries

> *"No place affords a more striking conviction of the vanity*
> *of human hopes than a public library."*
>
> —SAMUEL JOHNSON

Did that get your attention? At first this cynical quote perplexed me. Samuel Johnson (1709–1784) was an eminent English lexicographer and writer. He wrote a dictionary and is widely considered to be the greatest man of letters in English literature, so it is safe to assume that he used words correctly. One would also expect him to have greatly valued books and the places where they are kept. A dilemma.

Research reveals another Samuel Johnson (1696–1772)—this one a philosopher and clergyman—one of the founders of King's College, present-day Columbia University. His view was that the sensible world is made up of ideas man receives directly from God. That could explain the proposition that books are examples of man's vain hopes.

Yet more research finds that Samuel Johnson the writer was an expert on the subject of vanity, having written *The Vanity of Human Wishes*, a great poem about how all human efforts are as nothing without a proper regard for God. This Johnson used the word *vanity* in a more profound manner than is common today. He gets the nod as the source. *Bartlett's Familiar Quotations* agrees.

See what you can learn in a library?

Funding for rural libraries is often inadequate or entirely absent. My only serious country living regret is the distance to a large library. Our very modest county library is funded by donations and fund-raisers and is maintained and staffed by volunteers. Notable exceptions to these stark conditions are found in those towns that contain colleges and universities.

I will always treasure books. I can't imagine curling up with a good computer. Heavy and up-to-the-minute research is another matter. While I have a substantial library and read many periodicals, I also use electronic data sources, CD-ROM encyclopedias, online services. Once computers become ubiquitous and we all learn how to navigate the electronic information world, libraries will become less necessary. That may take a generation.

Services Equal Taxes

"The art of taxation consists in so plucking the goose as to obtain the largest amount of feathers with the least amount of hissing."

—Jean Baptiste Colbert

Most of us complain about one or another of our taxes. Here's where you get to choose your real estate taxes, state income taxes, and sales and excise taxes. And your services. Because, bureaucratic waste aside (now there's an oxymoron), the services and taxes go hand in hand, or hand in pocket. Although we can do nothing—legal—about federal income tax and Social Security tax, by carefully choosing the state and county that we will move to we can choose state income tax, state sales tax, county property tax, local sales taxes, use taxes and fees that we will pay.

Low taxes support minimal services but maximum freedom. Ideally, we buy only as much service as we really need. As one of my criteria, I listed low taxes. I got them. With the exception of the state conservation department, all fire protection in our county comes from volunteer departments that are funded by membership fees and fund-raisers such as recycled-materials sales and auxiliary activity. State roads are blacktop; county roads are gravel. There is no trash pickup beyond town boundaries. There is no planning commission and no zoning commission. If we choose to build a pyramid or a bowling alley in our front yard we are limited only by imagination, energy, finances, and common sense. Common sense seems to do the job just as well as if we had zoning laws. There is also no building inspector. I feel certain that you would not believe how low our taxes are.

The historical record shows that voters in our county almost always vote against new tax proposals. Our county commissioners understand from the get-go that they have a steep uphill battle trying to make any "improvements." Schools, roads, a small sheriff's department, a jail no sane criminal ever wants to return to, and the bare minimum number of county employees necessary to meet state requirements. That's it. I bought our land in 1976—the property taxes are lower today than they were back then.

Some rural areas, especially those close to cities, provide and charge for almost as many services as cities. Just remember: if you get more services, you pay for them. And in the case of planning, zoning, and building officials, you also pay for loss of freedom. Your choice.

Property taxes vary substantially from county to county. Unlike income and sales taxes, the lion's share of which go to state governments, revenues from property taxes are split 96 percent to local governments and only 4 percent to the state. Fees and miscellaneous revenues are more evenly split, with 57 percent going to local governments and the remaining 47 percent to the state (USDA, AR-31, June 1993).

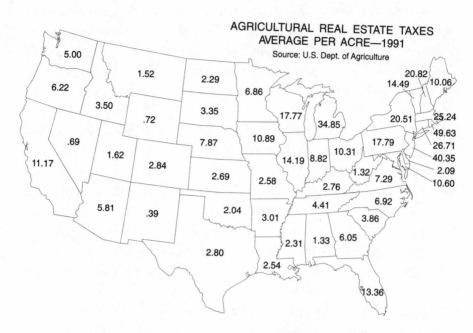

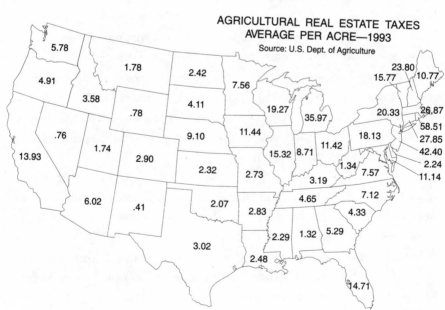

State sales taxes range from zero to 9 percent. Counties and municipalities often add to this. Local officials can give you the rates.

States that do not charge state income taxes have to make up that loss by charging more through another type of tax. New Hampshire is an example of a state that does not tax income or (most) retail sales. Sound good? In *Country Careers* Jerry Germer states that it is not uncommon to have a New Hampshire property tax bill of $3,600 or more on a $100,000 home.

Devolution

The Citizens for Tax Justice booklet offered below notes that the responsibilities of government "are being shifted from federal to state and from state to local governments." The tension between the demand for services and the desire for lower taxes will always be with us. This tax shift is certain to produce varying results across the country, as states and counties react to voter demands.

Mark your criteria list according to your specific needs and desires for services—and taxes. Remember: the best tax is the one not due. This is also the time to write your needs and preferences for electricity, telephone, and radio and TV reception. Review Chapter 11, "The Cost of Living," if necessary.

Resources

Citizens for Tax Justice
1311 L Street, NW
Washington, DC 20005
202-626-3780
E-mail: ctj@ctj.org; Web page: www.ctj.org

CTJ and the Institute on Taxation and Economic Policy published *Who Pays? A Distributional Analysis of the Tax Systems in All 50 States*, June 1996.

National Homeschool Association
P.O. Box 157290
Cincinnati, OH 45215-7290
513-772-9580

The people who run this nonprofit organization are unpaid volunteers. For information on homeschooling laws, call and leave a message saying which states you are interested in. A contact in that area will phone you. It will be less expensive for them if you send a note with a SASE. They also have a packet of information for first-time homeschoolers.

World Wide Web: There are several Web sites on homeschooling. Just search the subject.

"The income tax has made more liars out of the
American people than golf has. Even when you make [a tax form]
out on the level, you don't know when it's through if you
are a crook or a martyr."

—WILL ROGERS

— 20 —

To Build or Not to Build

*"At a certain season of our life we are
accustomed to consider every spot as the possible site of a house."*

—Henry David Thoreau

If your dream includes building a house, then buying bare land may be on your mind. An alternative that gives more property choices is to buy land with an old house on it that you can live in while you build. If the house is really humble it will not add appreciably to the property value, especially on a larger parcel. A caveat—the existing house may be sitting on the choicest building site on the entire acreage. That was my dilemma—take it down, move it, or rebuild it. I have vacillated on that issue for over twenty years. Beware of the charm of old shacks.

Another option is to buy a mobile home for temporary living during construction. Once your home is built you may be able to sell the mobile unit for nearly as much as you paid for it. If you choose this route you will have to provide temporary electric, telephone, water, and waste lines.

Buying undeveloped land requires additional research and inspections. Ensure the availability of water, electricity, and telephone service. Talk to local well drillers about the cost of a well and pressure system and the odds on finding good water within a reasonable depth. Verify this information by talking to adjacent landowners. If you are not yet comfortable with the concept of a composting toilet, local backhoe operators can tell you the cost and probable effectiveness of a septic system. Some soils have inadequate drainage character-istics; a percolation test answers that question and is required in many counties. Ensure that you will have legal ingress and egress rights. Inquire at county business offices for building permit costs and requirements. Check for zoning restrictions to make sure you can do with the land what you wish and to deter-mine cost and compliance requirements.

Part of the foregoing may not apply if you buy a lot in an existing subdivision or town. But you must check zoning laws for uses permitted, building codes, and whether there is an architectural review board that must approve your plans. In some subdivisions you must build within certain size and style guidelines and, for instance, you may only be allowed to paint your castle an authorized color. If any of these conditions exist you are probably not in real country.

In addition to getting the design you want, a big advantage of building a new home is that you can use modern materials and methods. Home energy conservation technology has made great progress in the last decade and can greatly enhance your comfort and substantially lower the cost of maintaining a comfortable climate inside your home.

Building materials will cost as much and maybe more than in the city because of trucking costs. The wages of rural craftspeople are less than their city kin and often less than they are worth. In our county, you can hire a good plumber or electrician for $15 per hour. Carpenters get between $8 and $15, depending on experience and skill level. If you are not ready to wear the hat of general contractor you will need to pay someone to fill this role.

Log homes are the quintessential country dream home. As we have seen, surveys show that nearly one third of Americans dream of a cabin in the woods. According to the Log Homes Council, a division of the National Association of Home Builders, 20,000 log homes were built in 1992 (*Harrowsmith*, September/October 1993); in 1994, an estimated 35,000 to 40,000 were built (*The New York Times*, 9-24-95). Most log homes are customized from stock plans offered by log home companies. The better ones are not only beautiful but energy efficient.

Rural residences range from ultramodern dwellings to old farmhouses unburdened with plumbing or wiring. Electricity did not make it to some rural counties until the 1950s. Inadequate and improper wiring is a serious fire threat and should be upgraded before use—rodents love old homes and attic wires are often found chewed free of insulation. Old heating systems, especially wood-burning, may preclude buying fire insurance.

Property with a well-designed modern home is most costly but will give you quality and convenience. The two primary reasons for buying land with old houses are low price and atmosphere. Old farmhouses are typically given little value by the local assessor, real estate appraisers, and sellers and buyers. In many cases that is appropriate, as the cost of bringing them up to modern standards can be substantial. Many old places are uninsulated, have inadequate electrical wiring, archaic heating, inadequate or nonexistent plumbing, may have a colony of bats living in the attic, and leak in the lightest rain. Most important, the foundation may be deficient.

Old houses also have architectural character, history, heart. The atmosphere of an old place can be steadying, reassuring, quieting, a powerful influence on how you feel about living in that place.

An existing house means that certain necessities are in place. An existing road saves the cost of paying a bulldozer or grader operator to put one in. A good existing water supply system takes away the possibility of drilling a dry hole and the costs of drilling, pump, pressure tank, plumbing, fixtures. Existing electricity

Essential Country Skill #4: milking a cow

Instructions: The small animals with feathers are chickens. The cow is the large animal with horns. The milk comes out of the cow's nozzles as illustrated. Place a milk bucket under the nozzles. Grasp one or two nozzles and squeeze. If milk does not come out, squeeze harder. If the cow kicks, you are squeezing too hard or should trim your fingernails. Apologize to the cow and replace the bucket. Squeeze with a top-to-bottom action. Squeezing with other actions may cause the milk to flow upward instead of downward—this will annoy the cow. Continue squeezing a few thousand times until the milk bucket is full. Thank the cow and go make some ice cream. (Note: When buying a cow the most important consideration is the nozzles. Keep searching and squeezing until you find a good fit.)

means a substantial savings over having to contract with the local utility to bring it in or buying and installing a home generating system. It also means the poles are in place so telephone lines may be installed if they are not there.

Where there is an existing house, there also are likely to be outbuildings. An old barn, garage, root cellar, or workshop adds to the utility of any property. There will often be other pleasures. Fences, bridges, paths. Existing or old garden spots. Flower beds. Fruit and nut trees.

As with much in life, making the decision to buy improved or unimproved land is something of a balancing act. Quality versus character. Convenience versus cost. The cost factor will change if you have construction skills and want to use them. Most important are your feelings. You probably already have a preference for building or buying an existing house. My purpose here is to alert you to the appropriate considerations so that your choice will be informed.

So now, on your criteria worksheet, write your preferences for property: bare land or improved property. And remember, you can always change your mind later.

Resource

Log Homes Council
National Association of Home Builders
1201 15th Street NW
Washington, DC 20005-2800
Phone: 800-368-5242, ext. 162; or: 202-822-0200

> *"No house should ever be on a hill or on anything.*
> *It should be of the hill. Belonging to it. Hill and house should live*
> *together, each the happier for the other."*
>
> —FRANK LLOYD WRIGHT

～ 21 ～

Prices

*"The price of that upward mobility of which
we have—as a people—for so long been so proud
has become too high."*

—Marya Mannes

The characteristics of value are demand, scarcity, transferability, utility. Land and home prices are affected by more; they are influenced by interest rates, fear, inflation, and greed.

Real estate price movement used to be pretty predictable—always upward. There was a time in the 1970s when we didn't worry about paying top price for any property because within a few months the market value was up by 10 percent. It was hard to go wrong. No longer. Since about 1990, prices in many rural areas have been rising while many urban and suburban areas have experienced fallen or stagnated prices.

The breathtaking urban and suburban price jumps of the 1970s and 1980s were initiated by the demand of 76 million baby boomers born between the mid-1940s and the mid-1960s. Schools overflowed and the biggest school building boom of all time commmenced. More high schools were built in America in 1967 than in any year before or since.

After finishing school the boomers got married and started rearing families. They wanted homes of their own just like Mom and Dad. Rural landscapes disappeared as pastures became sprawling subdivisions. During the 1970s the baby boomers created a huge demand so subdividers provided the supply. Soon speculators—which many of us became—bought anything they could get for a low down payment and rented it out, putting up with plugged-toilet-in-the-middle-of-the-night calls because they knew they were going to become wealthy if they hung on long enough. In the early 1980s we suffered a recession. Then in the middle and late 1980s the market went crazy as the last of the boomers and the speculators made a final run.

The fast-rising prices of the 1970s created a new home-ownership paradigm. A home was no longer a treasured place that would stay in the family for generations. A home was now an investment. Traditional home ownership values were replaced by portfolio enhancement considerations.

The population bulge that is the baby boom market force has moved to the right side of the graphs. As the millennial clock ticks over, boomers are mid-thirties to mid-fifties and most have already bought homes. Today's women are waiting longer to have children and are having fewer of them. The demand for

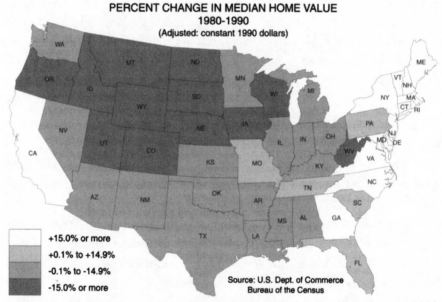

PERCENT CHANGE IN MEDIAN HOME VALUE
1980-1990
(Adjusted: constant 1990 dollars)

+15.0% or more
+0.1% to +14.9%
-0.1% to -14.9%
-15.0% or more

Source: U.S. Dept. of Commerce
Bureau of the Census

first homes, the foundation that holds up the house of real estate, has crumbled.

That's why part of the house has fallen down. That's part of the reason for record foreclosures and the S&L wipeout—that and greed and changing market conditions influenced by world forces. The world changed quickly in the late 1980s. All within a few years, the Berlin Wall thundered down, the world decided to take a well-deserved depression break, and the Cold War melted and evaporated. All but the fiercest hawks conceded that Star Wars was history. All but the blind noticed the national debt, the S&L depositor rape, a prolonged national recession, and the absence of an identifiable evil enemy. Desert Storm proved that the U.S. is more than adequately armed to deal with second-rate military forces. And so the feds closed military bases and canceled contracts for planes, missiles, military R&D. California, the seventh most productive political unit in the world, paid the price. The financial earthquake continues to rumble. Inflated home equities—paper fortunes—are disappearing like designer ice cubes in cappuccino.

Prices are not reacting equally throughout the land. Not all areas were dependent on defense. Certain hot spots like Washington, D.C., and Houston caught fire. Houston laid claim to becoming the capital of the world or something.

So where are we? Is nothing about the real estate market dependable anymore? Are all the old rules out the window? No. Everything still acts and reacts as it did before. It's all predictable. Not an easy task, but possible. It's still a matter of supply and demand, interest rates, inflation, greed. But today's market factors change much more quickly than ever before because of big business/government activities and so the predicting business has become more of a guessing game.

Rural Property Prices Today

The average value of U.S. farmland in 1995 was $832 per acre, an all-time high. Prices of marginally productive farmland in areas such as parts of the Great Plains are falling as irrigation costs rise, land is abandoned, and agribusiness forces more family farmers out of business. The trend today is to huge agrifactories, whether for grain or animal production, on land close to inputs and markets. This trend has created difficult conditions for family farmers but may be beneficial to urban refugees looking for old farmsteads at favorable prices.

Rural homes with acreage and unimproved land suitable for homesteads may be more or less expensive per acre than land appropriate for full-scale farming, depending on location, seller motivation, demand, and other local conditions. Following is a sampling of rural listings from Better Homes and Gardens Real Estate Service and Rural Property Bulletin, available in 1996:

- Arizona: 40 acres near Ash Fork; appraised value, $15,000, cash discount.
- Arkansas: 3 bedrooms, 2 bathrooms, central heat and air, 2-car garage, 25 acres, $95,000.
- California: 16-acre parcel, panoramic view of foothills, $55,000.
- Colorado: 1.9 acres with cabin, views of the Rocky Mountains, $68,750.

- Florida: 3 bedrooms, 2 bathrooms, on 10 acres, $39,000. Also, 20 acres, $36,000.
- Idaho: 20 acres, creek, trees and pasture, mountain views, $52,000.
- Illinois: Own your own island: 7-acre island, 2 cabins, great fishing, $28,500.
- Kansas: 157 acres, some tillable, some timber, rural water available, $65,000.
- Kentucky: 185 acres, rolling hills and hollows, hardwoods, some open, $59,500.
- Michigan: 40 acres, 3 bedrooms, custom barn with box stalls, indoor arena, $152,900.
- Minnesota: 16 acres, 4 bedrooms, 1 3/4 story, great outbuildings, fruit trees, $84,900.
- Montana: Cabin, 2.5 acres, over 400 feet of creek frontage, remote setting, $49,900.
- Pennsylvania: 89-acre farm, 4 bedrooms and 2 full bathrooms, barn and 2 outbuildings, $180,000.
- Rhode Island: 105-year-old Colonial on approximately 2.01 acres with pond, $89,900.
- Virginia: 84 acres, woods, springs and creek, wildlife, 3-room cabin, $58,500.
- Wisconsin: 158 acres, abandoned farmhouse, barn, 40 x 90 shed, $59,500.
- Wyoming: Ranch land 20 miles west of Rawlins, 640 acres, $41,600.

Here are some median housing prices that appeared in "A Small-Town Sampler," *Time*, 12-8-97:

- Randolph, Vermont, population 5,000: $85,000
- Lexington, Virginia, population 7,000: $90,000.
- Danville, Kentucky, population 15,500: $93,000.
- Nappanee, Indiana, population 5,500: $85,000.
- Pontiac, Illinois, population 11,500: $72,000.
- Chippewa Falls, Wisconsin, population 13,000: $65,000.
- Hannibal, Missouri, population 18,000: $70,000.
- Okmulgee, Oklahoma, population 13,500: $60,000.

• Georgetown, Texas, population 18,000: $108,000.
• Grass Valley, California, population 9,500: $135,000.

Californians are currently in love with the Rocky Mountain states. Prices of highly scenic land in Idaho, Wyoming, Montana, and Colorado are being driven up fast by the demand. Newcomers often bring with them the paradigm of buying homes with property for investment. Some longtime ranching families are selling out for premium prices, then buying much larger acreages in less scenic places. Dr. Tom Carlson, a veterinarian and rancher, sold his 600-acre horse ranch in Shell at the base of red cliffs in Wyoming's Big Horn Mountains. He then acquired 16,800 acres in the high plains near Medicine Bow and had money left over (*The New York Times*, 5-7-95).

Future Prices

Guessing the speed of real estate price movement is a high-stakes game intensely played by investors, bankers, developers. For instance, huge acreages are being purchased in parts of the West on speculation that land prices there will escalate. Heavy hitters might figure that Tarzan Ted Turner bought his 140,000 Montana acres with more in mind than just privacy for playing with Jane. My bet is there will be a ten- to twenty-year period of undulating adjustment while inflated urban prices meet the effect of rural migration, immigration, and the reality of global economic forces. Until NAFTA, GATT, the EC, and other alliances have shown their influence on American jobs, predicting urban prices is a crap shoot.

What's the future for rural real estate prices? Part of the answer can be found by studying the census reports of the last thirty years. The 1980 census showed that the forty-year movement from country to city had reversed. Now in the last part of the twentieth century, Americans increasingly find cities unhealthy, unsafe, too expensive. In "Rural Rebound Revisited" demographers Kenneth M. Johnson and Calvin Beale note that rural residents are typically staying put while metropolitan residents continue the migration to rural places (*American Demographics*, 7-95). It is reasonable to predict that the migration to rural America will continue. I believe that it will accelerate.

The pattern of population migration from city to country has become clear. The movement is incremental. Central city dwellers move out to the suburbs while suburbanites move out to small towns or to real country. Like the circular wave created by a disturbance in calm water, the movement is outward, ever outward.

University of Washington real estate professor Jack Lessinger studies this movement. He predicts: "Prices will rise in penturbia. They must, to reflect growing populations. . . . In newly developing counties, land values will rise, in metropolitan counties they will fall. Gradually, the two will become more equal in value."

Anticipating the demand for rural property, many people are now buying second homes as a hedge against higher prices and as a way of more easily making the city-to-country transition. Baby boomers are turning their backs on faded corporate dreams and are converting big-city equities into small-town cottages and rural businesses. Legions of ex-Californians are already growing gardens in Washington, Oregon, Arizona, Colorado, Nevada, Utah, Idaho, and Texas. East Coasters are filling Maine, Vermont, the Carolinas, Georgia, and Florida. Midwesterners are migrating to Wisconsin, Michigan, Missouri, Tennessee, Kentucky, Arkansas. So—are country prices going up? Do politicians break promises? Does a goose go barefoot?

Decision Time

For most of us, price is an important criterion, but not the most important. My advice is to identify the area that meets your requirements, check it out with both paper research and personal visits, and then buy as much land as you can afford.

If what you want is more than you can presently afford, a good compromise is to buy your country property now but then stay in the city at a high-paying job until the property is paid for. Every city refugee I have ever talked to agrees that having one's property paid for before moving to the country is a wise choice— often the one factor that determines the difference between a successful rural rooting or a retreat back to suburbia. Having forty acres and independence in a few years is better than instant gratification but the pain of making property payments from lower country wages.

Another answer to affordability is to buy farther out. Prices decline as miles to the nearest city increase. Really inexpensive property can be had where the utility lines have not yet appeared. Utility line extensions are expensive but photovoltaic technology makes generating one's own power a reasonable alternative. Cellular telephone service may soon make telephone lines unnecessary.

A common dilemma is choosing between less property now or more property later. The dilemma of buying more acres but then spending more time in the city to pay for them is a conundrum. Talk it over with your family. There is no right or wrong answer. Take your time. You will note that price is down at the bottom of the criteria worksheet. That's because all the preceding factors are best decided without a dollar consideration. To buy your ideal property may mean having to wait before moving to it. I've lived through that scenario and I think the goal is worth the price.

On your criteria worksheet, write what you now believe should be the maximum price you will pay for your property. Divide this price by the minimum number of acres you desire and you will have the per-acre price that you can pay.

Sources

Better Homes and Gardens Real Estate Service
2000 Grand Avenue
Des Moines, IA 50312
800-274-7654

Ask for a free copy of *Homes Away from Home* and a referral to brokers in your target areas, who can then send you information on available properties.

Rural Property Bulletin
P.O. Box 37
Sparks, NE 69220
402-376-2985
Web site: http://www.cnweb.com/rural

RPB is an independent national publication not affiliated with any real estate agency. $2 sample copy; $16 per year for 12 monthly issues.

Farmland price information is available from:

Environmental Indicators and Resource Accounting Branch
Natural Resources and Environment Division
Economic Research Service, USDA
1301 New York Avenue, NW, Room 532
Washington, DC 20005-4788
Phone: 202-219-0436; fax: 202-219-0477

PART III

Finding Your
Ideal
Country Home

— 22 —

Regions, Bioregions, States

*"In the United States there is more space where
nobody is than where anybody is. That is what makes
America what it is."*

—GERTRUDE STEIN

Economic-Cultural Regions

Calvin Beale, senior demographer at the U.S. Department of Agriculture, is said
to have traveled in well over half of the nation's 2,304 nonmetropolitan counties
(Peter A. Morrison, *A Taste of the Country*). Perhaps because of his habit of
getting into the field as much as possible he was the first demographer to notice,
in the late 1960s, that some metropolitan areas were losing population to the
countryside. This was the beginning of a return to the trend of the first two
centuries of our country's history—minus the 1940s, 1950s, and most of the
1960s. Beale developed the following map and designations of twenty-six
economic-cultural subregions.

Northern New England–St. Lawrence
Density and prices have stabilized. This area has been the primary destination of
young professionals, environmentalists, and homesteaders from the Boston to
New York area. The region gets a lot of media attention and has developed a self-
conscious rural/small-town culture. The main economic base is manufacturing,
but many urban professionals have begun small businesses, and tourism is
strong. Upper Maine has low prices, rugged winters. The Great Ice Storm of 1998
likely cooled the plans of some potential residents.

Northeastern Metropolitan Belt
The most densely populated nonmetropolitan area in the U.S. stretches from
southern Maine to northern Virginia, averaging about 140 persons per square

26 Economic-Cultural Subregions

Developed by Calvin Beale,
Senior Demographer, U.S. Dept. of Agriculture

1. Northern New England • St. Lawrence
2. Northeastern Metropolitan Belt
3. Mohawk Valley and New York • Pennsylvania Border
4. Northern Appalachian Coal Fields
5. Lower Great Lakes Industrial
6. Upper Great Lakes
7. Dairy Belt
8. Central Corn Belt
9. Southern Corn Belt
10. Southern Interior Uplands
11. Southern Appalachian Coal Fields
12. Blue Ridge, Great Smokies, and Great Valley
13. Southern Piedmont
14. Coastal Plain Tobacco and Peanut Belt
15. Old Coastal Plain Cotton Belt
16. Mississippi Delta
17. Gulf of Mexico and South Atlantic Coast
18. Florida Peninsula
19. East Texas and Adjoining Coastal Plain
20. Ozark • Ouachita Uplands
21. Rio Grande
22. Southern Great Plains
23. Northern Great Plains
24. Rocky Mountains, Mormon Valleys, and Columbia Basin
25. North Pacific Coast
26. The Southwest

mile. Most areas are within commuting distances of job centers. There are many second homes and vacation homes in this region.

Mohawk Valley and New York–Pennsylvania Border

Conditions similar to the above. Very little real country—dominated by major cities of Buffalo, Rochester, Syracuse, Albany. High-tech industrial plants. Finger Lakes region.

Northern Appalachian Coal Fields

Long history of polluting industrial and mining operations combined with uncertain economy creates negative environmental and employment conditions.

Lower Great Lakes Industrial

Between and beyond the cities of Milwaukee, Chicago, Indianapolis, Detroit, and Cleveland are many small cities and towns. Heavy industrialization near the lakes. Rural areas are primarily concentrated agricultural operations—farm sizes are increasing. Beware of pollution.

Upper Great Lakes

Negligible agriculture, continued resource-based economy. Strong water-based recreational activity by tourists, second-homers, retirees, previous residents. Northern half of lower Michigan is growing rapidly, creating typical growth problems, including water quality.

Dairy Belt

Stable, predominantly rural area of farms, influenced strongly by the Minneapolis–St. Paul metropolitan area.

Central and Southern Corn Belts

Over 85 percent of land is in farms. Many small towns. Moderate manufacturing. Population declining as farms are consolidated into larger agribusiness operations.

Southern Interior Uplands

Thousands of small tobacco farms. The region has lately been characterized by a reduction in agriculture and an increase in manufacturing. Recreational activities have been increased by development of the Tennessee and Cumberland rivers. Large areas of rural conditions. Strong immigration in central Tennessee is causing rising prices.

Southern Appalachian Coal Fields

Narrow, winding hollows and rugged hills, very little level land. Very rural, many small towns, poor. Beale notes that the deeply dissected Cumberland Plateau country of southern West Virginia, eastern Kentucky, and smaller parts of Virginia and Tennessee has been the classic area of white poverty in the United States. As coal prices go, so goes the economy. Heavily mined, the area has suffered severe environmental degradation. Stay far from water that may be contaminated by past, present, future mining operations. The other caution is: bring money with you—this is a very poor place to make a living.

Blue Ridge, Great Smokies, and Great Valley

Eminent countryman Wendell Berry said that if he were free to move, he'd look in the mountains of western Virginia (Donald McCaig, *An American Homeplace*). That's a high recommendation.

Southern Piedmont

Nearly half of all rural residents work in manufacturing. Economic emphasis is on textiles, furniture, new products. Agricultural activity is low and decreasing. Rural densities fairly high and rising. Atlanta is the dominant economic influence.

Coastal Plain Tobacco and Peanut Belt

Rapidly changing area. Emphasis has shifted from agriculture (tobacco, peanuts, soybeans) to industry, with substantial influx of companies seeking cheap labor pools. Wide distribution of business and residences. Nonmetropolitan population outnumbers the metropolitan population. North Carolina is sometimes held up as the example of where we are headed demographically as a nation.

Old Coastal Plain Cotton Belt

Predominantly agricultural. Substantial rural land with low population density. Beware: cotton is a high chemical-input crop and the soil and water of the region reflect this.

Mississippi Delta

Rich soil, high pollution, high poverty rates with distinct racial aspects.

Gulf of Mexico and South Atlantic Coast

Tobacco, peanuts, soybeans. This area has lost much population to industrial areas. High percentage of the widely distributed rural population is black and poor.

Florida Peninsula

More than one fourth of rural residents are sixty years old or older. Most of the area is dominated by retirement, recreation, attendant service industries. Fast population growth since 1960s has substantially raised rural land prices and living costs. High crime rates in metro areas. No letup in sight to continuing huge immigration rates by Americans, Cubans, Haitians, others. Rural land is disappearing.

East Texas and Adjoining Coastal Plain

Burgeoning Dallas–Fort Worth area in the middle and Houston in the south dominate socioeconomic conditions. Contrary to common perception, this area has substantial rolling, wooded farmland suitable for country living. Beware of mineral rights laws that allow surface intrusion, also use of eminent domain laws for private development.

Ozark-Ouachita Uplands

My beloved bioregion. The Ozarks area is the result of the last of several great uplifts from ancient seas. Hills and hollows, the latter carved by water over 250 million years. Hillsides are mostly covered with oak-hickory forest plus pine and cedar. Generally poor, rocky soil, but garden sites are available in all but rocky hilltops and glades. Except for bottomland fields, farmland is predominantly pasture/hayfield. Population was apparently higher in the past; there are many vacant or unfarmed old subsistence farms. Winters range from harsh in the north to mild in the south. Fast weather changes are common. "If ya don't like the weather, jist wait a bit." Rainfall averages thirty-nine to forty-five inches. Lots of springs, streams, ponds, man-made lakes. Historic atmosphere. "Even the land-scape fosters the feeling that you can simply glance over your shoulder into the past," wrote Phyllis Rossiter in *A Living History of the Ozarks*. Popular retirement destination especially around lakes. Low land and housing costs, both in small towns and boondocks. Negatives include low wages, rocky soil, fickle weather, late frosts, thunderstorms, ice storms, tornadoes, humidity, biting insects, venomous snakes, poison ivy. Don't say I didn't warn you.

Rio Grande

A mixture of semiarid to arid plateaus and mountains. About two fifths of the population are Mexican-Americans, one tenth Native Americans. Very low density. Water determines where agriculture is possible. Scattered mining activities. Economies are often supported by transfer payments. Southern New Mexico is attracting retirees. Santa Fe has social friction between poor natives and rich immigrants.

Southern and Northern Great Plains

Sparse and declining population. Small towns struggle to survive. Declining groundwater supplies for irrigation may dictate bleak economic future. Lots of empty houses. If you need low prices, can live with flat land, and make a living at home with a modem, this might work for you. The cost of houses is very low. The people are so nice it takes getting used to.

Rocky Mountains, Mormon Valley, and Columbia Basin

Dominant Morman influence in Utah and surrounding edges of other states is being diluted by continued inmigration. Economy is basically agricultural—

ranching, dairying, irrigated crops, and dry farming, plus coal, oil, gas, and uranium mining. Strong recreational economy around Lake Powell and national parks in southern Utah. Much of the region is very dry.

North Pacific Coast

*"Come and visit us again. . . . But for heaven's
sake, don't come here to live."*

Tom McCall (when he was governor of Oregon)

Heavy rainfall, mild climate, timber, lush ocean coast, valleys, mountains. Timber industry future is uncertain as lumbermen and environmentalists joust for control. Agriculture flourishes in Willamette River Valley. Cloudbelt image shows that Sunbelt is an imperfect synonym for population growth. Strong immigration has caused resentment among Washington and Oregon residents, who actively discourage immigrants, especially Californians, although one reader wrote to say that she found Oregonians to be very friendly.

The Southwest

Las Vegas growth continues at a very high rate in spite of obvious water dearth. Phoenix growth is also strong. Arizona, southern California, Nevada continue to attract sun seekers. California is, well, California—all superlatives and pejoratives fit—I recommend exhaustive research. All weather patterns available. Strong Asian and Mexican inmigration—substantial native-born American outmigration to Rocky Mountain area. Agribusiness operations in San Joaquin and Sacramento valleys continue to poison groundwater. North-versus-south water battles continue.

Bioregions

*"The valley in which we lived was
designed by nature as an isolated, self-contained
economic and social unit."*

—Helen and Scott Nearing, *Living the Good Life*

In *Dwellers in the Land: The Bioregional Vision*, Kirkpatrick Sale says the word "bioregion" was "first propagated by writer Peter Berg and ecologist Raymond Dasmann . . . working through an organization called Planet Drum [see Resources below] and a newspaper irreverently called *Raise the Stakes*, who brought the concept to a wider audience."

On the matter of definition, Sale says: "The natural region is the bioregion, defined by the qualities Gaea has established there, the givens of nature. It is any part of the earth's surface whose rough boundaries are determined by natural characteristics rather than human dictates, distinguishable from other areas by particular attributes of flora, fauna, water, climate, soils, and landforms, and by the human settlements and cultures those attributes have given rise to. The borders between such areas are usually not rigid—nature works of course with flexibility and fluidity—but the general contours of the regions themselves are not hard to identify by using a little ecological knowledge."

Sale wrote in 1985 that about forty bioregions had been identified across the North American continent. Examples of bioregions are the Ozarks Plateau, the Sonoran Desert, the Great Plains, and the Central Valley of California. Within bioregions are distinct ecosystems, each contributing to and overlapping other systems. Jim Robbins explains their process in *The Last Refuge*: "As charismatic as the grizzly bear is, however, there is a movement among conservationists and scientists to swing the spotlight away from animals with popular appeal, like the wolf, or bear or mountain lion, to recognize instead the myriad and intricately related life-forms—from microbes to fungus to insects to mammals—that make up an ecosystem. Research in the past few decades has shown just how dependent an ecosystem is on each part. Tiny microbial soil dwellers, like bacteria and fungi, decompose logs, grass and other organics into minerals that growing plants can use. . . . And so the goal of a sustainable ecosystem is not just to protect the grizzly bear habitat or wolf habitat, but to keep as much of the ecosystem intact as possible, to preserve biodiversity."

States and counties have artificial boundaries; bioregions have natural boundaries. This is readily apparent from an airplane; children (and perhaps a few urban adults) are confused to find no state boundaries on the ground. For our purposes here, we can use bioregions to identify our ideal area, but we use states and counties to gather information, as that is how we presently organize data.

The value of thinking on a bioregional level is that we consider natural conditions and natural laws. To fulfill our present mission—finding our ideal home place—we consider human conditions such as taxes, roads, utilities, services, but our greatest consideration should be for the natural conditions of climate, landform, soil, vegetation, and water. Thinking in these terms will allow us to think beyond political boundaries during our search. This is a big change for most, so I include the following information classified by states.

States

> *"States, like men, have their growth, their*
> *manhood, their decreptitude, their decay."*
>
> —WALTER SAVAGE LANDOR

Every state has something special to recommend it but certain states are attracting most city-to-country migrants. Fast growth drives up prices, creates growing pains, creates resentment by natives. Oregon, Washington, and Colorado residents most notably have lashed back at Californians invading their states. North Carolina natives are upset with the Florida "halfback" migration (retirees moving halfway back to where they came from originally). It is to be expected that natives or longtime residents of other states will have similar negative feelings against those whom they perceive are negatively affecting the quality of their places.

Since the 1960s, homesteaders and other back-to-the-landers have been moving to rural parts of Missouri, Tennessee, Arkansas, North Carolina, Kentucky, Oregon, Washington, Wisconsin, Michigan, Oklahoma, Maine, Vermont, New York, West Virginia, Virginia, South Carolina, Minnesota, and Georgia. The Sunbelt—California, Arizona, Nevada, New Mexico, Texas, and Florida—has been attracting retirees for decades. The Texas economy rollercoasts with energy prices but the Hill Country still attracts urban refugees. Florida has become expensive and crowded and is humid in summer—still the sun lovers flock there.

Colorado is the favorite destination of Californians looking for a Rocky Mountain high. Many of those seeking big open spaces are choosing Idaho, Montana, and Wyoming. Most other states have pockets with outstanding geographic features. Water concerns are growing in the West; with the exception of western Oregon and Washington, most western states have inadequate water except along rivers, and even there water rights may preclude use by new settlers.

California is a special state. Blessed with multiple climates, landforms, and features, it seems an ideal place. It was. California is perhaps our clearest example of what happens to a place when too many people move there—over 31 million humans have turned Eden into a teeming quagmire. "Californication" is an epithet now used to describe high prices, social disarray, and urban sprawl caused by overpopulation. Businesses and individuals are leaving the central and southern parts of California for the same reasons—a souvenir postcard says it all: "Earthquakes, Riots, Wildfires, Droughts, Mudslides, Smog, Gridlock, Overcrowding, Rampant Crime, High Cost of Living—Enough Is Enough . . . I'm Out of Here!!!" Northern California has some beautiful low-density country but residents there pay high fees and taxes to keep the floundering state financially afloat.

Consider carefully the characteristics of your bioregion: the shape of the land, water resources, the plants and animals (including human), the nature of the soil, the action of the sun. These features will influence the rest of your life.

Use the states map to outline your initial regional preferences—those states that fit your topographic and climate criteria. You may find you are attracted to several. Mark them all.

Resources and Recommended Reading

Chambers of Commerce

The *World Wide Chamber of Commerce Directory* is out of print but is available in many libraries. For a nominal fee you can purchase a directory of the chambers for each state from the U.S. Chamber of Commerce, 1615 H Street NW, Washington, DC 20062, or phone 202-659-6000. Most state and local chambers will send you packets of information including maps and real estate company listings. Also, the annual *World Almanac and Book of Facts* gives addresses and phone numbers for each state's chamber or department of tourism.

States, cities, even small towns have created sites on the Internet. Use your browser's search capability, type in the name of the place you want to investigate, and, voilà, you will have substantial information on that place.

State chambers and tourism departments are usually located in the state capital. They are good sources of maps, tourist guides, demographics, climate information, industry, taxes, and so forth. Tell them what you want. The volume of material you receive will show the priority placed on attracting tourists and residents, an indication of growth probability.

Real Estate Company
Several real estate franchise companies deal in rural property. I conducted cooperative sales with various Better Homes and Gardens Real Estate offices for many years and have observed their operation since they started in 1978. They have offices in all of the states—over 1,400 offices nationwide. Their computerized referral center gives you quick access to agents in any area. Use them as research resources for area information as well as listings. After you identify your ideal area, call the referral center. Ask your referred agent to send you information on all available properties meeting your criteria. It will save headaches to both sell your city home and buy your new place using BH&G agents. A big advantage of using BH&G agents on both ends is that each agent will constantly be checking with the other, so selling and buying transactions can be coordinated. Escrow closings can be coordinated even to the extent of having funds automatically transferred from your sale escrow to your purchase escrow.

Better Homes and Gardens Real Estate Service
International Referral Service Center
Phone: 800-274-7654; fax: 800-274-7680

Bioregional Organization
Planet Drum Foundation
P.O. Box 31251
San Francisco, CA 94131
Shasta Bioregion
415-285-6556

Source for information on bioregions and bioregional movement.

Books

Downing, Joan, editor. *America the Beautiful*. Chicago: Children's Press, 1990. This is a set of books, one for each state. Although they are classified as juvenile literature, I found them in the adult book section of a library, and the ones I have used appear to be well researched, written, and designed, totally suitable for adults. Of course I'm just a large, semi-old child. Subjects include geography, history, government, economy, industry, culture, and population density, distribution, and growth.

Sale, Kirkpatrick. *Dwellers in the Land: The Bioregional Vision.* San Francisco: Sierra Club Books, 1985.

Shattuck, Alfred, *The Greener Pastures Relocation Guide: Finding the Best State in the United States for You.* Englewood Cliffs, NJ: Prentice Hall, 1984.

"A strong sense of identification with a particular place means making a bond with the other people who live there—whether you always agree with them or not. Common ground in the geographic sense creates common ground in the social sense."

—Daniel Kemmis, Mayor of Missoula, Montana

~ 23 ~

Real Country, Boondocks, and Old Subsistence Farms

"I am speaking to city people. This leads me to say that there are two kinds of country and country life—the country of the city man and the country of the countryman. These prospects are wholly unlike, for the country is seen from opposite points of view, and with different preconceived ideas. The city man looks outward to the country: it is his respite and release. The countryman is part of the country: it is his realm and his support."

—LIBERTY HYDE BAILEY, *The Outlook to Nature*

Real Country—A Condition of the Mind

Real country for some is the land just beyond the last urban bus stop, or the last suburb beyond the previous last suburb, or the single field of grazing cattle between two towns that have not yet grown together. For many it is the area variously called exurbs, rhuburbs, slurbs, fringe areas, the edge. For others, it is far beyond all city influence—outback, bush, boondocks, indeed, what urbanites might call wilderness.

Your concept of real country is unique to you and likely denotes not merely distance from city but certain conditions and features. Population density, size of property holdings, types of human activities, and evidence of the natural world are all factors that contribute to a sense of real country.

Jack Lessinger coined the word "penturbia" to describe the fifth area of American development: "small cities and towns, and subdivisions, homesteads, industrial and commercial districts interspersed with farms, forests, lakes and rivers." In regions such as the Northeastern Metropolitan Belt the interspersion

229

has become thin. The so-called farm country in Massachusetts has a density of between 100 and 250 people per square mile, only 2.5 to 6.4 acres per person. Bostonians may consider that to be real country.

Most of us would agree that real country means an area of sparse population. Then we would debate the definition of sparse. For my wife and me, it is being surrounded by hundreds of acres of forested hills and hollows, the nearest small town fourteen miles and thirty minutes away and the nearest shopping center a one-hour drive. (In addition to our garden we have a pantry, freezer, and root cellar.) There is nearly a half mile of thick woods between us and our nearest neighbor's house.

The state maps in Appendix B show the sparsely populated areas in each state. Areas indicated by shading have a population density of less than fifty people per square mile, even less in some cases, which equates to at least 12.8 acres per person. For some of us this is too crowded. For others, after living in a concrete jungle it may feel like the wild frontier.

Why did I set the limit at fifty people per square mile? Well, that's how I found the data in *America the Beautiful*. How the people who produced that wonderful set of books acquired that data is a mystery to me—census takers could never create those noncounty lines. I envision a wide line of trustworthy Boy Scouts dutifully marching through each county, honestly counting people. "Good morning, ma'am, you're eighty-seven!" "What! How impertinent!" (Courtesy is in the mind of the oath taker.)

As urban areas have sprawled, country has become closer to more people. Real country today may be less than an hour's drive from towns with major schools, hospitals, shopping centers, cultural facilities. Some of the best of these towns are small state capital and college towns.

Boondocks

Boondocks—what a wonderful word. In Tagalog, the primary Austronesian language of the Philippines, *bundok* means mountain. Etymologists persuade that *bundok* was combined with *sticks* (as in "out in the sticks") to get *boondocks*, which now means a remote rural area. And you thought you were only going to learn geography here.

Boondocks is a challenging word to work with. Is it: boondocks are serious country, or boondocks is serious country? It's at moments like this that I wish the girl in front of me in English class had not been so devastating. Well, they/it are/is. In the boondocks, four-wheel-drive vehicles are appropriate, as are supplies adequate for extended periods. Water is an issue. Considerations include lack of electricity and telephone lines. Other than wood, energy for heating and cooking is often imported. Photovoltaic charging systems currently available can make living in the boondocks quite comfortable. Lights, refrigerators, tools, radios, even computers may now be powered by batteries recharged by the sun.

Boondocks land prices are usually very low. If you are proudly independent with a high level of country skills and your idea of adequate space is similar to that expressed by Daniel Boone—"If I can see the smoke from my neighbor's fire, it is time to move"—then the boondocks may be the place of your ideal home.

Unless you have lived in a primitive manner before, you might try camping in a remote area for a few weeks, better a few months, best a full year. Expect procuring potable water to be a challenge. Without a well and electric pump, water sources may be limited to springs, streams, lakes. Plan to purify. Take tools, food, a lot of books. Take a very close friend.

Abandoned Small Farms

According to the U.S. Department of Agriculture, the number of farms has dropped every year since 1950, from 5.6 million then to 2.059 million in 1997. Regrettably, none have dropped onto politicians' heads. In prime soil areas, extensive farm consolidation has occurred and around cities many former farms are now shopping centers and subdivisions. Still, there are thousands of old subsistence farms in real country just waiting to be discovered. The former owners were often too poor to use chemical fertilizers, herbicides, and pesticides, so the land is probably clean, although the family dump site will typically be found in some low spot.

These abandoned farms are often ideal country home places. Many may be found in Michigan, northern Wisconsin, southern Missouri, northern Arkansas, Kentucky, Tennessee, and other southeastern states, particularly in hilly areas. They are often owned by city people who only occasionally visit "Grandmother's farm."

I especially like old subsistence farms for many reasons:

• They have land too poor and/or too hilly for agribusiness operations.

• They have established water sources.

• They are in communities of small farms.

• They are often reasonably priced.

• They have a set of buildings which, even if ramshackle, can be used for temporary shelter and storage.

• They have old garden sites and fruit and nut trees.

• They have history.

• They have nostalgic surprises: remnants of stone walls or split-rail fences; family cemeteries; old-fashioned rose bushes; daffodils that in spring appear in a row where a long-ago fence protected a farm wife's flower garden from chickens, cows, horses, hogs, and dogs. Ours bloom every spring.

If all of the above is too wild for you, the next chapter on small towns and villages may include your definition of country.

"The new heartland can be seen on the outer fringes of metropolitan areas; around small towns far removed from the large cities; along rivers, coastlines, and reservoirs; near recreation and retirement areas; on marginal farmland; along country roads; and on remote land that is barren except for its physical beauty."

—JOHN HERBERS, *The New Heartland*

— 24 —
Small Towns and Villages

"Where all the women are strong, all the men
are good-looking, and all the children are above average."

—GARRISON KEILLOR

If your vision of an ideal country place is a small town or village, then this chapter is for you. The quality and the character of small towns, the likelihood of change, and the nature of small-town communities are all factors that bear consideration.

Small-Town Change

"The price of a good community is eternal vigilance. You get
the master plan and you think it's done. But it isn't done. It's a living
document. The community is changing every day and somebody has
to be paying attention all the time."

—TERRELL J. MINGER, Robert Redford Institute for Resource Management

Norm Crampton, author of *The 100 Best Small Towns in America*, wrote under the title "Small Is Beautiful" in *USA Weekend*, 12-3-95: "Today, something surprising is happening in America: Small towns are growing again. More people who grew up in them are staying put. More people who left them are coming back. And more people from big cities are being drawn to small-town life."

It is tempting to romanticize small towns and life therein—easy to be influenced by nickel-ice-cream nostalgia. Some of us grew up in a small town;

most of us are only a generation or two away from one. Memories persist of clean, uncrowded, crime-free communities, of warm evenings on front porches, of shy boys kissing giggling girls behind lilac bushes. Those who are a generation or more away have heard family stories about small-town life, commonly, "the good old days."

"For any American who had the great and priceless privilege
of being raised in a small town there always remains with him nostalgic
memories of those days. And the older he grows the more he senses what he
owed to the simple honesty and neighborliness, the integrity that he
saw all around him in those days."

—DWIGHT D. EISENHOWER

I find it difficult to generalize about small towns. I'd like to say that they reflect our heritage, our roots, from whence come the values that are the foundation of our national soul. I'd like to say that they exude a sense of community. I'd like to point out that small-town inhabitants can be counted on to smile and wish us a good morning or good afternoon—and mean it. I'd like to say that small towns are like good parents and grandparents, a dependable source of trust, support, encouragement. In my nostalgic dream list small towns change their human faces with births and deaths, but their hearts keep the same predictable beat.

Well, some do, some can, some are, and some will. But many small towns are no longer trustworthy. Too often today, in the time a person gets to know one well, it changes to another identity. Osha Gray Davidson reviewed two books relating to the dilemmas of small towns ("Mixed Media," *Utne Reader*, May/June 1993). In the first we are presented with part of the picture: "Some rural communities are being destroyed by economic decline, others by infusions of prosperity" (Raye Ringholz, *Little Town Blues: Voices from the Changing West*). In the second another image: "Once-stable villages in New Hampshire, Connecticut, Vermont, and upstate New York are being 'pureed by progress'—blended into an increasingly diffuse, culturally ambiguous, and urban-influenced mass" (Ron Powers, *Far from Home: Life and Loss in Two American Towns*).

Change is inevitable, destruction of community is not. The lifeblood of a small town, of a community, is the people. As with marriage and friendship, good conditions prevail when the participants are motivated by love and respect to protect, preserve, enhance. Small towns preserve their heart and their health when residents care enough to make it happen. Many communities have adopted slow-growth or no-growth laws, but that's only part of the solution. Any community is composed of all its factors and features and unless attention is paid to them all something inevitably will go awry. The destruction of small-town qualities has become widespread but it is far from universal.

> Q: *So, do you think that small town life in America is disappearing?*
> A: *No! Oh, no . . . oh, no! Communities such*
> *as these can be found all over the United States. I mean, it sure*
> *as hell is shrinking, but it's still out there.*

—PAUL NEWMAN (Interview by Jonathan Cutler in *Venice* magazine, December 1994)

The characteristics of small-town life are passed from elders to children. Ron Alexander's "Metropolitan Diary," *The New York Times*, 1-14-96, included a letter from Mary Anne Christofferson: "In the small town of Port Crane, N.Y., where my grandchildren live, neighbors toot their horns as they drive by and family members look up from gardens, swings, lawn chairs or snow shovels to wave hello or to call out a greeting. Here, in New York City, I walked with Daniel in his stroller and was not surprised by angry drivers blasting horns impatiently. Daniel, almost two, smiled, looked up, waved and said, 'Hi.' Bless his country heart."

Bona fide small-town atmosphere is the result of generations of people who have lived by the demanding natural rules of their place. The elements of small-town quality are natural and man-made beauty, stable economy, strong community, low population density—and time. Only in low-density beautiful, natural places is the human spirit preserved and nourished. Compacting people causes certain social disease. Again—never forget—all cities once were villages.

"Christopher Alexander, the author of *A Pattern Language*, a primer on architecture and urban design, recommends between 5,000 and 10,000 as the ideal population for small towns; like Aristotle before him, Alexander bases this figure on the number of people that can effectively govern themselves" (Witold Rybczynski, *City Life*).

The one small-town quality that does not change:

> *"A small town is a place where everyone knows*
> *whose check is good and whose husband is not."*
>
> —SID ASCHER

There is one thing that is constant in all small towns. It was true in Ben Franklin's time and it will be true when our great-great-grandchildren are smoothing their lawns with automatic, preprogrammed, solar-polared, satellite-position-guided, laser-zapping grass trimmers. The one thing that is constant in all small towns, and will last longer than anything of which I can conceive, is this: small-town life is not very private. Someone once noted that in a small town a car with the wrong directional signal blinking endangers no one because everybody knows where the driver is really going.

When everyone you meet smiles and greets you, when the bank employees all address you by your name, when your neighbors put out your trash cans because you forgot, it is not because these are members of a superior species living on a higher plane than mere humans. It is at least partly because everyone knows that the least slight, the most minimal of neighborly indiscretions, will become instantly known by everybody in town and remembered for at least three generations. "Why yes, my dear, don't you know—he's the grandson of Robert Booboo—you remember, he's the one who didn't even notice poor old Mr. Wretched struggling with his stuck gate that bad winter of ought-seven, and poor old Mr. Wretched like to have had a heart attack. Mmm, yes, that was his grandfather."

> *"So live that you wouldn't be ashamed to sell the*
> *family parrot to the town gossip."*
>
> —WILL ROGERS

In many ways our county (about 9,000 population) functions rather like a small town. A friend of ours once appeared on a national television show featuring his wood carvings. A few weeks later he received a letter from a viewer in Arizona addressed to "The wood carver" at the wrong post office—but in our county. That was enough information for the postal clerks.

We live fourteen miles from our nearest town. We do our banking there and buy as many things as we can, considering selection and prices. I get to that town on average about twice each month. I know few people there. Yet I have been stopped on the sidewalk and addressed by name by total strangers. The ensuing conversations left no doubt that the strangers knew much more about me than my name.

I can't say that I mind living in a place with these conditions. Now, if I lived right in town, I might. Think about it. If you cherish anonymity for your virtues or your vices, you may not be comfortable in a small town.

Suburbs in Disguise—"Towns" to Avoid

"Everybody when they come to the suburbs they want the trees
and bunnies and birds, okay? And that's why we put two swans
out there and feed the damn ducks so all the frigging geese and ducks come
around and people say, 'Gee, I work out in a place where they have paths
and running tracks, ponds, birds. Do you have a running track
where you work?'"

—DEVELOPER TO AUTHOR JOEL GARREAU, in *Edge City*

Caution: New Towns are designed to seduce you. The face is pretty but superficial. The concept is ancient; the dream of creating a perfect human environment in a natural setting has persisted throughout history. The most famous recent attempts began with Reston, Virginia, in 1962, continued with Columbia, Maryland, in 1963, and include Jonathan, Minnesota, and Irvine, California—a town fast becoming a city. The idea of planned cities goes back at least to Miletus, Greece, which was planned during the fourth century B.C. During the Middle

Ages, over 400 new towns were built in England, Wales, and Gascony, as well as about a dozen in Switzerland and Germany.

The current craze in urban planning is the effort to "villagize" the suburbs. San Francisco architect Peter Calthorpe is impressing his Transit-Oriented Development design on Laguna West, an Apple computer facility near Sacramento. Calthorpe advocates dense communities where cars are passé. He envisions linking workers to their jobs with light rail transportation. A noble plan. But the number of riders a light-rail system needs per day to be cost-effective is 7,000 and the probable number of car commuters who will change to rail has been determined to be 12 percent. So to make light rail cost-effective requires 14.5 million square feet of office space—more than downtown St. Louis or Cincinnati.

Miami architects Andres Duany and Elizabeth Plater-Zyberk, of Seaside, Florida, fame, promote their Traditional Neighborhood Development, codes that any jurisdiction might adopt. TND mandates mixed-use developments designed as small towns. On paper the effort is laudable: deemphasize the auto; build paths so people can walk to work and shopping; create small parks where inhabitants can talk and play chess. To ensure atmosphere, the codes require white picket fences and ornamented front porches. The imagery is beguiling, a developer's dream. Nostalgia sells, and big investment money is betting that the concept will reap profits.

These are designer towns, suburbs with psychology, homes with chutzpah, nouveau nostalgia, yuppie high camp. The purported goal is to deemphasize the automobile and encourage a village atmosphere. The result is artificial villages—the product of a "you can have a brand-new 'grandma's town' and we're prepared to give it to you for a price" marketing strategy.

The homes are expensive. And there part of the absurdity is found. These counterfeit communities are being built for those who yearn so strongly for the qualities of small towns that they are willing to enslave themselves to large monthly mortgage payments to fake it in a suburb. To parody an old song—I owe, I owe, so off to work I go. How can there be high-quality life with employment slavery? There cannot be. And the "quality" is a veneer.

Developers and bureaucrats say New Towns are grand attempts to create a quality environment. However clever the words, the primary goal is profit. The analogy with agribusiness is compelling—give consumers what they have been conditioned to want: a colorful, blemish-free product—and to hell with nutrition. In *New Towns: Another Way to Live*, Carlos C. Campbell states: "Planning commissions and zoning boards are nothing more than smoke screens for the real decision makers—bankers, politicians, and bureaucrats." Reflecting their fathers, New Towns tend to be heavy on control. They often embody numerous associations, councils, and institutions to control social conditions. In the view of New Town progenitors, the ideal town has ideal control of its less-than-ideal citizens.

Main Street is another consumer hot button—witness the success of Main Street at Disneyland. Duany and Plater-Zyberk transformed Mashpee Commons, a Cape Cod shopping mall, into an old-fashioned Main Street. In Kentland, Maryland, they redesigned a regional shopping center to emulate the nature of a traditional town square.

The allure of small-town ambience is irresistible. Millions of tourists travel to small towns each year to absorb the atmosphere. Quick quiz question: how many artificial villages will become tourist destinations? Joel Garreau suggests some guiding questions: "Will we ever be proud of this place . . . will we ever feel—for this generation and the ones that follow—that it's a good place to be young? To be old? To fall in love? To have a Fourth of July parade? Will it ever be the place we want to call home?"

New Towns and edge cities, like suburbs of any name, exacerbate the serious issues of habitat destruction, water scarcity, sewage treatment, social tension. They are the yuppie hot spots of today, the slums of tomorrow. Inner-city sickness spreads outward in expanding concentric shock waves; suburban sprawl is the leading edge of city cancer; artificial villages are simply compacted suburbs more prettily packaged.

With regard to suburban development, Jack Lessinger is clear: "In our vast inventory of land, suburban real estate is the one type least suited to the emerging consensus. . . . Suburbia will go down with the ship—along with the entire system of the Little King's consumption economy. . . . We will see miles of 2,500-square-foot behemoths, their wide windows broken and patched, their many rooms divided and subdivided into nondescript apartments, and, betraying the indignities of poverty, the former proud front lawns will be littered by junk automobiles and broken furniture."

Another example of an inspired effort to build perfect-town is Arcosanti. Visionary architect Paolo Soleri has designed and, with the labor of student workers, is building a self-contained community in the desert north of Phoenix. An apse-shaped foundry, housing, restaurant, gift shop, swimming pool, gardens. A "town" as a sprawling concrete monolith. I visited Arcosanti three times over the last twenty-five years. It doesn't seem to be happening very fast. The main source of funds appears to be tour admissions, student-worker fees, and the beautiful bronze wind chimes the workers cast. It takes a lot of chimes to build future-town.

The Disney Company doesn't sell chimes, yet, but it has the do-re-mi to build about anything it wants. A cattle pasture near Orlando is becoming the new town of Celebration. The lucky winners of a drawing were allowed to write checks for their choice of housing: Estate, Village, Cottage, Townhomes, Apartments. All commercial buildings vill be owned by Disney. The population of Celebration vill be 20,000. The houses vill be painted approved colors. There vill be no clothes on lines in der yards. Achtung!

Avoid Fast Change

Change is irresistible and small towns are susceptible. If you desire an old-fashioned small-town atmosphere that will persevere, then research population trends and growth plans before committing to any place. Ask the mayor, county clerk, newspaper editor, bank president if they know of any companies considering a move to your chosen hamlet. If large companies move in they will cause rapid change. It is a matter of percentages. If your target town has a present population of two or three thousand and a big company builds a factory or headquarters there that will employ several hundred, the odds are great that the essence of that place will quickly change. Talking to key people in town will help you gauge local inclination toward fast growth, especially company head-quarters, factories, and shopping malls—developments that can change and dominate the atmosphere of a small place.

Prosperity begets change. L.L. Bean brought excessive success to little (6,905) Freeport, Maine. The mail order giant's 90,000-square-foot store first only attracted shoppers and tourists. But the crowds attracted what locals call "Bean sprouts," over 100 new stores hawking everything from perfume to furniture. Today, more than 2.5 million shoppers a year produce traffic jams, thick exhaust, escalating real estate prices.

Where to Look for a Small Town

The North Central region has more small towns than any other U.S. area. Glenn Fuguitt of the University of Wisconsin has compiled data on nearly 5,600 incorporated towns of fewer than 2,500 population located in nonmetropolitan counties in this region. That is 30 percent of all incorporated places of all sizes nationwide.

Away from "megalopoli" (my perception of megalopolis after magalopolis ad nauseam), the Northeast is composed of hundreds of small towns, each separated from the next by woods and farms. The South and the Midwest have numerous towns that once served as commercial hubs for farms in their area. In many cases their role has changed but those that have survived often have great character. In the mountainous West, many old mining towns have survived the depletion of the minerals that created them.

There are still small towns with traditional values, strong community, and a warm atmosphere created by nature, design, and the character of good people. The best choices are insulated from fast growth by distance, inferior roads, or topography—for instance, by being in a small valley with hills impossible to develop (but note Aspen and Vail, Colorado), or backed up to a river or lake with steep hills on the other side. Those that have very limited space for growth and a real reluctance for growth by influential citizens are most likely to retain their present qualities.

College Towns

Change is less likely in towns where the economic base is one of long-term commitment. Some of the nicest small towns are college towns. They have stable economies based on the college, allied "intellectual" enterprises, service businesses. The country immediately surrounding these towns is often an excellent place to live. Population ebbs and flows with the scholastic year. The intellectual climate of the college generally sets the tone for the community. It's a great place to rear children.

State Capitals, County Seats

Small state capitals tend to be conservative and stable. An employment base exists from the multiple state departments and with the various service industries that support them. To a lesser degree, the same is true of county seats.

Looking

> *"There are towns*
> *That are not on a map;*
> *But can be located*
> *By the smell of coffee,*
> *The casual conversation*
> *Across a laundry line,*
> *And where concern*
> *Is never an intruder,*
> *But a way of life."*
>
> —ELLEN FUCHS

A super way to discover small towns and villages is to spend time driving the roads of your preferred area. Take your time. Once you find a town that appears ideal, talk to everyone you see. Have lunch. Use your criteria list and rate the town on how well it meets your needs. If it looks good, subscribe to the local paper. Drive the surrounding area. Get lost; ask for help. Keep talking to people—beyond the natural beauty and architecture, the essence of a place is found in its people. If there is a library, read back issues of the newspaper; nothing will more quickly give you a picture of the social character of a place.

If you are unable to go to an area but would like to begin your search, write to the state chamber of commerce or board of tourism and tell them you may be interested in moving to their state. They will send you an information packet which will include a map. You can also contact real estate people in your areas of interest. Real estate agents will send you brochures on available properties. If you would like to know more about a specific town, order a newspaper subscription. It will probably be a weekly. The local news, letters to the editor, social calendar, and political campaigns will give you instant insight into the values of that place.

Resources and Recommended Reading

Chambers of Commerce

Find local chambers through the phone company, or through the U.S. Chamber of Commerce, 1615 H Street NW, Washington, DC 20062; phone: 202-659-6000. Most chambers will send you packets of information including maps and real estate company listings. Some rural chambers are so small they can't afford to mail information packages—perhaps an indication of a superior place to live.

Newspapers

Subscribe to the local newspaper and you will be able to quickly check the pulse of the area. The best source for subscription information about each of the U.S.'s 1,651 daily newspapers is *Editor & Publisher's International Yearbook*. For information on the nearly 7,000 weekly papers, check out the *IMS Directory of Publications* or *Gale's Directory of Publications*.

Placing an ad in the Personals section of the classifieds requesting contact with others who have moved there from the city is a way to get information and maybe make friends—possibly a place to stay when you visit. Expect to hear from every real estate agent in the area.

Books

Campbell, Carlos C. *New Towns: Another Way to Live*. Reston, VA: Reston Publishing Company, 1976.

Crampton, Norman. *The 100 Best Small Towns in America*. New York: Macmillan General Reference, 1995.

Fuguitt, Glenn V., David L. Brown, and Calvin L. Beale. *Rural and Small Town America*. New York: The Russell Sage Foundation, 1989.

Garreau, Joel. *Edge City: Life on the New Frontier*. New York: Doubleday, 1991.

Ringholz, Raye C. *Little Town Blues: Voices from the Changing West*. Layton, UT: Gibbs Smith, 1992.

*"In the country town we gain in contact with
our neighbors. We know people by the score, by the
hundred. . . . Our affairs become common with one another,
our joys mutual, and even our sorrows are shared. . . . It
all makes life pleasantly livable."*

—WILLIAM ALLEN WHITE

~ 25 ~

Subdivisions

"A few miles off the road is the site of a planned community dating from the nineteen-sixties. It was to have wide streets and a fountained square, but construction was delayed and then indefinitely postponed. Ghostless ghost town, it had been named Neptune City."

—John McPhee, *Basin and Range*

Land Subdivisions

Rural land subdivisions are typically very large acreages purchased by corporations and then subdivided into parcels, usually from one-half acre to ten acres in size. During the 1960s and 1970s, thousands of subdivisions were created on poor mountain, desert, or swamp land in Florida, California, Nevada, and other states. Land companies used slick advertising and powerful sales methods to sell the parcels to naive city people longing for a piece of country. The lots were priced at only a few thousand dollars and liberal terms were part of the sales appeal. With few exceptions these lots were essentially useless.

"I just got wonderful news from my real estate agent in Florida. They found land on my property."

—Milton Berle

The Rockefeller Brothers Fund released a report in 1973 called *The Use of the Land*. It revealed: "In 1971 an estimated 625,000 recreational lots were sold by over 10,000 subdividers. . . . For the nation as a whole, at least six recreational lots were sold in 1971 for each second home constructed. . . . In California, between 50,000 and 100,000 acres of rural land were subdivided annually in the late 1960s and early 1970s by recreational lot sellers. By 1971, however, houses had been built on only 3 percent of the lots sold in the previous decade."

The pitch was: "You're getting in on the ground floor—this area is going to boom—in a few years you'll make a killing!" Promised roads, utilities, services, and escalating values almost always failed to materialize. The lots, sold with enticingly low down payments and modest monthly payments (those of us in legitimate real estate at the time scoffed: "Five dollars down and fifty dollars a month—forever!"), often were abandoned and sat vacant, available to anyone who paid the back taxes. As soon as the development company had taken the easy money, and before spending any of it on improvements, it either declared bankruptcy or simply disappeared. Today some of these rip-off developments can be seen from interstate highways in the western desert—they're the ones with big faded signs, barely discernible dirt roads, sometimes one or two small houses far out in the sagebrush.

Well, the feds received complaints—whew, did they ever!—and it is now more difficult for unscrupulous developers to make a dishonest buck. That is not to say that some aren't trying to relive their lucrative wayward youth. If you are tempted to buy land in an undeveloped subdivision, do twice the amount of checking as for any other property. Beware of slick promotional material with "artist's rendition" clubhouses, lakes, marinas, golf courses. And just don't believe sales claims that values are going to rise substantially and soon.

Consumer Protection

The Department of Housing and Urban Development (HUD) enacted legislation to protect subdivision property buyers from misrepresentation, fraud, and deceit. Many states have similar statutes. The federal law requires that purchasers of certain properties must receive a property report disclosing such items as availability of utilities, soil problems, distance to schools and firehouses, restrictive covenants, oil and mineral rights, special assessments for roads or other improvements, and payment terms. Properties that are usually exempt from this law include lots with buildings, subdivisions with fewer than 100 lots, and lots of twenty acres or larger.

Please note that the property report is not an indication of government approval of the project, it simply reveals pertinent information supplied by the developer. If you are interested in this kind of property be certain to read the property report carefully. The law requires that a purchaser sign a statement that he has received the report and it gives a seven-day cooling-off period during which the buyer may cancel the purchase agreement (in writing) and receive his deposit back. This law could change; verify the length of the cooling-off period on the papers provided at the sales office.

There is a solid reason for the right-to-cancel-law. Real estate salespeople in subdivisions know they will probably only get one shot at buyers, so they are trained and conditioned to be very aggressive—to make the sale today. Do not be persuaded by the glib "You have a seven-day right to cancel; make your decision today while it's convenient; you can always change your mind later." Other pressing matters may interfere, and later becomes too late.

Housing Subdivisions, Retirement and Recreational Developments

"Many old people think of retirement communities as large compounds of the elderly living among themselves with little contact or interest in the native population around them, the kind of places found in Arizona or Florida. In the Ozarks and other regions where elderly people go to live, the retirees are likely to be segregated by neighborhoods, but so pervasive are the natural surroundings and the native culture that their influence cannot be escaped in the low-density settings which have sprung up in recent years."

—JOHN HERBERS, *The New Heartland*

There are many housing subdivisions that may be attractive to country home seekers. Retirement communities are sometimes found in small subdivisions of homes on large lots or small acreages surrounded by forests and hills. Ski resorts, fishing lakes, and man-made facilities center many new communities that can exist only because of transfer payments such as retirement checks. These areas are often far removed from urban centers, so they offer year-round service employment for younger people. The names of such places often indicate what was dispossessed to create them: Pheasant Run, Quail Meadow, Grizzly Crossing.

When considering any subdivision, which may also be called a development, project, retirement community, planned unit development, or destination resort (new sobriquets appear yearly), be sure to receive and carefully read a copy of the covenants, conditions, and restrictions (CC&Rs). This is not the same thing as the property report. CC&Rs frequently are spelled out in a thick packet of pages with small print. It's tough reading—great stuff for insomniacs—but you do not want to miss details such as, for instance, requirements that resales must be made through the development company, that you must build a house of at least a certain square footage, or that you must paint your house every two years—the exact color that the architectural review board dictates. You also need to find out what fees owners must pay for common area maintenance, insurance, accounting, security, and so on.

Some subdivisions, especially condominiums and planned unit developments, are aimed at retirees and second-home buyers. Many of these places end up with a substantial number of renters—who will not share owners' attitudes. While it is impossible to predict how new developments will go, local property management people or real estate agents will be able to tell you what the score is with a project more than a year old.

Yet another type of development has been dreamed up—developing old towns. Pity tiny Rico, population 150, the last undeveloped town in the San Juan Mountains of southwestern Colorado. A high-powered tax shelter lawyer from Manhattan and his investor buddies bought up nearly all of Rico. As he and his partners envision hundreds of new homes in the hills, he claims to be concerned: "How is it that we can prevent ourselves from spoiling any of this beauty?" Well, Jack, duh, don't start the bulldozer. I think we need a twelve-step program for the greed-impaired.

Shadow Governments

When considering any planned community beware of the power of shadow governments. Usually spelled out in the CC&Rs, homeowner associations may control most aspects of life within their jurisdiction, down to the color of the curtains in the windows fronting a street. These shadow governments have the power to levy taxes (assessments), legislate (create rules and regulations), and enforce (police power to force homeowners to obey their edicts). And the officers are often elected by votes with a dollar basis, rather than the democratic one-person-equals-one-vote concept.

Shadow governments regulate the nature of landscaping. They decide how many pets are allowed and what size. They decide the age of inhabitants. Many forbid anyone younger than forty-five; if your adult child and spouse die, you may be prohibited from taking in your grandchild. In some places shadow governments have become virtual dictatorships. Owners who sue them usually find that courts uphold their actions.

If you purchase property in a planned-unit or condominium development, about the only way you can have any real effect on how things are run is to become active in homeowner association affairs. If you like politics and meetings you'll fit right in.

Tax Sales

If you feel you would like to acquire tax sale property, visit the county courthouse and ask to see the delinquent tax list. Subdivision lots are listed most frequently. If you feel that these lots are a good investment you can often buy them for the back taxes. Be aware that even after a tax sale, within a specified time period the previous owners can come forward, pay the back taxes, interest, and expenses, and regain title. Ask the tax collector what the laws are in that county.

Resources

If a subdivision is promoted in interstate commerce, it must be registered with the following agency. Ask for the free booklet HUD183H(10), *Before Buying Land . . . Get the Facts*. Request a list of other available materials regarding buying land.

U.S. Department of Housing and Urban Development
Interstate Lands Sales Registration Division
451 Seventh Street SW
Washington, DC 20410
Phone: 202-708-1422, ext. 5; fax: 202-708-2313

State real estate commissioners have information on subdivisions within their jurisdictions. Planning commissions and real estate boards will have appropriate addresses and phone numbers.

– 26 –

Intentional Communities and Ecovillages

*"We can be grateful for what one person can create, but when we see
what abundance we can create together, it will baffle the intellect and arouse
our spirits to celebrate the oneness of humanity and the need for
cooperating in sustainable community."*

—KEN NORWOOD, *Rebuilding Community in America*

Intentional communities range in size from two or three people to several
hundred. Their physical sites range from city houses to 5,000 acres of country
land; the average is perhaps twenty people on eighty acres. Early communities
were often founded to promote a particular philosophy or religion; the majority
of modern communities are open to and accepting of diverse personal beliefs.
Most communities are located on rural land and are ecologically oriented, with
energy-efficient housing and organic food production. The emphasis is on group
support and cooperation. All ages are represented. Many intentional communities provide schooling and communal nurturing for resident children.

Many intentional communities have evolved from the counterculture
communes of the 1950s, 1960s, and 1970s. The communities of today, while still
usually at odds with business-as-usual politics and social norms, are generally
more conservative in their approach to right living. Those I have visited are
populated by people with the same motivations described in this book's Chapter
4, "Who Are You?" Intentional community residents are much like the rest of us
who choose to live in the country, but they prefer to live with others in a
supportive group environment.

People in intentional communities typically live more peaceably than the rest
of society. Most communities make decisions by consensus, and are continually

working to improve skills in noncompetitive conflict resolution. Group needs are balanced with individual members' needs.

Three Examples of Intentional Communities

Founded in 1937, Celo Community is the oldest land trust community in America, and one of the most successful. It comprises some thirty family units living on 1,200 acres of North Carolina land owned by the community. Members purchase "holdings" which are confined to the realistic needs and uses of each family. Celo Community members are diverse in background, occupation, and religion, and make their livings independently (membership includes crafts-people, farmers, teachers, doctors). A number of successful projects, services, and schools have been developed, some with a national clientele. Celo has a two-year waiting list of potential new members.

Perhaps the best-known intentional community is The Farm, founded in 1971 by Stephen Gaskin and 320 San Francisco hippies seeking to create, as spokesman Albert Bates says on The Farm's Web site, "a cohesive, outwardly directed community which could, by action and example, have a positive effect on the world." Today, approximately 250 residents and about forty businesses flourish on its 2,550 acres in southern middle Tennessee. Most of the land is held as a conservation trust to "encourage natural biodiversity." The community is described as "full featured," and has all the facilities of a thriving village: grocery store, post office, medical clinic, pharmacy, gas station, water system, many homes and businesses. A school offers basic skills plus foreign languages, fine arts, and apprenticeship training. Businesses include the Soy Dairy, Mushroompeople, Tempeh Lab, Solar Electronics, the Book Publishing Company, the Birth Gazette, Total Video, WUTZ-FM, and the Dye Works. The Farm is home to the Midwife School—babies are delivered regularly, only 1.8 percent cesarean, versus 20 percent cesarean for mainstream hospitals. Its Kids to the Country program maintains a nature enrichment program for urban children.

Situated on 1,000 acres of south-central Washington, Ponderosa Village is a subdivision that was intended and advertised to be an intentional community. The stated organizing concepts are self-responsibility, voluntary cooperation, personal growth, individual spiritual values, respect for each other and the environment, and a place of security in case of serious problems. Those who have bought lots are community-oriented. With the exception of a seven-acre park site, the property is comprised of five-acre lots. Lots were first sold in 1980; by March 1996, all but seventeen lots were sold, with thirty-five homes built, many of alternative design. Ponderosa Village has seventy-five residents aged from a new baby to a ninety-four-year-old. There is a community water system, but sewage handling is the responsibility of individual homeowners. Visitors are welcome and camping is available, but call or write before visiting. Seminars on subjects as diverse as soap making, gardening, straw bale construction, and wilderness skills are conducted for varying fees.

INTENTIONAL COMMUNITIES LOCATIONS, 1995

From *Communities Directory, Second Edition,*
© 1995 Fellowship for Intentional Community.
Used with permission.

Ecovillages—Redesigning Human Habitat

Ecovillages are cooperative communities embodying current technology that aim to live in sustainable harmony with nature while growing their own food, generating their own energy, handling their own wastes. Housing often consists of duplex, triplex, or higher-density units clustered in small groups, all oriented toward common buildings, open areas, parking, office facilities. The ecovillage concept allows inhabitants to buy individual living units, have access to common land and facilities, and have wide latitude in how collective or private they choose to be. From my ex–real estate broker perspective, ecovillages are small, energy-efficient, ecologically designed, planned-unit developments. They are very progressive and are oriented toward social and environmental sensitivity. This is high-quality, light-on-the-land living for those who wish to live in a modern village atmosphere.

EcoVillage at Ithaca, New York, is affiliated with Cornell University. About 20 percent of its 176 acres will be used for housing, the rest for gardens, ponds, orchards, and nature preserve. A common parking lot is planned with paths leading to the clustered homes. Residents will share such items as lawnmowers, snowblowers, washing machines. Private, semiprivate, and public areas are designed to help create strong social networks. The mission statement reads: "The ultimate goal of EcoVillage at Ithaca is nothing less than to redesign the human habitat. We are creating a model community of some five hundred residents that will exemplify sustainable systems of living—systems that are not only practical, but replicable by others. The completed project will demonstrate the feasibility of a design that meets basic human needs such as shelter, food production, energy, social interaction, work and recreation while preserving natural ecosystems." The first neighborhood of thirty homes (fifteen duplexes) was completed July 1997 and includes a common house overlooking a pond. Home sizes range from a one-bedroom (922 square feet) unit to a four-bedroom (1,642 square feet) unit. All homes will be super-insulated and airtight and have large triple-paned, south-facing windows; yearly heating bills are projected at $200 per household. Initial owners were involved in design decisions. Two EcoVillage residents operate on-site West Haven Farm, a community-supported agriculture operation (see Chapter 13), which provides organic vegetables, herbs, and flowers to shareholders from early June through mid-November.

Albert Bates, spokesman for The Farm, reported in 1995 that "The Farm will launch the Ecovillage Network of North America (ENNA), to be headquartered initially at The Farm Ecovillage Training Center. ENNA will link together the efforts of a wide variety of green communities, Eco-City projects and incipient ecovillages to make the way easier for future ecovillagers and to lay the foundation for a major shift in Western consumer lifestyles across the broader culture."

Resources

The Eco-Village Network of the Americas
Albert Bates
The Farm
556 Farm Road
Summertown, TN 38483-0090
Phone: 615-964-3992; fax: 615-964-2200; e-mail: albert@gaia.org

Celo Community
Route 5, Box 79
Burnsville, NC 28714
704-675-5525

Ponderosa Village
195 Golden Pine
Goldendale, WA 98620
509-773-3902

For information about EcoVillage at Ithaca, contact:

Cornell University
Ithaca, NY 14853
Web site: http://www.cfe.cornell.edu/ecovillage/

Eco-village resource list with online links:
http://www.gaia.org/links/northsoutham.html

The Shared Living Resource Center published in 1995 *Rebuilding Community in America*, by Ken Norwood and Kathleen Smith. The book has excellent background, examples and plans on community and eco-villages. The Center is at 2375 Shattuck Avenue, Berkeley, CA 94704; phone: 510-548-6608.

Fellowship for Intentional Community
Route 1, Box 155
Rutledge, MO 63563-9720
Phone/fax: 816-883-5545; e-mail: 5012004@mcimail.com

FIC provides quarterly journals, newsletters, audiotapes, and referral services. It also published *Communities Directory*, second edition (1995), a 440-page reference guide with detailed listings of 540 communities across North America (and seventy international), thirty-one in-depth articles about various aspects of community living, and an extensive resources section. It's available for $23 postpaid (check payable to Communities magazine) from: Directory/Communities, Route 4, Box 169, Louisa, VA 23093.

> *"The common complaints of our time—loneliness,*
> *loss of values and meaning, lack of personal fulfillment,*
> *emptiness, disillusionment, powerlessness, and fear—are all symptoms*
> *that reflect our loss of community."*
>
> —KATHLEEN SMITH, *Rebuilding Community in America*

～ 27 ～

Places and Conditions to Avoid

"Everyone has gone back to a place that they remember from childhood and seen an apartment complex or a K-mart. When I was growing up, we were on the edge of the Everglades. Now we're in the middle of mall hell."

—CARL HIAASEN

The pervasive stench of an intensive hog farm/factory at mealtime, the airborne drift of pesticides into your child's room, incessant traffic noise while you attempt to read, work, or sleep, thousands of cars suddenly passing your house each day because of a new casino down the road—these are but a few of the potential conditions that could ruin an otherwise ideal country home place.

Those who promote or sell real estate rarely point out all the negatives of a property, much less the surrounding area. Natives of a place may have over many years become so accustomed to a negative condition that they simply don't even notice it anymore. Longtime residents are often inured to eyesores, smells, sounds, pollution. Chambers of commerce do not send out brochures about such conditions. In this chapter we explore those negative conditions of place that, once discovered, may remove that place from your consideration.

Places That Boom and Bust

Calvin Beale reported that many mining, resort-retirement, and exurban fringe counties grew by 40 to 50 percent or more in population from 1970 to 1980, especially in the West and Florida. He observed that growth at these rates is next to impossible for a small community to endure without negative results. Water and sewer facilities, schools, medical and social agencies, crime rates, roads, and other issues and services are impacted hard, with local agencies often unable to cope. He noted that it is important to determine what part of the growth cycle a place is in.

The boom and bust syndrome common to mountain towns that are dependent on mining employment first causes fast demand for services and then later closes stores and empties schools. In *Country Careers* Jerry Germer wrote: "In the last century, mining towns like Virginia City, Nevada, or Park City, Utah, became ghost towns practically overnight when their single economic base was exhausted." Areas heavily into agriculture also have an uncertain future. The current trend is for fewer people using larger machines to farm more acres. Meat production is moving to factorylike operations. So agricultural areas are likely to continue to decrease in population.

Any place where one company or a military base dominates the employment scene is a disaster waiting for a layoff or federal budget cut. The exception is when a company is very stable, for instance Hershey Chocolate Company, in Hershey, Pennsylvania, population 11,860. Given the human penchant for anything sweet, Hershey will be selling kisses for a very long time.

Not just small places boom and bomb. Joel Garreau relates how during the 1980s New England was electrified by an economic boom so strong that in one decade it lifted New England from the poorest region in America to the richest. The extraordinary business growth used up prime space so fast that growth stopped, then nose-dived. In the early 1990s the Massachusetts Miracle became the Massachusetts Massacre. Wyoming's population soared 41 percent in the 1970s, based on coal and oil demand. In the 1980s worldwide oil prices dropped and thousands of Wyomingites lost their jobs and left the state.

City Fringe Areas

Part of the difficulty of measuring city-to-rural migration patterns is that cities have annexed suburban areas and even rural areas and continue to try to increase their official metropolitan area. In *Where to Make Money: A Rating Guide to Opportunities in America's Metro Areas*, G. Scott Thomas reports that "The federal government has given the metropolitan designation to some areas that are decidedly unmetropolitan, places like Grand Forks, ND, Casper, WY, Enid, OK."

The purpose is power—salaries and profits fed by votes, taxes, government largesse. Revenues generated by expansion areas will partly be used to mollify inner-city residents as living conditions continue to decline. The fringes of these metropolitan areas may appear rural but they are often adversely affected by city regulations and city taxes. Buy land far from city fringes disguised as country.

Towns between cities less than four hours apart often become bedroom communities that then become cities. Some are planned that way. Columbia, Maryland, located midway between Baltimore and Washington, was founded in 1963 as a planned community on 14,000 acres of farmland. In 1967 the buyers moved into the first of ten planned villages, named Wilde Lake. (Putting an "e" on the end of a place name adds cachet—and dollars to the price. Ye Olde Towne Taverne would be worth a fortune.) By 1995 Columbia had almost 100,000 inhabitants.

Unsafe at Almost Any Speed—Growth and Development

"Economic growth is not only unnecessary, but ruinous."

—ALEKSANDR I. SOLZHENITSYN

During my search in the 1970s I consciously avoided areas close to major highways or railroads, two criteria for major manufacturers. If you treasure open space, and peace and quiet, you will also avoid small towns and their surrounding areas that have locations and features attractive to large corporations in their quest for lower wages and taxes and fewer regulations.

When developers and preservationists clash, the latter often lose. In *Edge City*, Joel Garreau says developer John Tilghman Hazel, Jr., has so rapidly transformed entire northern Virginia landscapes that his vanquished opponents have been "reduced to describing him in satanic terms—no less than the Prince of Darkness and the Father of Lies."

I can imagine the outcry: "This guy is anticapitalism!" Nope, just anti-growth for growth's sake and especially for ideal country places. Yeah, I know our economy is based on the growth theory. And the next dictum is that the government must keep growth happening. That's part of why economists' predictions are worthless—too much meddling with natural laws. To know where the economy was going we have watched where the politicians were going. But through overuse, they seem to have worn out the steering mechanism—money.

Politicians appear to believe that human laws are more intelligent than natural laws. I once accepted an invitation to a luncheon with our visiting congressman. The conversation was mainly on the agricultural economy and the various new government programs being considered. The congressman and the others lamented at length that "nothing seems to work anymore." The devil made me do it—with manifest naïveté, I observed: "Supply and demand used to work quite well." Instant silence and lowered eyes. Forks pushed salad around. I boldly pushed forward: "Perhaps we should consider having fewer, not more programs." Well, that was that—I was never invited again. Damned troublemaker.

It's not that simple, of course. Strict supply and demand would result in the super-rich lions and us poor lambs. Alas, until the Golden Rule becomes universally genetically implanted, we humans will continue to need some traffic signals to keep us from tromping all over each other.

Growth does not equal progress or health. And fast growth can destroy the good qualities of any place or community. I will keep reminding you that cities once were villages and small towns, ideal places now ruined by growth.

Finding a place that is growth-resistant will help ensure that the qualities that attracted you will remain. There are some land characteristics that restrain or retard growth, like scarce water, or huge deserts with no valuable minerals underground. Those are not what we're looking for. The ideal country place has highly desirable features for our purposes but is a place that no industrialist or developer would give a second look. A developer's or manufacturer's list of negatives includes poor transportation routes, insufficient work force, anti-growth laws, land parcels too small to be profitably developed, wild-eyed obstructionists, snail darters, and spotted owls—all of which indicate a potential ideal home place.

It is not uncommon to find small-town citizens who honestly believe that growth will raise their quality of life. Calvin Beale, in a 1985 talk titled "Rural Development in Perspective," told of a billboard outside a small Wisconsin town.

The sign read:

> ## WELCOME TO
> ## GALESVILLE
> ### The Garden of Eden
> ### Industry Invited

Said Beale: "Here, in a nutshell, the basic modern dilemma of rural America is expressed. On one hand there is the ardent assertion of the idyllic, fulfilling quality that life in a small community can have, but then tempered by the necessity to invite the serpent of industry into the garden if people are to have the means to live there."

If you are considering living in or near a small town, talk to the people there who make growth happen—bankers, bureaucrats, businesspeople. Act like you might favor some growth and check their reaction. If you want things to stay the way they are as long as possible, avoid places with growth-oriented chambers of commerce. If they persist, they will get growth—but they may destroy the soul of their town.

People in wonderful small towns often just don't understand how quickly growth can destroy the qualities of their community. Following the lead of states, many low-population areas are wooing business. Typical is the following ad from the *Los Angeles Times* of February 13, 1994:

OHIO COUNTY—KENTUCKY

Our community is the best-kept secret in America. An abundance of talented, friendly labor to help you reach the potential you deserve. Labor costs are favorable because of the area's low cost of living. We need small to medium size expansion or developing industries. Let us help you help us. Incentives, training, quality of lifestyle. Contact:

Judge Larry Whitaker, 502-283-3213
Judge Dudley Cooper, 502-298-4400
or Wayne Evans, 1-800-844-3553

By the way, I suspect the two judges in the ad are county judges, citizens elected to administer county business affairs; in some Midwest counties they are called county commissioners, in others, judges. Some even do settle minor legal disagreements.

Unchecked economic growth can quickly become a curse. Paradise can be found and lost in short order, especially if it is within commuting distance of cities and therefore desirable to large corporations. Tyson's Corner, Virginia, went from country crossroads to sloppy suburb in a single decade. Controlled-growth programs are the typical response of town planners. I recommend a town too small to afford or need a planner.

I expound on this theme of avoiding potential development because I know the pain it can cause. Once you find and buy your ideal country home place you will likely make substantial improvements. You will invest yourself in your property and in the community. Inevitably that place will become even more special to you. A friend in Arlington, Texas, told me of an elderly couple evicted from their home by the eminent domain proceeding used to create space for the Texas Motor Speedway. For decades the family had planted a tree to commemorate each significant family event, the birth of each child and grandchild, graduations, marriages. The price given them for their modest home did not allow buying in the same area, let alone the cost of transplanting many mature trees. Where their beloved trees once grew is now a barren parking lot.

In 1932 Helen and Scott Nearing purchased a remote Vermont maple farm and then spent nearly twenty years building gardens and stone buildings. In 1947 a paper company began denuding the mountain above them. Once the trees were gone, ski slopes were developed and advertised. By the fall of 1951, those activities plus unannounced drop-ins so destroyed their lifestyle that the Nearings moved to Maine and, at advanced ages, started over.

I have advised against buying too little land. Even moderate-size parcels may provide inadequate protection of peace and quiet. In *An American Homeplace* Donald McCaig finds farmer/writer Wendell Berry contemplating the possible need to leave his cherished seventy-five acres of Kentucky land because a developer had bought the acreage next door and planned to "erect and sell dozens of tacky weekend camps." When the plan faltered, Berry was able to buy the land and preserve the nature of his place.

A really large parcel next door is a gilt-edged invitation to developers. In the Afterword of *Maine Farm*, Stanley Joseph writes: "Developers have subdivided the four hundred acres bordering our land [part of Helen and Scott Nearing's place] into forty lots, and million-dollar houses are going up." One can imagine what that will do to the peace and quiet. And the taxes. Beemers and polo ponies. There goes the neighborhood.

Development typically moves out from cities and towns in more or less concentric rings, often burgeoning at highway intersections. Sometimes it takes big jumps. Features such as rivers, lakes, and other tourist attractors are like magnets to developers. Beware of buying near large plots held by speculators waiting for the right time to build new communities or commercial developments. Staying far from main highways and railroads helps ensure low development potential but is no guarantee by itself. If a development is announced near your private Utopia, about all you can do is prepare to suffer the sights, sounds, traffic, and increased taxes, sell and move, or loudly announce your own plans—a large skunk ranch operation. Put up a big sign: Skunks Bought, Sold, Traded.

*"Growth for the sake of growth is the
ideology of the cancer cell."*

—EDWARD ABBEY

Sounds

*"One good thing about living on a farm is that you can
fight with your wife without being heard."*

—FRANK MCKINNEY "KIN" HUBBARD

Sounds seem to travel farther in the country, where background covering din is reduced to bird songs and wind through the trees. When our winds reverse their normal pattern I sometimes hear the sounds of a gravel dredging operation many miles away.

One way to discover potential negative sounds is to camp on the property. In *Goodbye City Hello Country*, Julie Hayward and Ken Spooner relate the experience of a family who had fallen in love with a beautiful piece of land in northwestern

Arkansas. After making a deposit and signing a contract, the family camped on the property. That night, "As they tried to sleep they heard the roar of trucks on Highway 70." The next day they walked away from their deposit and bought another property, one with appropriate country night sounds—hooting owls and yapping coyotes.

Theme Centers, Recreation Resorts, Reservations

Yep, reservations. Who would have thought that activity on Native American reservations might one day destroy surrounding settlers' rural atmosphere? Well, at least one has and others are trying. Some might consider the situation poetic justice. Some might include me.

It all started after Congress passed a 1988 law enabling tribes to open casinos. Poor tribes saw hope and went into action. Now 140 tribes operate gambling establishments in 22 states (Internet), 123 tribes in 24 states (*Business Week*), or 126 tribes in 19 states (*Time*, 4-1-96), take your pick.

Foxwoods Resort Casino has current annual revenues estimated to be at least $850 million. Nevada? Nope, southeastern Connecticut, an area of tiny villages, rolling hills, and centuries-old farms. The Mashantuckett Pequot, a Native American tribe numbering about 350, found financing in Malaysia and a management team in Atlantic City. Agreeing to pay the state 25 percent of slot machine revenues or $100 million per year, whichever is greater (about $135 million during fiscal year 1994–1995) bought state approval. In three years the casino went from an entrepreneurial dream to an enterprise that dominates the area, employing nearly 10,000 and clogging roads with 25,000 cars a day.

The Pequot and local non–Native Americans are now engaged in a modern Indians-versus-settlers war on the issue of annexing more land to the 1,230-acre reservation. (Pequot is from Pekawatawog, "the destroyers." They were the most feared tribe in New England until the colonists massacred most of them in 1637. Two reservations were created in 1655 on Connecticut's Mystic River. Now they're getting even.) The weapons today are referendums and zoning laws. Things look bad for the white man. Future tribal plans include building two golf courses, a theme park, tennis courts, a skeet-shooting range, and a $100 million museum and research center.

Foxwoods has become a model for other reservations across the U.S., which to a certain extent are "nations within a state," hoping to cash in on the gambling bonanza. States see gambling as the least objectionable way to raise revenue since the creation of sin taxes. Not everybody is happy about the Native American edge. Donald Trump is pursuing legal avenues to try to stop the drain on his Atlantic City revenue.

Reservations are attractive venues to those who want to do things that would have tough sledding if proposed for nonreservation land. Prairie Island on the Mississippi River near Minneapolis is owned by the Mdewakanton Sioux. Northern State Power (NSP) wants to expand the nuclear waste depository on the island. It seems that NSP has finally offered enough wampum. *The Twin Cities Reader* (1-24-96) reported: "In 1994, during a heated controversy, the Legislature limited to 17 the number of casks NSP could build for dry-cask storage at the site. The legislation also required NSP to search for an alternative storage site in Goodhue County, away from the Mississippi River. . . . 'First it was a health and safety issue and now it's a monetary issue,' says one insider, who expects that the agreement will roll out in the form of a new legislative proposal by the end of the week."

PRESENT-DAY LOCATIONS OF NATIVE AMERICAN TRIBES
(Not to scale)

• States with heavy outlines have Indian casinos (TIME, 4-1-96).
• Oklahoma has no reservations, although 35 tribes have been forced to live there.
• Please consult state road maps for precise locations.

Based on information in "A Guide To America's Indians," by Arnold Marquis, Univ. of Oklahoma Press.

A caution is in order regarding the preceding map of Native American locations. Many state reservations can be located only by studying large-scale maps in an atlas—and I advise you to do so. For instance, the Pequot are mentioned in various books but their location is not mapped. About 4 percent of California's 200,000 Native Americans live on one of eighty-three reservations. Altogether, the U.S. government recognizes 555 tribes. In an April 1994 speech, President Clinton reiterated the government's commitment to self-determination and sovereignty for tribal governments. Remote locations may preclude development—reservations most likely to be successful as casino locales are those situated within easy driving distance of large population centers.

While Disney World, near Orlando, is the largest U.S. theme park and attracts the most visitors, Dollywood in Pigeon Forge, Tennessee, Silver Dollar City in Branson, Missouri, Six Flags over Texas in Arlington, Texas, and other states, and the many Lion Country Safari and other theme parks attract millions of tourists each year. Theme parks initially need a large parcel of low-priced land—read rural. Once established, the parks generate other businesses, higher prices, higher taxes, high traffic volume. Goodbye country.

Disney's proposed historical theme park at Manassas, Virginia, near Civil War battlefields has failed, at least for now. Mickey's corporate masters bought a big plantation, quietly bought options on a total of 3,000 acres, won the governor over, and were confidently working their way past zoning challenges and outraged citizens. The "little guy" property owners in Prince William County got testy. They felt pretty sure that the projected 77,000 cars per day would have a negative effect on their peace and quiet. One nearby landowner referred to the proposed development as "Disneyopolis." Sometimes you can beat city hall. So many people fought the plan that politicos feared for their jobs. Pluto finally left town with his tail between his legs.

Places that are just too beautiful may create the small-town-turned-resort syndrome that has become a paradigm in the West. Tourism is often seen as economic salvation for small towns losing their people to other places with more jobs. A touch of tourism may leave a town intact but spectacular natural features often bring big development and big change. In *Little Town Blues*, Raye Ringholz shows how tourism has drastically changed Sedona, Arizona; Jackson Hole, Wyoming; Aspen, Colorado; and Moab, Utah—in all cases started by locals seeking to increase the number of jobs. Ringholz writes: "If there's a mountain to hike or ski, redrock backcountry to explore, a waterway to play on, or a desert oasis to green into a golf course, it's being developed by entrepreneurs with hordes of tourists and recreationers hard on their heels. Within a few short years, the immigrants follow and authentic mining camps, rustic cow towns, pioneer farming communities—historical signatures of the American West—succumb to cosmetic changes that leave them little resemblance to their original selves. Even worse, they all start to look alike."

Development of all kinds increases traffic, taxes, prices. It inevitably increases the number of land-use laws and regulations. While casinos, theme parks, recreation resorts, and other tourist attractors may be fun to visit, they all have the potential to drastically change an area, perhaps destroying the community that drew you there. Whether such development will occur depends on local attitudes, natural features, and proximity to transportation routes. The combination of seductive scenery and aggressive local businesspeople almost guarantees that such development will occur.

Military Installations

Military bases are often major polluters with no one to keep them in line. A case in point: *Time*, 2-12-96, under the head "Chemical Time Bombs," noted there have been 2,100 reported incidents of leakage inside the chemical weapons "igloos" used for storage on military bases. In 1995, sixty workers at the Anniston Army Depot in Alabama were evacuated and one was hospitalized after the nerve gas sarin leaked from an M-55 rocket. Military bases should not be considered a stable employment base. And their male personnel should not be allowed near your daughters without a chaperone. (Just kidding—I was one and I was nice. Honest.)

Flight Paths—The Invasion of Paradise

Modern jet airports require large amounts of space. New ones are typically built away from cities in sparsely populated areas. Living under a designated flight path is enduring a soundtrack from hell. As you narrow your search you will want to determine if your chosen area includes airports and their attendant flight paths. I recommend you make a very thorough investigation. From maps and conversations with locals, find out where the nearest airport is located. Find

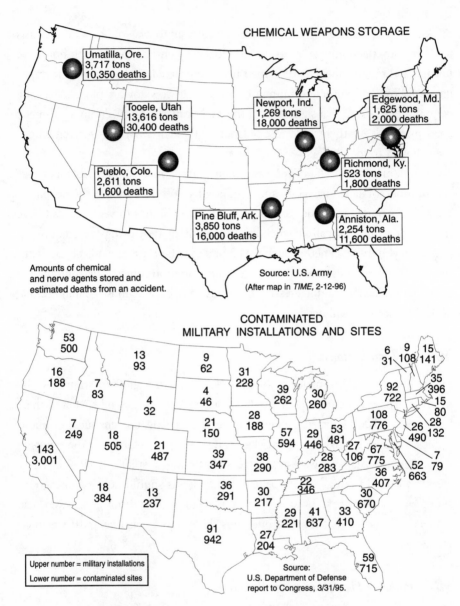

CHEMICAL WEAPONS STORAGE

Umatilla, Ore.
3,717 tons
10,350 deaths

Tooele, Utah
13,616 tons
30,400 deaths

Newport, Ind.
1,269 tons
18,000 deaths

Edgewood, Md.
1,625 tons
2,000 deaths

Pueblo, Colo.
2,611 tons
1,600 deaths

Richmond, Ky.
523 tons
1,800 deaths

Pine Bluff, Ark.
3,850 tons
16,000 deaths

Anniston, Ala.
2,254 tons
11,600 deaths

Amounts of chemical
and nerve agents stored and
estimated deaths from an accident.

Source: U.S. Army
(After map in *TIME*, 2-12-96)

CONTAMINATED
MILITARY INSTALLATIONS AND SITES

Upper number = military installations
Lower number = contaminated sites

Source:
U.S. Department of Defense
report to Congress, 3/31/95.

someone there who can show you on a map where the local flight paths are. Talk to your potential neighbors. Contact the Federal Aviation Administration. If you can't get the information you need, call your congressperson. Call the President. Unless you love airplanes more than life itself, call God if necessary, but do get the facts on all flights in your chosen area, including those used by military aircraft, upon which no requirement for noise control is imposed, so their roar is greater than that of commercial aircraft. It is that important. While my experience may be out of the ordinary, I have visited people who live under flight paths. Conversation necessarily stops when a jet goes overhead. I like airplanes. They are a safe, efficient way to travel. But over a residence and a garden they are noise pollution and air pollution.

I had lived on my place for several weeks and was working in the garden one morning when an earthshaking roar came up the hollow. The hair on my neck stood straight out as the roar materialized into a very-low-flying bomber painted dull gray with no identifying marks, with what appeared to be metal shutters covering the windshield. It came directly at me. I staggered, my intellect did a full stop. I braced myself to die (your life does *not* flash before your eyes). A cerebral neuron finally fired and I realized that I was experiencing the beginning of the end of the world. This Darth Vader–like apparition was from the evil empire, sneaking in under radar, committed to vaporize some nearby secret military target. My world would end with a blinding nuclear explosion. The monster thundered by directly overhead, its bomb doors clearly visible.

Time passed. Surprised that I still lived, I staggered inside and used the telephone. A neighbor calmed me. Somewhat. It was one of ours. It was a training mission. A pilot was being trained to fly under Russian radar. More would come. They practiced 500 feet above the ground, inches above my airspace. They practiced using instruments only. None had crashed—yet. They came, I was told, from a Strategic Air Command base up near Kansas City. They came on an infrequent, unpredictable, but endless basis. Yes, calls had been placed, letters had been written. There was, I was told, nothing to be done about it.

It was for more than the usual reasons that I celebrated the end of the Cold War. And I freely admit that I experienced selfish thoughts when military budget cuts were announced.

Still they came over, stopping phone conversations in mid-sentence, spewing jet fuel exhaust onto our organic garden.

Finally we found a phone number that reached a radar tracking station sergeant who reported our situation to his captain who contacted a major at the squadron where the bombers are based. Someone who works for the major called. He said they would come soon with a global positioning device that would pinpoint our location so they could instruct their pilots to avoid us. We waited. The day they were supposed to be here they called and said the weather was going to be windy so they couldn't fly down to see us. I guess Air Force guys don't drive. Do wars stop because of wind? "Hello, General Swinekiller, this is General Goodguy. Our weather people say the wind will be up tomorrow. What say we take a day off? Great! Give my regards to the missus."

I recently learned that aeronautical charts showing established flight corridors may be found at any good map store. Yet another example of how I am too soon old, too late smart.

The National Priorities List (Superfund Sites)

"Radiation leaks are caused by fools like me,
but only God can build a nuclear reactor 93 million miles
from the nearest elementary school."

—STEWART BRAND

EPA Administrator Carol Browner stated that nearly 73 million people live within four miles of the more than 1,300 toxic sites on the federal priority list for decontamination (report to U.S. Senate, 9-4-97). In the last fourteen years, with an expenditure of nearly $9 billion by government and billions more by private industry, the Superfund program has concluded cleanup on 220 sites. (Please see Superfund map at end of Chapter 28, "Toxic Pollution.")

Nuclear Power Plants

Following is a list of the 109 operable nuclear reactors in the United States as of December 31, 1994. Seven additional units had received construction permits by the end of 1994. Rising costs, lower electricity demand because of energy conservation, regulatory delays, and citizen opposition may preclude new construction of nuclear reactors.

Alabama—5

Browns Ferry 1, 2, and 3, Decatur; Joseph M. Farley 1 and 2, Dothan

Arizona—3

Palo Verde 1, 2, and 3, Wintersburg

Arkansas—2

Arkansas Nuclear 1 and 2, Russellville

California—4

Diablo Canyon 1 and 2, Avila Beach; San Onofre 2 and 3, San Clemente

Connecticut—4

Connecticut Yankee, Haddam Neck; Millstone 1, 2 and 3, Waterford

Florida—5

Crystal River 3, Red Level; St. Lucie 1 and 2, Fort Pierce; Turkey Point, 3 and 4, Florida City

Georgia—4

Hatch 1 and 2, Baxley; Vogtle 1 and 2, Waynesboro

Illinois—13

Braidwood 1 and 2, Braidwood; Bryron 1 and 2, Bryon; Clinton 1, Clinton; Dresden 2 and 3, Morris; La Salle 1 and 2, Seneca; Quad Cities 1 and 2, Cordova; Zion 1 and 2, Zion

Iowa—1

Duane Arnold, Palo

Kansas—1

Wolf Creek, Burlington

Louisiana—2

River Bend 1, St. Francisville; Waterford 3, Taft

Maine—1

Maine Yankee, Wiscasset

Maryland—2

Calvert Cliffs 1 and 2, Lusby

Massachusetts—1

Pilgrim 1, Plymouth

Michigan—5
Big Rock Point, Charlevoix; Donald C. Cook 1 and 2, Bridgman;
Fermi 2, Newport; Palisades, South Haven

Minnesota—3
Monticello, Monticello; Prairie Island 1 and 2, Red Wing

Mississippi—1
Grand Gulf 1, Port Gibson

Missouri—1
Callaway 1, Fulton

Nebraska—2
Cooper, Brownville; Fort Calhoun 1, Fort Calhoun

New Hampshire—1
Seabrook 1, Seabrook

New Jersey—4
Hope Creek 1, Salem; Oyster Creek 1, Forked River; Salem 1 and 2, Salem

New York—6
Indian Point 2 and 3, Buchanan; James A. Fitzpatrick, Scriba;
Nine Mile Point 1 and 2, Oswego; Robert E. Ginna, Rochester

North Carolina—5
Brunswick 1 and 2, Southport; McGuire 1 and 2, Cowens Ford Dam;
Shearon Harris 1, New Hill

Ohio—2
Davis-Besse 1, Oak Harbor; Perry 1, North Perry

Pennsylvania—9
Beaver Valley 1 and 2, Shippingport; Limerick 1 and 2, Pottstown;
Peach Bottom 2 and 3, Lancaster; Susquehanna 1 and 2, Berwick;
Three Mile Island 1, Middletown

South Carolina—7
Catawba 1 and 2, Clover; H.B. Robinson 2, Hartsville;
Oconee 1, 2, and 3, Seneca; Summer 1, Jenkinsville

Tennessee—2

Sequoyah 1 and 2, Daisy

Texas—4

Comanche Peak 1 and 2, Glen Rose; South Texas 1 and 2, Bay City

Vermont—1

Vermont Yankee, Vernon

Virginia—4

North Anna 1 and 2, Mineral; Surrey 1 and 2, Surrey

Washington—1

WNP 2, Richland

Wisconsin—3

Kewaunee, Carlton; Point Beach 1 and 2, Two Creeks

Nuclear Waste Shipment Routes

Buy property well away from interstate highways. Federal regulations require that nuclear waste shipments by truck must use the interstates. If Yucca Mountain, Nevada, becomes the national nuclear waste repository, 77,000 tons of "spent"

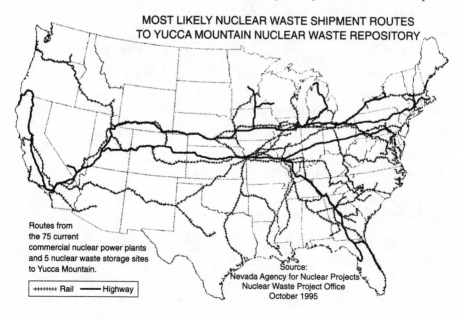

MOST LIKELY NUCLEAR WASTE SHIPMENT ROUTES
TO YUCCA MOUNTAIN NUCLEAR WASTE REPOSITORY

Routes from
the 75 current
commercial nuclear power plants
and 5 nuclear waste storage sites
to Yucca Mountain.

++++++ Rail ——— Highway

Source:
Nevada Agency for Nuclear Projects
Nuclear Waste Project Office
October 1995

fuel from seventy-five sites in thirty-four states (most are in the East) will travel our highways (see map). An official quoted in *The Denver Post* (9-20-95) stated that he was "not as concerned" about shipment of four million cubic feet of transuranic waste in barrels through Colorado to the Waste Isolation Pilot Project in Carlsbad, New Mexico. Beginning in 1998, the material, plutonium-laced clothing and lab equipment, will be shipped there from Rocky Flats, Idaho, and Hanford, Washington. Nevada transportation adviser Robert Halstead said Nevada may be more worried about transportation of the high-level fuel rods than their actual storage underground. States around Nevada should also be worried, he said. "It benefits us for people to know what happens in Nevada does affect them. There are two very real concerns—terrorist attacks and accidents."

Factories, Power Plants, Paper Mills

In case you become too depressed to read the entire following chapter on toxic pollution, be advised to stay far upwind and upstream from any factory that discharges fumes or fluids into the air or water or dumps hazardous wastes nearby. And remember that wind directions occasionally reverse.

Power plants use enormous amounts of water for cooling and change local aquatic and marine ecosystems. Power plants burn various fuels and can emit huge plumes of noxious smoke. Even the most advanced flue scrubbers occasionally fail.

Paper mills create a smell that must be experienced to be believed. White paper is bleached by a chlorine process that releases deadly dioxins into waterways. And the particulates produced can combine with precipitation to create an acidic rain that will literally melt the rubber of your car's windshield wipers. It's not wonderful for your car's paint either. Or your eyes, skin, or lungs.

In addition to pollution, factories generate equipment sounds which, in the quiet of country, may travel substantial distances.

Agribusiness, Cropland, and Meat Production

Small family farms add much that is good to the atmosphere and quality of a community. Big operations—corporate farms—tend to use large amounts of fuel, chemical fertilizers, herbicides, and pesticides. Pesticide spraying may result in drift, airborne toxins floating over to your property. U.S. cotton farmers use over

16 million pounds of pesticides each year. Feed lots and other intensive livestock operations generate substantial animal wastes and smells. Groundwater pollution is common near these facilities. Being downwind from feedlots discourages breathing. Some specific horror stories were presented in Chapter 13, "Farming and Market Gardening." If you have a pet dog, be aware that most farmers and ranchers have the legal right to shoot any dog bothering livestock. And right-to-farm laws properly protect farmers from lawsuits by people who move to the country, then complain about manure smells and the noise generated by all-night machinery operation.

LULUs

Locally undesirable land uses—LULUs—are those enterprises and practices that our current society supports but that no one wants in their neighborhood—the NIMBY syndrome. Wastes—from household garbage to radioactive spent fuel rods from nuclear power plants—are being sent from affluent metropolitan areas to poor, low-population places. Waste management companies target vulnerable counties, then gain permission to dump their refuse by making political donations, creating a few jobs, and spreading dollars around schools and other high-profile community services.

Northeastern municipalities increasingly are paying for the privilege of dumping their garbage in inland states hundreds or even thousands of miles from their own backyards. Wendell Berry reports that eastern states are trucking garbage to his home state of Kentucky. Tiny Sierra Blanca in western Texas receives daily boxcarloads of sewage sludge from New York City. It will soon become the dump site for radioactive waste from Vermont and Maine. The waste management company expects to make a $168 million profit over the next five to eight years—a crumb of which is being fed to locals to override citizens' protestations that the practice is poisoning their land. *The Toronto Star* (12-21-95) reported that three of the four companies bidding for Toronto's garbage disposal contract hope to haul the garbage south to sites in the United States, "leaving us liable for damages in the future."

Check with the county clerk, county health office, planning department, and state waste management permit officials to determine if this is happening or being considered in your targeted areas. Frankly, quite aside from pollution considerations, I would avoid buying property in any county where elected officials would consider letting such a thing happen.

A hazardous waste dump is a landfill's brother-gone-bad. These facilities are often simply ponds lined with clay into which toxic liquids are poured. Often uncovered, rains fill and overflow the ponds. Vegetation downwind from these places often dies. I know of a San Francisco Bay Area housing subdivision that was constructed within a quarter mile downwind of one such pond. The women there experienced a high rate of pregnancy problems and babies were born with abnormalities. Landscaping vegetation routinely died. The waste dump owners of course denied responsibility.

Prisons

At the end of 1996, the federal prison system was estimated to be operating at 25 percent overcapacity, while state prisons were estimated to be operating at 16 to 24 percent over their highest rated capacity. Not surprisingly, the current trend is to build more prisons. According to *Corrections Compendium*, ninety-nine new prisons were built in 1993; another fifty-two were planned for the 1994–1995 fiscal year. With an average of 5.8 new prisons built or planned per state, Texas is keeping its steel and concrete contractors happiest—it built fourteen in 1993 and has plans for another thirty. Runners-up are North Carolina with thirteen, and Florida with ten. Over forty states are building new prisons or expanding existing ones. Oregon plans to build seven new prisons for $1 billion. The political response to escalating crime is "three strikes and you're out," which will require ever more prisons—presumably until all of us are either in prison or guarding those who are (the Department of Justice, 6-22-97, reported that one of every 118 American males is behind bars). Most new prisons are built in rural areas. Check with someone at the state level to determine sites being considered for new prisons. The governor's staff can direct you to someone who knows. Be persistent.

Laws, Codes, and Regulations

Freedom is one of the basic tenets of high-quality life. We have lost many of our original freedoms guaranteed by the Constitution. This has occurred gradually over a long period of time and we don't think about it much anymore. We just accept the condition as one of the many features of modern life to which we must submit.

One of the most pleasurable conditions I found in my adopted county was the almost total lack of laws, codes, and regulations for building. There is no zoning commission to say what must go where; there is no building inspector to demand fees or sets of plans and to make surprise inspections. The only "enforcement" I have experienced came from the local electric co-op, whose lineman inspected the rewiring work I had performed in our house. It was more of a free service to be sure the wiring was safe. I welcomed the inspection; had a recommendation been made I would gladly have made the appropriate correction.

The downside to lack of codes and enforcement is that buildings may be built using unsafe methods and designs. While a bad floor plan may merely be inconvenient, a badly designed or constructed flue could kill you.

The farther you locate away from cities the more likely you are to find such conditions as in my county. Beware of "rural" counties that lie within metropolitan areas where city codes and regulations are enforced. Such enforcement is not only degrading of personal freedom, it requires taxes to pay for it. Paying salaries and overhead for people to enforce city rules and regulations is not a part of high-quality country living.

Eminent Domain

Eminent domain law allows the state to condemn and take your property for the public good, as for a park or a new highway. Most of the many dams built by the Corps of Engineers created lakes on land once owned by individuals, land often in the same family for generations. In some cases, whole towns were moved.

Besides outright taking (through mandatory sale), some state laws also allow use of the power to obtain rights-of-way. The March/April 1992 issue of *Harrowsmith Country Life* reported the story of an artist who bought land in Wyoming's Owl Creek Range, looking forward to peace and quiet. That ended when a judge upheld an obscure state law to let a Denver oil company commandeer, widen, and use a road through the middle of her property to move well-drilling equipment to a site on U.S. Bureau of Land Management land.

That article exposed the fact that condemnation laws in most western states give private companies eminent domain powers normally reserved only for governments. The purpose is to encourage natural resource development by private firms.

The most egregious use of eminent domain I have heard of was to obtain land for construction of the previously cited Texas Motor Speedway in the Dallas–Fort Worth area. Apparently the great State of Texas assigns its eminent domain power to private development companies. Approximately 100 home-owners were forced to sell their homes so the speedway could be built. The same tactic is being used to create space for sports stadiums. Another Texas caution regards mineral rights. In Texas, those who hold mineral rights to your land have surface development rights—the right to come onto your land and, for instance, drill for oil. Beware, the drilling may take place very close to your house. And the drilling company has no obligation to clean up its mess when it leaves. If it leaves.

Backing up to or being surrounded by national forest or other government-owned land seems like a good thing. Often it is not. If the federal government or its lessees need access for a logging operation, forest improvement, oil drilling, or any other authorized activity and the shortest route is across your land, guess what? They will go across your land. If you object, an eminent domain pro-ceeding almost certainly will be decided in favor of the government. That may mean that you will endure the noise and dust of logging trucks rumbling past your house from sunup to sundown, or worse. And after the forest is denuded or the oil rigs are in operation, your view will be not nearly as pleasant as before. Another reason to not buy land adjoining government land is that you will likely never have the option of buying it, should you wish to enlarge your acreage.

Eminent domain proceedings are rarely to private property owners' satis-faction. The potential threat of eminent domain can destroy your peace of mind. Absent great overriding advantages, avoid buying property with discernible eminent domain potential.

Fire-Prone Areas

The arid West is generally more fire-prone than the moist East. But even here in the Ozarks, which receives between forty and forty-five inches of rain each year, we have a fire season for several weeks in late winter. Fire typically burns upward, so higher elevations are at greater risk than valley bottoms, but fire can occur anyplace with adequate fuel, oxygen, ignition. Not only forested land is at risk. Chaparral and brush burn even faster than coniferous forests. Droughts exacerbate fire danger conditions.

"In the northeastern Sierra region, trees killed by the recent seven-year drought and subsequent bug infestation are stacking up, creating fuel ladders much like what you build in your fireplace or woodstove. . . . The pervading fear is the vast amount of fuels on these forests will catch somewhere one day and be anything but controlled. In fact, the runaway Cottonwood fire nearly burned down the town of Sierraville last year" (*Timber*, a Feather River Publishing Company supplement, 9-20-95).

In early 1996, grass fires consumed nearly 50,000 acres of parched grassland in Texas, Kansas, and Oklahoma. Hundreds of homes were burned, many people were injured, and hundreds were evacuated to safe areas. In 1997 there were 66,196 fires that consumed 2,856,959 acres.

Beyond the danger of living in a fire-prone area, fire insurance rates reflect the zone assigned your area by insurance underwriters and the quality of fire-fighting services available as well as the type of heating unit in the house.

Only about 10 percent of fires are lightning-caused, so the amount and type of human activity in an area is an important factor. Should you decide to buy or build in a fire-prone area, establish and maintain a substantial fuel-free area around your buildings. Note, however, that such zones are little protection from airborne burning material.

Information on fire incidence and type can be obtained from volunteer fire departments, paid town departments, state conservation departments, and state or federal forestry departments.

Floodplains

We discussed floods in Chapter 9. Any low area that receives runoff from a large area can flood. The greater the watershed, the greater the possibility of flooding. In hollows and small valleys evidence of flooding can often be easily found. Leaves, twigs, and other plant detritus several feet up in shrubs and small trees along a bottom are strong evidence of flooding, but their absence should not be taken as proof that the area is flood-free. Talk to conservation agents, emergency personnel, newspaper employees, and residents of your target area for flood history.

Isolation

"And I'll say further that many back-to-the-landers listen for and can hear a UPS truck when it's five miles out and if UPS doesn't stop at the back-to-the-lander's place that he charges the truck and tries to bite the tires. And that is also true of me."

—BRITT LEACH, *Country Connections* (May 1995)

This is more an alert about the downside of isolation than a condition to avoid. I am not quite an isolationist but I do relish more privacy than most people seem to require. The caveat to being way out in the boonies is this: while isolation and peace and quiet go hand in hand, a personal subjective result may be loneliness. If you usually stay busy and you attend to your social needs on a regular basis you may never become lonely. But if you are accustomed to the hubbub of city activity you may find country seclusion almost overwhelming, especially after you get settled in. And be aware of the danger of having an accident and needing help when there are few people nearby.

Local Conditions

Your contentment will be affected by the lifestyle and values of those who already live where you will go. Consider the nature of a place. Cattle, hog, sheep, and poultry producers have different values than vegetarians. In wild areas, old-timers still kill hawks, eagles, coyotes, and wolves on sight—laws be damned. This may merely sadden most of us but would wound passionate birders and environmentalists. If these people become your neighbors, how will their activities impact your values and lifestyle?

Specific Places and Conditions to Avoid

(In all cases, places downwind or downwater from pollution sources are at greatest risk.)

   • Retired and active landfills, toxic and hazardous waste sites. No matter how well built—and many were not—they all eventually leak or overflow.

- Toxic waste incinerator vicinities. Smoke and ash from these devices can be deadly.

- Mining areas. Toxic tailings and water-filled mines contaminate groundwater and surface waterways.

- Agribusiness areas. Pesticide drift and groundwater contamination, stench from intensive meat production operations, potential for huge excrement floods. (It has already happened.)

- Near major highways. The Wisconsin propane spill that forced evacuation of a town underscored again the danger that shipping routes pose.

- "In addition to the San Joaquin Valley in California, there are major concentrations of pesticide use throughout the Midwest, especially Iowa and Illinois, as well as along the Mississippi River, in a band across the Southeast coastal plain, and in the states of Florida and Washington. Iowa, Illinois, Minnesota, Indiana, and Ohio all account for larger shares of pesticide use than does California" (Benjamin Goldman, *The Truth About Where You Live*).

- Near active or retired nuclear reactors.

- Industrial areas. Western Pennsylvania. Wherever there is industry there are hazardous wastes. Three quarters of all hazardous waste produced in the United States originate in chemical factories and laboratories.

- Near paper mills. Paper mill effluents contain deadly dioxin compounds and sulfites. Dioxin's effects on laboratory animals are so lethal that some scientists rank it among the most poisonous substances known.

- Along major rivers with industry or agribusiness upstream. Jim Robbins (*The Last Refuge*) reports that a billion gallons of waste pour into the Columbia River every day from agricultural and municipal sewage.

- "The world's largest hazardous waste site sits between Geiger and Emell [Alabama]" (Fred Setterberg and Lonny Shavelson, *Toxic Nation*).

- "*National Wildlife* magazine once called Triana, Alabama, the 'unhealthiest town in America'" (Setterberg and Shavelson).

- Yucca Mountain, eighty miles northwest of Las Vegas, may become the nation's nuclear waste disposal place. So far, $3 billion have been spent "studying" the site. A large packet of information, including "Why Nevada Is Opposed to Yucca Mountain," is available from: State of Nevada, Agency for Nuclear Projects, Nuclear Waste Project Office, Capitol Complex, Carson, NV 89710.

Other Places to Avoid

- Towns with parking meters—the people who run the town either have a parking problem, a tax problem, or a values problem—all conditions to stay away from.

- Places with a strong chamber of commerce pushing for growth.

- Places with a planning board or commission. If there are none and also no building department to torment you with fees, regulations, quadruplicate plans, and inspections you may have hit the jackpot.

- Any place within sound of a highway or commercial business.

- Developments that have displaced serious wildlife. The State of Montana now has an official form: The Mountain Lion Response Form. The form asks: "What action did the lion take?" Answer choices: "1) Watched person; 2) Growled; 3) Hissed; 4) Showed teeth; 5) Lip curl; 6) Fled; 7) Crouched; 8) Attacked; 9) Other."

And, from writer Richard Todd: "You should be able to drive away from your farm in either direction and reach a tractor dealer before you come to a fast-food outlet" ("A Place in the Country," *Harrowsmith Country Life*, January/February 1992).

Resources and Recommended Reading

A Livestock Producer's Legal Guide to Nuisance, Land Use Control, and Environmental Law costs $12 from:

American Farm Bureau Federation
225 Touhy Avenue
Park Ridge, IL 60068

For more information on contaminated military installations, contact:

Environmental Research Foundation
P.O. Box 5036,
Annapolis, MD 21403
Phone: 410-263-1584; fax: 410-263-8944

Books

Garreau, Joel. *Edge City: Life on the New Frontier*. New York: Doubleday, 1991.

Goldman, Benjamin A. *The Truth About Where You Live: An Atlas for Action on Toxins and Mortality*. New York: Times Books, 1991.

Setterberg, Fred, and Lonny Shavelson. *Toxic Nation: The Fight to Save Our Communities from Chemical Contamination*. New York: John Wiley & Sons, 1993.

And for a more sane solution to prison overcrowding than simply building more prisons, read *Ain't Nobody's Business If You Do: The Absurdity of Consensual Crimes in a Free Society*, by Peter McWilliams, Los Angeles: Prelude Press, 1993.

~ 28 ~

Toxic Pollution

*"Can anyone believe it is possible to lay down
such a barrage of poisons on the surface of the earth without
making it unfit for all life?"*

—RACHEL CARSON, *Silent Spring* (1962)

Toxic pollution is a depressing subject but it is one that must be addressed in our search for the ideal home. We can avoid fouling our own nest, but first we must avoid making our nest in a foul place.

The grim news is that pollution exists in every state, probably in nearly every county. The good news is that there are still places where we can live on clean soil, breathe clean air, drink safe water. If we become aware of how to live properly we can keep it that way. If we are discerning in our product purchases, we can help clean up the rest of the world.

Most contamination is in the form of chemicals. The U.S. chemical industry is a huge, capital-intensive business, a major player in the U.S. economy. It has changed the source of consumer products from wood and iron and cotton and wool to petroleum products. It has made possible pipe that won't rust, shirts that won't wrinkle, shoes that help athletes jump. Its technology is high science, transforming crude oil into molded dashboards and designer sunglasses. It has caused artificial to become accepted as natural. And we are killing our children and ourselves with its by-products.

It is impossible to maintain a safe human environment in the presence of the large numbers of toxic chemicals now in common production and use. There are laws governing the production, transport, use, and disposal of chemicals, products of chemicals, and chemical wastes. They are inadequate. We know this because of the sickness and death these materials and their use are causing. Our most basic requirements for life—air, water, food—are poisoning us.

It is uncomfortable to admit, but each of us is responsible for toxic pollution. We all buy products whose production and disposal create pollution. We all buy, use, and dispose of poisonous products. Household cleaning items, painkillers, and cosmetics are leading sources of accidental poisonings in the home. Our carpet, our furniture, and our vehicles emit toxic fumes. Not only do chemicals permeate our food, our clothing, our homes, our cars, they *are* our food, our clothing, our homes, our cars. Chemical consumption and exposure are major causes of high rates of cancer.

Tragically, our children suffer most from toxic contamination. In *Toxic Nation* Fred Setterberg and Lonny Shavelson report: "Beyond the paradoxical attractions of toxic dumps, kids come into greater contact with dangerous chemicals simply because they eat more than adults in proportion to their body weight—including more pesticide residues from fresh vegetables, fruits, and juices. The EPA classifies as possible carcinogens over 65 percent of the 560 million pounds of herbicides and fungicides sprayed annually on U.S. crops. The average child consumes four times the amount of these suspect chemicals than an adult."

Setterberg and Shavelson quote Dr. Herbert Needleman, "the nation's foremost researcher on childhood lead exposures. 'We're twenty years behind on the study of pesticides. . . . There is no question that pesticides impair children's brain functions as insidiously as lead. I will tell you without fear of contradiction that exposing children to excessive levels of pesticides is impairing their health, eroding their mental abilities, and shortening their lives."

DDT is bioaccumulative, that is, it is retained within the body of the consuming organism and is concentrated with each ensuing level of the food chain. Rachel Carson's *Silent Spring*, published in 1962, warned of the danger from DDT. Its use was banned in the U.S. in 1972. End of story? Hardly. American chemical companies still produce and export DDT to other countries, knowing full well that food products produced there using the poison will be exported—to American grocery shelves. Profit at any price. Laws are not enough; greed is too strong. We need to stop rewarding these companies by buying their products.

Pesticides and herbicides are designed to kill food crop pests. Arsenic is part of their recipes. Like lead and mercury it accumulates in the body. Like the wife who fed her husband small quantities of arsenic until enough accumulated to kill him, our chemically treated foods are slowly filling us with lethal residue.

The resistance to elimination of chemical sources of toxic poisoning reminds me of how information presented thirty years ago about the link between cigarettes and lung cancer was dismissed as "inconclusive" by smokers and tobacco companies. The former continue to die of lung cancer. In spite of billion-dollar legal settlements, the latter continue to put profit above life, aiming seductive advertising at susceptible young people, providing cigarettes to those who will not or cannot quit smoking. It is not a stretch to consider that tobacco companies modus operandi is: Give us dollars; give them death.

Air Pollution

"The thoughts of Plato and Machiavelli . . . don't seem quite
enough armor for a world beset with splitting the atoms,
urban guerrillas, nineteen varieties of psychotherapists, amplified
guitars, napalm, computers, astronauts, and an atmosphere
polluted simultaneously with auto exhaust
and TV commercials."

—JOHN FISCHER

Air pollution is caused by emissions from power plants, solid waste incinerators, factories, vehicles. The six major types of air pollutants are carbon monoxide, hydrocarbons, nitrogen oxides, particulates, sulfur dioxide, and photochemical oxidants. Air pollution on a regional scale is in large part the result of city and industrial air pollution that has spread out to encompass areas of many thousands of square miles. Meteorological conditions and landforms influence air pollution concentrations at any given place.

Even natural areas far downwind from pollution sources are affected. Jim Robbins wrote about the Grand Canyon in *The Last Refuge*: "Air pollution from coal-fired power plants and places like Los Angeles gets caught up in prevailing winds and makes its way to the Grand Canyon, where, because of temperature differences, it often sinks and stubbornly sits. 'The canyon,' says Carl Bowman, an air quality specialist for the Park Service, 'is a catch basin for pollution.' He has a picture on his office wall of the canyon filled to the rim during a haze episode."

Acid Rain

Acid rain is created when sulfur dioxide and nitrogen oxides combine with atmospheric moisture to form rain, snow, or hail containing sulfur and nitric acids. Coal burning produces carbon monoxide and sulfur dioxide. In 1980 in the United States, more than 60 percent of the man-made sulfur dioxide emissions was attributed to coal-fired electrical generation plants. Antipollution regulations have caused sulfur dioxide emissions to decrease substantially, but acid rain has diminished only slightly, because the incidence of acid-neutralizing substances has also dropped.

Acid rain raises the acidity (lowers the pH level) of surface water to a level that kills freshwater aquatic life and marine life in coastal waters. It kills trees and other vegetation. It damages croplands, erodes structures, and contaminates drinking water. In the beautiful bayou country of Louisiana, air pollution and acid rain have killed the Spanish moss on many of the giant oak trees. Jim Robbins relates that "ozone and acid precipitation show up in high levels in Sequoia and Kings Canyon. Ozone has contributed to the death of Jeffrey pine trees in Sequoia and has caused visible damage to ponderosa pines."

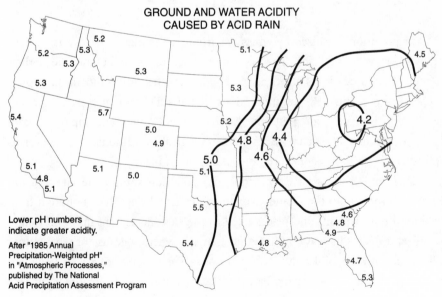

GROUND AND WATER ACIDITY
CAUSED BY ACID RAIN

Lower pH numbers indicate greater acidity.

After "1985 Annual Precipitation-Weighted pH" in "Atmospheric Processes," published by The National Acid Precipitation Assessment Program

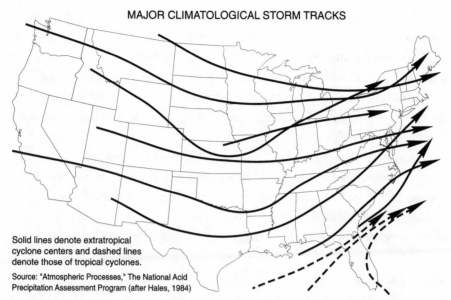

MAJOR CLIMATOLOGICAL STORM TRACKS

Solid lines denote extratropical
cyclone centers and dashed lines
denote those of tropical cyclones.

Source: "Atmospheric Processes," The National Acid
Precipitation Assessment Program (after Hales, 1984)

The major factors controlling transport and dispersion are the character and movement of meteorological systems. Winds can carry pollutants thousands of miles from their source. Greatest acid rain damage in the U.S. exists in streams, lakes, and forests of the Northeast but is also found in forests of the South and Midwest.

Pollutants move both with strong air movements—storm centers that gather them quickly—and with weak, slow-moving high pressure systems that allow sufficient time for thorough mixing to take place. The major storm track map from Chapter 9 is duplicated here so you may easily compare storm patterns with acid rain incidence.

Radiation Pollution

Radiation pollution is any form of ionizing or nonionizing radiation resulting from human activities. The best-known radiation is from the detonation of nuclear devices and the controlled release of energy by nuclear power plants. Other sources of radiation include spent-fuel reprocessing plants, by-products of mining operations, and experimental research laboratories. The 1979 accident at the Three Mile Island nuclear power plant near Harrisburg, Pennsylvania, and the 1986 explosion at Chernobyl in the former U.S.S.R. clearly illuminated radiation danger.

The environmental effects of exposure to high-level ionizing radiation have been extensively documented through postwar studies on Japanese survivors of the Nagasaki and Hiroshima bombings. Some forms of cancer show up immediately, but latent maladies of radiation poisoning have been recorded from ten to thirty years after exposure. The effects of exposure to low-level radiation are not yet agreed upon by scientists, many of whom are dependent upon grants from large companies.

Radioactive wastes cannot be disposed of in the same manner as chemicals. They must be stored in heavily shielded containers in areas remote from living things. The "safest" of current storage sites are allegedly impervious deep caves and abandoned salt mines. Some radioactive wastes have half-lives of thousands of years and no storage method has been found that is certainly safe.

Water Pollution

In the Great Lakes and St. Lawrence Seaway area, water quality is an oxymoron. The Great Lakes are polluted by toxic chemicals called organochlorines from agricultural pesticides and industrial wastes. Fish from the Great Lakes are so full of chemicals and heavy metals that states have banned them for human consumption. Beluga whales in the St. Lawrence River are dying from eating fish and eels full of toxic substances. PCBs were almost completely banned in 1979, yet in 1993 dead belugas still showed such high concentrations of PCBs that their corpses could be classified as hazardous waste.

The Mississippi River Delta region is one of the most polluted areas in the world. The Mississippi drains 41 percent of the contiguous forty-eight states. A legacy of chemical agriculture and industry, the river is a gruesome brew of over 100 toxic chemicals, increasingly worse downstream. There is a 6,000-square-mile area at its mouth called the "dead zone"—so distinct that it shows up on photographs from outer space.

The huge San Joaquin and Sacramento valleys of California are intensively farmed using chemical fertilizers, herbicides, and pesticides. Setterberg and Shavelson state in *Toxic Nation* that "potentially cancer-causing chemicals had already seeped into almost one-third of the [California] state's drinking water wells *at levels deemed safe*" (my emphasis).

Thus far, agribusiness lawyering and lobbying power has evaded responsibility for numerous cases of childhood cancer in these areas. As Gregg Easterbrook, author of *A Moment on the Earth: The Coming Age of Environmental Optimism*, noted in his review of Jonathan Harr's *A Civil Action*, "in any contest between personal injury lawyers and corporations, the corporate side holds what is by far the most important advantage, namely the funds with which to finance a stall defense" (*The New York Times Book Review*, 9-10-95).

Thermal (Heat) Pollution

Thermal pollution is the discharge of waste heat into cooling water and subsequently into nearby waterways. The major sources of thermal pollution are fossil fuel and nuclear power facilities and cooling operations associated with industrial manufacturing, such as steel foundries, other primary-metal manufacturers, and chemical and petrochemical producers. An estimated 90 percent of all water consumption, excluding agricultural uses, is for cooling or energy dissipation.

The discharge of heated water into a waterway often causes major fish kills near the discharge source. The increased temperature accelerates chemical-biological processes and decreases the ability of the water to hold dissolved oxygen. Thermal changes affect the aquatic system by limiting or changing the type of fish and other water life able to live in the waters.

Land Pollution and Destruction

> *"When an agribusinessman hires an expensive crop duster to spray*
> *for alfalfa weevils, he may increase this year's alfalfa production.*
> *He may also kill his neighbor's bees and his own earthworms and beneficial*
> *insects. He may pollute well-water downslope from his fields. If*
> *he is not very careful, he will do all these things."*
>
> —DONALD McCAIG, *An American Homeplace*

Land pollution and destruction is the contamination and degradation of the land surface through misuse of the soil by poor agricultural practices, mineral exploitation, industrial waste dumping, and indiscriminate disposal of urban wastes.

Soil erosion—primarily a result of poor agricultural practices—removes rich topsoil developed over many years through natural processes and strips the land of valuable nutrients. Strip mining for minerals and coal ruins thousands of acres of land each year, subjecting the area to widespread erosion and pollution. Clear-cutting hillside forests destroys the soil's water-holding ability; sediment loads in adjacent streams may increase as much as 500 to 1,000 times.

Radon

Radon occurs more from natural conditions than from man-made ones, but you need to be aware of it, know how to avoid it, and know how to deal with it if it enters your home. Radon is the second most prevalent cause of lung cancer; the EPA estimates that radon causes about 14,000 deaths per year. It is an invisible, odorless gas naturally produced from decaying radium, which comes from uranium, which is found in about 150 minerals. Among these are granite, phosphate, and shale. In *Radon: The Invisible Threat*, Michael LaFavore notes that "large deposits of uranium ore, pure enough to mine for atomic fuel, are located in parts of western Colorado, eastern Utah, northeastern Arizona, northwestern New Mexico, Wyoming, Texas, and western Canada."

Uranium mine tailings emit huge quantities of radon. Heavy rains leach radioactive particles out of mine tailings and contaminate groundwater. Before radon was publicly recognized as a health threat, tailings were used to make concrete products and even as landfill under and around new homes. In *The Menace of Atomic Energy*, Ralph Nader and John Abbotts report that as many as 3,300 homes were built on radioactive tailings in Grand Junction, Colorado. At least one school was built of masonry composed of tailings.

Most U.S. areas have "safe" low levels of radon. While the presence or absence of certain minerals indicates greater possibility, homeowners should satisfy themselves as to safety by having a radon test performed. Uranium concentration can be very narrow—the absence or presence of radon in one home may not be repeated in a neighboring home. How a house is built can increase its risk. If high levels of radon are found, corrective work can be performed but it may be costly if excavation work is needed to place vent pipes.

In addition to the resources listed at the end of this chapter, state health departments often have radon contact agencies. These agencies and the regional offices of the EPA (see Resources) are good sources of general information about the health risks of radon, radon measurements in your home, and correction of radon problems.

RADON POTENTIAL AREAS

Based on radioactivity map in "The Geology of Radon" by U.S. Department of the Interior

I drew the radon map based on a color radioactive map in *The Geology of Radon* published by the U.S. Department of the Interior (see ordering information at end of chapter). The following numbered comments are also those of the department. Note that No. 10 and No. 16 are areas of *low* radon potential.

1. Great Salt Lake: Water absorbs gamma rays so it shows as no data area on the map.
2. Nebraska Sand Hills: Wind has separated the lighter quartz sand from the clay and heavier minerals that usually contain uranium.
3. The Black Hills: A core of granites and metamorphic rocks high in radioactivity is surrounded by less radioactive sedimentary rocks and gives a distinctive pattern.
4. Pleistocene glacial deposits: The area has low surface radioactivity, but uranium occurs just below the surface. Thus it has a high radon potential.
5. Deposits of glacial Lake Agassiz: Clay and silt from a prehistoric glacial lake have higher radioactivity than glacial drift surrounding it.

293

6. Ohio Shale: Uranium-bearing black shale with a narrow outcrop zone was scooped up and spread over a large area in west-central Ohio by glaciers.

7. Reading Prong: Uranium-rich metamorphic rocks and numerous fault zones produce high radon in indoor air and in groundwater.

8. Appalachian Mountains: Granites contain elevated uranium, particularly in fault zones. Black shales and soils above limestone also contain moderate to high levels of uranium.

9. Chattanooga and New Albany Shales: Uranium-bearing black shales in Ohio, Kentucky, and Indiana have a distinctive outcrop pattern clearly defined by radioactivity.

10. Outer Atlantic and Gulf Coastal Plain: This area of unconsolidated sands, silts, and clays has one of the lowest radon potentials in the United States.

11. Phosphatic rocks, Florida: These rocks are high in phosphate and associated uranium.

12. Inner Gulf Coastal Plain: This area of the Inner Coastal Plain has sands containing glauconite, a mineral high in uranium.

13. Rocky Mountains: Granites and metamorphic rocks in these ranges contain more uranium than sedimentary rocks to the east, resulting in high radon in indoor air and in groundwater.

14. Basin and Range: Granitic and volcanic rocks in the ranges, alternating with basins filled with alluvium shed from the ranges, give this area a generally high radioactivity.

15. Sierra Nevada: Granites containing high uranium, particularly in east-central California, show as red areas [on the USDI map].

16. Northwest Pacific Coastal Mountains and Columbia Plateau: This area of volcanic basalts is low in uranium.

Sewage, Oil, and Mining Pollution

Most cites have sewage problems because sewage volume and ingredients exceed the capabilities of treatment facilities. Untreated and partially treated sewage from municipal systems and rural septic tanks puts significant quantities of nutrients, suspended solids, dissolved solids, oil, and heavy metals into waterways. More than 13,000 oil spills occur in the U.S. yearly. Thousands of environmentally untested chemicals are routinely discharged into waterways. An estimated 400 to 500 new compounds are marketed each year. In addition, strip mining for coal releases acid wastes that poison the surrounding waterways.

Beware of western mining towns inundated and surrounded by toxic mine tailings. In *The Last Refuge*, Jim Robbins reports: "All but a small part of the city of Butte is a Superfund site, and around town there are three million cubic yards of old mine tailings, rocks, dirt, soil and other mining detritus, filled with high levels of such toxic elements as arsenic, lead, cadmium and mercury. . . . The six-thousand-acre site where the Anaconda smelter separated the [gold] metal from the ore for ninety-six years is number forty-eight on the national Superfund list. . . . There are 185 million cubic yards of poisoned tailings here. . . . Arsenic is also widely scattered across the countryside near Anaconda. . . . One rancher twelve miles downwind lost a thousand cattle, eight hundred sheep and twenty horses to arsenic poisoning in a single year. . . . High levels of arsenic have been found in children in the area.

"Butte is not the only place where miners have been replaced with toxic-waste remediation workers. Toxic-waste sites can be found near any number of western mining towns, waiting like huge, festering wounds to be treated. Bunker Hill in the Silver Valley of northern Idaho. The Yak Tunnel on the headwaters of the Arkansas River near Leadville, Colorado. . . . The copper wastes near Miami and Globe, Arizona, east of Phoenix. Telluride, Colorado. The Bingham Canyon Mine, near Salt Lake City. It's estimated that twelve thousand miles of American rivers and streams have been polluted by mining."

Solid Waste

U.S. municipal wastes—the solid wastes from households and businesses sent to local landfills and other waste-disposal facilities—measure about two billion tons per year. Additional solid wastes amass from mining, industrial production, and agriculture. Although municipal wastes are the most obvious, the accumulations of the other types of wastes are far greater, in many instances are more difficult to dispose of, and present greater environmental hazards.

The most common and convenient method of disposing of municipal solid wastes is in sanitary landfill. Sanitary landfills work reasonably well for domestic waste cleared of hazardous materials. But industrial wastes are often commingled with domestic wastes, leading to groundwater contamination from toxic chemicals. Space for landfills is running out and all landfills eventually leak, so a saner system must be embraced.

Toxic industrial wastes, although often in liquid form, are generally treated the same as solid wastes. Hazardous waste disposal sites are often simply clay-lined ponds. No one has solved the problems of leakage and overflow from rain. Perimeter shallow wells are promoted as adequate for testing for leakage and pumping contaminated water from the ground but to where can we pump if the cesspool is full? William T. Cahill was one of the first to phrase the obvious: "We now understand that we can no longer throw our wastes away—because there is no 'away.'"

Incineration

Incineration is touted as an efficient method for disposing of solid wastes by those who hope for a simple solution. Incinerators use solid wastes as fuel, burning refuse and using the heat to make steam for electricity generation. Wastes must be burned at very high temperatures and incinerator exhausts must be equipped with sophisticated scrubbers and other devices for removing dioxins and other toxic pollutants. There are serious flaws with incineration: incinerator ash contains concentrations of heavy metals, becoming a hazardous waste itself, scrubbers sometimes fail, and incinerators discourage the use of recycling and other waste reduction methods. The U.S. Supreme Court ruled in May 1994 that municipal garbage-to-energy plants must treat the resultant ash as hazardous waste. Let's hear it for the Supremes.

Toxic Pollution—Just How Widespread Is It?

In *Toxic Nation*, Setterberg and Shavelson offer compelling vignettes from all over the country. Here is a sampling:

"In Pilcher, Oklahoma, abandoned copper, lead, and zinc mines overflowed during heavy rains, bubbling up from 'a 10 billion gallon vat of subterranean poison.'. . . The extruded acid water burned grasslands, scalded horses' hooves, and ate through a five-gallon metal bucket. 'Fish had open sores,' recalled one Pilcher resident, 'like somebody took a knife and cut a chunk out of them.'

"In Toone, Tennessee, several farming families spent four years in what seemed to be chronic depression, until they discovered chloroform in their drinking water.

"In Brookhurst, Wyoming, residents abandoned their chemically contaminated homes, turning the neighborhood into a ghost town and leaving their houses marked with anti-toxics graffiti.

"In Oxnard, California, Linda Paxton moved away from her two-story duplex after learning that it had been built upon a field of underground liquid toxic waste pools; she painted one side of her abandoned home with a huge skull-and-crossbones, announcing: Oxnard's Love Canal. Our Home Toxic Dump.

[Love Canal refers to a neighborhood in Niagara Falls, New York, where homes were built on land poisoned by toxic waste disposal. After a huge fight, the government bought most of the homes.]

"In Pompano Beach, Florida, tiny white particles of vinyl chloride descended from the skies like snow. . . . This extremely powerful carcinogen was being pumped into the air from a nearby polyvinyl chloride pipe factory. A health study organized by the local residents found high incidences of liver, heart, and kidney disease and cancer.

"In Pearland, Texas, the chances of contracting cancer are calculated as being the highest in the nation—with industrial pollution factored as a leading cause.

"In Springfield, Vermont, the residents of a mobile home park didn't realize they were sitting on a vast wasteland of arsenic, benzene, cyanide, and lead— what the regional EPA administrator called 'a chemical time bomb'—until 'there were people in white suits and rubber gloves and rubber boots walking around' testing the soil."

In *The Truth About Where You Live*, Benjamin A. Goldman tells of the 400 Ponca City, Oklahoma, families who were successful with a class-action suit against Conoco Oil Company, which had poisoned the community's groundwater. The company paid $23 million to buy the homes so the residents could start new lives elsewhere.

It may be impossible to locate far enough downwind to avoid all chemical drift. In "Troubled Waters Run Deep" in the 1993 *National Geographic Special: Water*, Michael Parfit wrote: "At Lake Laberge, way up in the Yukon Territory, a study of fish flesh turned up a variety of chemicals, including the insecticide toxaphene, which has been widely used in Russia. It probably blew east, and rain raked it in."

Don't even consider buying property near agribusiness operations. Setterberg and Shavelson reported the heart-wrenching stories of parents losing children to various cancers, from California's San Joaquin Valley to Yellow Creek, Kentucky, to New York. Interminable bureaucratic jungles, chemical company personnel, and agribusiness owners thwart efforts to end the horror of children born with no hands or feet or with impaired mental ability. In many places, even though tests of well water show contamination from various chemicals, current allowed concentrations preclude decisive action.

Recent media reports show that even so-called clean industries are creating health hazards. High rates of miscarriages and low-birthweight babies have become evident in California's Silicon Valley. Suspected are water supplies fouled by the solvents used to clean computer chips.

> *"Our ideals, laws, and customs should be based on*
> *the proposition that each generation in turn becomes the custodian*
> *rather than the absolute owner of our resources—and each generation*
> *has the obligation to pass this inheritance on to the future."*
>
> —Alden Whitman

Part of the Solution to Pollution—Recycling

Recycling is practical for much municipal and some industrial waste materials, and a small but growing proportion of wastes is being recycled. When wastes are mixed, recycling becomes far more difficult and costly. New processes for sorting ferrous and nonferrous metals, paper, glass, and plastics have been developed, and many communities with recycling programs now require refuse separation. Crucial issues in recycling are devising better processing methods, inventing new products for the recycled materials, and finding new markets for those products.

Composting is increasingly used to treat some agricultural wastes, as well as such municipal wastes as leaves and brush. Composting systems can produce usable soil conditioners, or humus, within a few months.

Although the movement toward recycling and energy production from wastes may help contend with waste disposal loads, it is not expected to reduce them so long as our high-consumption, throwaway society continues to generate increasing quantities of discarded material. The most sane plans for managing the solid waste dilemma are to reduce consumption, eliminate waste, make all containers recyclable, and require all producers to take back their used products and recycle them into new ones. The solution to pollution can begin with more responsible consumer buying practices. Each of us must be part of that solution.

Final Thoughts

Even with increased EPA regulation, new pesticides and hundreds of other new compounds are marketed each year. Many are not intended to enter the environment, but through waste disposal and accidents most eventually do. The EPA attempts to ensure safe management of an estimated 303 million tons of hazardous waste produced annually in the U.S. The agency has compiled an inventory of 32,000 sites that may contain hazardous wastes.

Prediction: Americans will increasingly turn to organically grown produce. Chemical-farming areas will be shunned by informed moderns turning to rural life. Eventually, such land will only be used for food exports to other, hungrier nations. Even farmers are turning against the throw-poison-at-it mentality. Angry cotton farmers in the Rio Grande Valley of Texas are saying no to the government recommended aerial spraying of malathion to eradicate the boll weevil. The farmers say the spraying has also killed beneficial insects, which, in turn, caused the outbreak of the beet armyworm, another cotton enemy that has now caused one of the worst harvests of this century. "This thing isn't a boll-weevil eradication program," said one leader of the recall drive. "It's a cotton-farmer eradication program" (*The New York Times*, 1-28-96).

Land without chemical contamination is still available. Most subsistence farmers were too poor to use the expensive products of the chemical companies so their old homesteads often make good home sites. Land far removed from industrial and agribusiness areas is available in many parts of the country.

Organic certification programs require soil tests to prove the absence of chemical poisoning. If ground has been subjected to chemical products it may take decades before it is clean of chemical residue. Uncontaminated land is becoming increasingly more valuable and more jealously protected.

Check with local planners to see if incinerators, landfills, or hazardous waste sites exist or are being considered for the area. Determine local attitudes toward recycling. Someone at the local recycling center may know the answers or will direct you to someone who does.

Resources and Recommended Reading

The 1984 Union Carbide chemical leak disaster in Bhopal, India, which killed more than 2,500 nearby residents, and the much less serious chemical release in West Virginia shortly thereafter prompted Congress to pass the Emergency Planning and Community Right-to-Know Act. A brochure is available which explains the Act, including how to get information on chemical releases in any community. To order *Chemicals in Your Community: A Guide to the Emergency Planning and Community Right-to-Know Act*, call the EPA Right-to-Know Hotline: 800-535-0202. An information specialist will direct you to a state agency that can give you information about toxic conditions in specific locations.

EPA Hazardous Waste, Superfund Hotline: 800-424-9346. Provides information and interpretation of federal hazardous waste regulations. Will provide referrals regarding other hazardous waste matters.

EPA Pesticide Hotline: 800-858-7378. Provides information on health hazards, cleanup, and disposal of pesticides. Will refer callers to human and animal poison control centers in their states if necessary.

EPA Drinking Water Hotline: 800-426-4791.

EPA Radon Hotline: 800-SOS-RADON for free radon information, including a copy of *Reducing Radon Risks*, which includes state radon contact phone numbers.

The Geology of Radon includes a radioactivity map and is available free from:
U.S. Geological Survey
Branch of Distribution
P.O. Box 25286
Denver, CO 80225

A different radon map produced by the U.S. Geological Survey may be viewed at http://sedwww.cr.usgs.gov:8080/radon/rnus.html.

The National Priorities List (Superfund sites) is available from the EPA. As of April 1995, there were a total of 1,227 Superfund sites nationwide; as of September 1997, 1,347 sites.

Environmental Protection Agency
Public Information Center, 3404
401 M Street SW
Washington, DC 20460
Phone: 202-260-2080; e-mail: Public-Access@epamail.epa.gov
Web site: http://www.epa.gov/superfund/oerr/siteinfo/index.htm

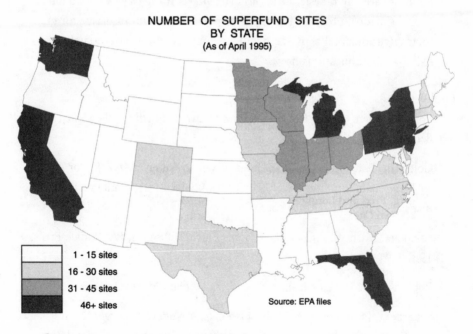

NUMBER OF SUPERFUND SITES BY STATE
(As of April 1995)

1 - 15 sites
16 - 30 sites
31 - 45 sites
46+ sites

Source: EPA files

Greenpeace
1436 U Street NW
Washington, DC 20009
Phone: 202-462-1177; fax: 202-462-4507

Large number of environmental publications available. Ask for catalogue.

Citizen's Clearinghouse for Hazardous Wastes
P.O. Box 6806, 119 Rowell Court
Falls Church, VA 22040
703-237-2249

For most people, a crisis center, helpful in dealing with community environmental problems. Source of plain-language publications.

Environmental Research Foundation
P.O. Box 5036
Annapolis, MD 21403-7036
Phone: 410-263-1584; fax: 410-263-8944

Publishes weekly newsletter *Rachel's Hazardous Waste News* (named after Rachel Carson), provides free rapid-response information service for grassroots environmental activists, maintains online computerized database. Ask for the publications list.

Books

Ford, Norman. *The 50 Healthiest Places to Live and Retire in the United States*. Bedford, MA: Mills & Sanderson, 1991.

Goldman, Benjamin A. *The Truth About Where You Live: An Atlas for Action on Toxins and Mortality*. New York: Times Books, 1991. Contains many maps showing unhealthful counties.

LaFavore, Michael. *Radon: The Invisible Threat*. Emmaus, PA: Rodale Press, 1987.

Robbins, Jim. *The Last Refuge*. New York: William Morrow, 1993.

Setterberg, Fred, and Lonny Shavelson. *Toxic Nation: The Fight to Save Our Communities from Chemical Contamination*. New York: John Wiley & Sons, 1993.

*"It is impossible to divorce the question of what we do
from the question of where we are—or, rather, where we think we
are. That no sane creature befouls its own nest
is accepted as generally true. What we conceive to be our nest,
and where we think it is, are therefore questions
of the greatest importance."*

—WENDELL BERRY

This is what happens when essential country skills are not taken seriously. These boys failed to learn **Essential Country Skill #44: driving a horse**. They have ignored **Instruction #1: At all times insist on being in charge**. If the horse disagrees with you, pull over to the side of the road and talk to the horse in a calm manner until it is mutually understood that you are in charge. Talk as long as necessary.

-29-
Finding Your Ideal Area

"The method of the enterprising is to plan with audacity,
and execute with vigor; to sketch out a map of possibilities;
and then to treat them as probabilities."

—CHRISTIAN NEVELL BOVEE

The United States of America is comprised of fifty states, 3,098 counties, 19,083 municipalities, 16,083 townships, and thousands of towns smaller than 2,500 residents. Climate zones range from arctic to subtropical. Topography flows from seashore to desert to mountains to great plains to rolling hills and forests. We have land bordering two oceans, a huge gulf, great lakes, medium lakes, small lakes, ponds, rivers, streams, creeks, and springs. It is reasonable to believe that within all this there is for each of us an ideal place. Let's find yours.

The Path to Your Ideal Area

Now that you have pondered all the components of place and completed your criteria worksheet, it is time to identify your ideal area. If you study pertinent research materials and cover each point, no disaster will befall you if you proceed in a casual, meandering fashion. However, I believe the following guidelines will save you time and prove most pleasurable and successful.

If you have already decided on an area, this is the time to use your iron-willed discipline. Calm down—or chill out, depending on your age group's vocabulary—and work your way through these steps. You may end up choosing what you have already identified. That's fine, but you will feel good forevermore knowing you have objectively, logically, intelligently arrived at your decision.

1. Using your criteria worksheet, make your criteria list. You may wish to weight each item or to arrange all items in order of importance to you.

2. Use the national maps in this book to identify the regions that meet your criteria for place-related lifestyle, climate, topography, and water quantity. The state maps show low-density areas. Write down all of the appropriate states in those regions—this is your beginning list. Don't be alarmed if this list is fifteen— or only one. After all, there's only one Everglades, and if you want panthers, alligators, and swamp, well, that's it—you're headed for Florida.

3. Order materials from the private and public sources listed in this book for those states that appear to most satisfy your needs. Study those materials, plus atlases and encyclopedias to eliminate states that do not meet your demographic criteria. Ask reference librarians for help—they are worth their weight in databases.

4. Apply your financial criteria: prices and economic opportunities. Reduce the list to no more than three states.

5. Apply the remaining criteria for lifestyle, air quality, water quality, and health. Narrow your list to a subregion or bioregion. This is your target area.

6. Using Chapters 27 and 28 on places to avoid and toxic pollution, contact the appropriate sources and get potential negative information about the area.

7. Choose towns in areas most free from pollution. Subscribe to their newspapers to check the pulse of the area. Newspapers are excellent sources of cost-of-living figures. In addition to real estate firms, local markets and retail stores often advertise in the local paper.

8. Place an ad in the Personals section of the classifieds requesting contact with others who have moved there from the city. This is a way to get information and maybe make friends—possibly a place to stay when you visit. Expect to hear from every real estate agent in the area. Treat them as a resource—use their area expertise to further inform yourself.

9. Find out about local conditions, taxes, and services. In addition to those listed after each chapter, sources of information for local weather, prices, taxes, pollution, crime, density, politics, and economic conditions are real estate agents, chambers of commerce, and bank officers, plus the agriculture extension agent, sheriff, tax assessor, and tax collector.

10. Experience the area. Walk towns. Drive the countryside. Listen to local radio stations. Talk shows quickly reveal local attitudes and concerns. Talk to all you meet. Interview the owners or managers of your bed and breakfast, motel or campground. Eat in local restaurants. Visit schools. Get lost several times and ask for help each time.

If an initial visit indicates that the area is ideal, the very best way to learn all about local conditions is to rent or caretake for one year a property similar to what you want. Living through all four seasons will allow you to see the area at its best and its worst. To find a vacant property whose owners want caretakers, place an ad in the local newspaper similar to the one successfully used by our friends shown in Chapter 18 or subscribe to *Caretaker Gazette*.

Consider living at an intentional community for a year. This is a way to experience the seasons and conditions and to learn country living skills. A directory is listed at the end of Chapter 26.

A way to experience an area for a shorter term is to utilize a home exchange service. For a fee, participants' home information is published. Exchangers trade homes with others for holidays or extended vacations. Two such services are listed below.

Resources

Caretaker Gazette
2380 NE Ellis Way, Suite C16
Pullman, WA 99163-5303
509-332-0806

HomeExchange.com
P.O. Box 30085
Santa Barbara, CA 93130
E-mail: prince@west.net
Web site: http://www.homeexchange.com/

Intervac U.S./International Home Exchange
30 Corte San Fernando
Tiburton, CA 94920-2014
Phone: 415-435-3497; fax: 415-435-7440; e-mail: intervacUS@aol.om
Web Site: http://www.intervac.com

– 30 –
Real Estate Law and Real Estate Agents

*"For identification, California merchants ask check writers
for their real estate license.
Not everyone in California has a driver's license."*

—Dennis G. Blair

Real Property Versus Personal Property

All property is either real property or personal property. Buying real estate requires knowing the difference. For example, such items as rose bushes, fences, and satellite dish antennas may appear to be real property but may in fact be personal property.

Real property is primarily land and that which is attached to it. In the case of the above-mentioned items, they may be real property or personal property depending on their method of attachment to the land and depending on the intention of the owner. These factors are considered by courts in case of dispute.

Typically, the only time these questions become an issue is when a property is sold and the buyer takes possession, only to discover a hole where the prize-winning rose bush and its buried container were removed, the portable split-rail fence has been loaded and hauled off, the satellite receiver has been unbolted and removed from the site.

There is only one certain item that will prevent misunderstanding about what will and will not remain with the real property—a written contract, spelling out what is included in the sale price. My advice is this: have your agent write and attach to the sales contract a personal property addendum listing all items of personal property that you would like to have stay with the property and especially list all items that are in the gray area between personal and real property. These include but are by no means limited to television antennas, FM antennas, window coverings, bedspreads that match window coverings, fireplace inserts, freestanding dishwashers, built-in refrigerators, chandeliers, and other special light fixtures, stained-glass windows, ceiling fans, window air conditioners, and mailboxes on posts in old milk cans. If in doubt, list it.

Laws of Agency

Agents

The basic law of agency is that an agent owes the principal (in real estate that has usually been the seller) a fiduciary responsiveness founded on trust and confidence. The agent must at all times act in the best interests of the principal. The agent has an obligation to disclose all known facts which the principal may use to make a decision. The agency relationship between seller and agent is established by the listing contract.

Buyer's agents are becoming more common. A buyer can retain a real estate broker to find a suitable property. The buyer agrees to pay a fee to the broker upon performance. The terms of the agreement should be in writing to eliminate misunderstanding and to be enforceable. A buyer's broker may not receive compensation from the seller without the buyer's permission and only upon full disclosure to the buyer.

Agency laws are finally changing to resolve the long-standing question of how an agent could be a subagent of the seller through the multiple listing agreement and still represent the buyer effectively. On January, 1, 1995, Illinois real estate law created the presumption that licensees are the agent of the consumer with whom they are working. The Chicago Association of Realtors president, Sid G. Woods, said that, "This means that when a buyer goes to an agent to find a property, that agent will be truly representing the buyer, and not acting as a subagent for the seller." I would expect other states to soon follow the example of Illinois.

Conflict of Interest

Until all states change their laws, in most cases a real estate agent, through the listing agreement, is legally working for the seller. Some believe this means that the buyer is on his own and is likely to be mistreated by the agent. Let's examine this.

First, in most states there are laws that require full disclosure to buyers of all known conditions that affect the value of the property. That's right, no secrets. If the basement becomes a swimming pool every spring, the seller must disclose that fact to the agent and the agent must disclose it to the buyer. If the roof leaks, if the well runs dry every September, if the neighbor is a retired general who drives a Sherman tank up and down the road early every morning, if the dishwasher dances into the middle of the kitchen every Thanksgiving evening, these conditions must be reported to the buyer. If they are not, both the seller and the agency may be liable for damages. Judges take a dim view of willful nondisclosure and even have the power to set a sale aside, in addition to assessing damages and criminal penalties. And the agent could lose his or her real estate license.

While the agent gets paid by the seller (with money from the buyer), guess who really makes the deal work or not? The buyer. And in most cases the agent gets not one dollar until the transaction is successfully completed. So an agent is highly motivated to help everybody get what they want, so that the sale closes and the commission gets paid. Also, after the transaction is closed, the buyer/owner is now a prospective future seller for the agent. Keenly aware of this from the beginning, it is understandable that the agent wishes to impress the buyer.

A full-time agent who has operated in an area for at least a year or two and who enjoys a good reputation in the community is succeeding in a demanding business by helping people get what they want. As to the information source of reputations, sellers often leave the area; buyers are the "reputation community."

Agent Motivation

Real estate licensees live with the pressure of uncertain income, as do all who are paid only by commission. Let's be candid—like anyone who works for a living, an agent wants to be paid. So the agent wants to make the deal work. The agent wants the buyer to make an offer that the seller will accept. If the buyer makes a low offer, then the agent wants the seller to either accept it or to make a counteroffer that the buyer will accept. A good agent will continue to write counteroffers rather than accept rejections as long as the seller wants to sell and the buyer wants to buy. The agent will continue to do everything legally possible to help the seller and buyer find agreement and complete the sale. That's how agents get paid.

Real Estate Agents

"Real estate agent" is a generic term used to describe anyone who, for a commission, lists, sells, exchanges, rents, or leases real property. This generally means brokers and salespersons licensed by the state in which they do business. Brokers can conduct business on their own; salespersons must work under the supervision of a broker, who is responsible for their actions. A salesperson may be an employee or an independent contractor in the view of the IRS.

Each state sets its own licensing requirements for education and continuing education for salespersons, and education, experience, and continuing education for brokers. Required salesperson education ranges from none in Maine, Montana, New Hampshire, Rhode Island, and Vermont, to 180 classroom hours in Texas. Broker experience (as a salesperson) requirements range from none in Wisconsin to five years in Delaware.

Persons exempt from real estate agent licensing laws include property owners dealing with their own property, lawyers conducting a transaction as an incidental part of their duties as an attorney, trustees and receivers in bankruptcy, legal guardians, administrators, and executors handling an estate, government agency employees dealing in agency business, and persons operating under powers of attorney.

Realtors ®

According to the National Association of Realtors®, there are about one million real estate agents in the U.S. Not all real estate agents are Realtors. Realtors are licensed agents who belong to the National Association of Realtors (NAR) and subscribe to a strict code of ethics. This is not to say that Realtors are inherently more ethical than non-Realtors, but the NAR provides an extra layer of protection for the public, namely the local real estate board's ethics and arbitration committee and the hearings it conducts. Hearings are available at low or no cost to any seller or buyer who believes a Realtor has done them wrong. During my years as ethics and arbitration committee chairman and as board president I monitored many such hearings. My experience is that Realtors tend to hold their peers to a higher standard than does the public. Realtors are highly motivated to upgrade their image. Complainants therefore receive fast and fair justice—always faster and oftentimes fairer than with the courts, which is where the public must go for justice with a non-Realtor.

Ethics hearings address questions of conduct; arbitration hearings adjudicate money matters. Ethics hearings are most commonly brought by one Realtor against another. Arbitrations typically settle client complaints against a Realtor regarding financial matters, although Realtor versus Realtor is not uncommon. A court of law will uphold the decision of a properly conducted arbitration hearing. If you ever feel you have been wronged by a Realtor, do not hesitate to register a complaint with the local real estate board. A complaint must be in writing.

Country real estate agents are less likely to be Realtors than city agents because of distance considerations. I do not downgrade country agents for not being Realtors if there is no real estate board within a reasonable driving distance. I bought my ideal country home using a non-Realtor.

As in any profession, education, experience, ability, and integrity are the qualities of excellence. For the first months I was in real estate, I expected someone to notice my naïveté and ask me how long I had been an agent. No one ever did. They should have. Country real estate agents typically do not handle as many transactions per year as their city cousins, so experience does not equate on a year-for-year basis.

Part-time Agents

From extensive personal experience I am biased against part-time agents. Of the many part-time agents I have known, only one was top-notch. When part-time agents are at their regular jobs they are not available to take care of their clients' business. Some part-time agents partner with another agent who covers for them when they are not available. As with doctors and dentists who have others cover for them while they are on vacation, this does not provide optimal personal service for the client, and it is very hard for the backup person to know all details of each case or transaction. Part-time agents rarely handle a high volume of sales, which is the only way to gain and maintain a high level of competence in this profession. My recommendation is to work with an experienced full-time agent.

Of course even some full-time agents are not worth their salt. Others are invaluable. What you want is a professional person who is very knowledgeable about properties, financing, laws, contracts, conditions, values, and procedures in your target area.

Why I Recommend Using an Agent

Agents are valuable not only for their specialized knowledge and experience but because they are third parties, emotionally removed from the egos, desires, and fears of the principals. Agents who specialize in a given field will always be more knowledgeable and effective than sellers or buyers who try to represent themselves. Buyers and sellers are emotionally involved and may damage or destroy a transaction due to temperament. Athletes, movie stars, writers, attorneys, and many others use agents to represent them on important matters. A buyer who represents himself may not have a fool for a client but he will likely have unprofessional representation.

Real estate agents are experts in real estate transactions in their area. They know local values, financing, escrow procedures, laws, customs, and who best provides all the needed inspections and services. Agents are strongly motivated to have a successful transaction and are experts in making that happen.

You may feel I recommend using an agent because I am an ex-Realtor. Although I had nearly eight years' full-time experience as a real estate agent, including six years as broker of my own office at the time, I used an agent to handle the purchase of the property that is now my permanent home—the most important real estate transaction of my life. I did so for all of the above reasons. And, in case you are wondering, I neither asked for nor received any special consideration or commission referral fee. I did, however, write the purchase contract.

How to Choose an Agent

Judging integrity is like guessing the weight of an elephant—it's easy to be fooled by presence. Therefore ask many people in your target area who is good and who is not. Certain names will recur in both categories.

Ask for recommendations from escrow officers and bank loan officers. You are likely to be in an area where you know no one. Certain criteria are useful. Is the agent a Realtor? Does she subscribe to a multiple listing service? Not all rural areas have one, but if there is one and an agent does not use the service, that agent cannot show you all of the listings available in the area. How long has he been in real estate? Is she full-time? Ask for a list of estimated purchase costs—if the agent hems and haws, excuse yourself and go on to the next office. Ask about local financing, title, and escrow customs. Ask how the agent feels about being the seller's agent and serving you at the same time. Ask for a list of the buyers' names and phone numbers for the last five closed transactions. Call some of them and ask for their feelings about how the agent handled their transaction. Glowing recommendations from past clients are indicative of competence but are not a guarantee; those transactions may have been much simpler.

Observe how agents handle themselves. Careful interviewing is a sign of a professional agent, as the process saves everybody's time. Good agents will take the time to clearly understand what you want and what you wish to pay. If you will need a loan to finance your purchase, they will determine your qualifications, either themselves or through a loan agent who will take your information. Agents will make a list of appropriate properties to show you and will call for appointments with the owners—at the same time making sure that the property is still available and price, terms, and conditions have not changed.

Don't go out looking at properties with an agent you are not comfortable with—for any reason. Looking at country property is time- and fuel-consuming. Although you are not legally obligated to stay with a particular agent, once that agent has spent considerable time, energy, and fuel showing you properties, you are both going to feel pretty bad if the relationship abruptly ends. Make sure you are satisfied with an agent's qualifications before looking at listings. If the vibes are bad, state honestly that you'd like to interview other agents.

Take your time and use your very best judgment choosing an agent. Do not feel obligated to agents just because they have spent time talking to you. Like any professional, an agent needs to earn your respect and support. Once you decide on an agent, treat him or her with the same respect that you desire and that you would give to any other professional.

Open Listings—A Country Condition

In my experience, country agents operate similarly to city agents but differently in one practice that is notable. For sound reasons many city brokers and multiple listing services will not accept open listings. Country agents often do.

An open listing is a nonexclusive listing given by a seller to one or several real estate brokers. A commission is paid only to the broker procuring a buyer, and the seller reserves the right to sell the property with no obligation to any broker. Unscrupulous sellers sometimes try to cheat brokers out of a commission by dealing directly with potential buyers brought to the property by the broker. This act is called "going around the broker." Brokers cannot justify spending time and advertising dollars on a listing that may be sold any day by another broker or the seller, with no compensation to the first broker. In spite of these dangers, in many rural areas agents regularly take open listings, especially in those areas without a multiple listing service.

Open listings and the lack of a multiple listing service (MLS) create a negative condition for buyers. Under such conditions, buyers must visit several brokers to be sure they are aware of all available properties, which can be very time-consuming. There is no way around it; if you find that in your target area agents do not have or belong to an MLS then you will have to use multiple agents to be sure of seeing all available properties.

Exclusive Listings

Exclusive listings come in two flavors: *exclusive agency* and *exclusive right to sell*. An exclusive agency listing means that the seller agrees to pay a commission to the listing broker even if another broker provides the buyer. In that case, the listing and selling brokers usually split the commission according to their prior agreement. Exclusive agency listings allow sellers to sell their property and not owe a commission. An exclusive right to sell listing is where the seller agrees to pay the listing broker a commission no matter who sells the property, including the seller. The advantage to the broker is obvious. The advantage to the seller is that the broker will spend money on advertising, will submit the listing to the MLS, and will generally expend all possible effort to sell the property because of the certainty of getting paid if successful.

FSBO

If you happen to find a property for sale by owner (FSBO, pronounced fizzbow) and you wish to buy it, I recommend that you use an agent to draw the contract according to the terms you dictate, to advise you on financing, and to recommend termite, structural, and other inspectors if you want them, appraisers, surveyors, lenders, escrow agents, and title companies. Negotiate a fee with the agent, to be paid from escrow upon successful closing of the transaction. Have the agent type up a simple agreement stating what services will be provided and the fee you will pay. Once you both sign, it is an enforceable contract. Get a copy.

If You Choose to Act as Your Own Agent

Educate yourself. Learn the language of real estate; start with the Glossary in this book. Study real property descriptions (U.S. Survey method, metes and bounds, and lot and block, all of which may be used for country property), rights-of-way and easements, title insurance and title opinions, escrow procedures and customs, types of financing and instruments used with each, mechanic's liens, appraisers and methods of appraisal, surveys, and inspections—health inspections of wells and septic systems, soil tests, structural inspections, termite inspections, energy-efficiency inspections, and so on.

Know that all matters pertaining to real estate contracts, agreements, and understandings are rarely enforceable unless they are in writing, so study contract law and learn to write contracts. Basic contract forms are available but rarely include room for the appropriate conditions and addendums often needed in country property transactions.

Expect your real estate education to take time. If you are willing to spend the time educating yourself, if you learn the customs and procedures appropriate to your target area, and if you intend to pay cash for your property, then you will only be restricted by your available time, ego, patience, and competence.

Be sure to have the property appraised by a licensed appraiser. This will probably cost between $250 and $500 but is the most reliable estimate of value you can get without using an agent familiar with area values.

Expect real estate agents to be uncooperative—they are not keen on helping novices who are cutting into their business. You will probably have to find properties that have not been listed, which means that most properties will not be available to you. You will likely be limited to FSBOs and properties you find yourself the same way real estate agents do, by making a lot of phone calls.

Expect something to go wrong. If you would like to know most of what can go wrong, spend some time talking to an experienced escrow officer. She (most often female) can turn your hair gray with real estate horror stories.

On Using a Lawyer to Help with a Real Estate Transaction

I am biased against lawyers being involved in most residential and rural land real estate transactions because of my experiences where they caused deals to be lost through their insistence on some contract condition that caused one of the principals to back out of the deal, or because they caused needless delays.

Some lawyers specialize in real estate and are competent to help buyers or sellers in their area. But unless they are very active in real estate, lawyers are rarely knowledgeable about property values, and price is usually the most important factor in any real estate transaction. I have expressed my feelings above on the subject of part-time real estate agents; lawyers who occasionally handle real estate transactions belong in the same category.

Lawyers are good for reviewing contracts that an unrepresented buyer or seller has written. In their effort to protect their client they tend to unnecessarily complicate contracts. In real estate transactions, time is of the essence. Lawyers sometimes cause transactions to be delayed and made more difficult by taking too long to do their work. And they add to the cost of the transaction.

Lawyers are not supposed to act as real estate agents except as an incidental part of their work for a client, for instance as part of their duties as trustees or executors/executrixes. In my opinion, lawyers who want to be real estate agents should first obtain a real estate license. Then they should handle a large number of real estate transactions each year so they stay informed as to local values and conditions.

> *"George Washington was a surveyor. He took the exact measure*
> *of the British and surveyed himself out about the most*
> *valuable piece of land in America at that time, Mount Vernon.*
> *George could not only tell the truth but land values."*
>
> —WILL ROGERS

～ 31 ～

Looking at Country Property

"We didn't look enough."

—THOUSANDS OF BUYERS

It is finally time to find your ideal country place. Do try to exercise patience—you've come too far to make a mistake now by hurrying. Take your time—look at a lot of properties before you make a decision. Yes, it is possible that the first one you look at will be the right one, but keep looking anyway, or you will always wonder. In this case, resist falling in love before the marriage.

We have a neighbor who, after seeing our place, expressed the common buyer's lament: "We didn't look enough." He and his wife have a sound house on forty acres, garden space, plenty of forest for firewood, and at the back of their property the downstream part of our creek. They are very nice people and we hope they stay, but his statement needs little interpretation.

When to Do It

"The great French Marshall Lyautey once asked his gardener
to plant a tree. The gardener objected that the tree was slow growing
and would not reach maturity for 100 years. The Marshall replied,
'In that case, there is no time to lose; plant it this afternoon!'"

—JOHN F. KENNEDY

We Americans have a cultural quirk to take actions according to the calendar. In the doldrums period following Christmas and New Year's Day we fret about who, what, and where we are and we resolve to initiate change. Our social conditioning programs us to refine ourselves, to be more bold, to do things that we have been putting off—and to do them at the beginning of a week, a month, or a year. Imagine the intensity of energy that will occur on the first day of 2000. Stand back!

Throughout my real estate career in the San Francisco Bay Area I found that the first four months of each year registered the heaviest sales activity. In northern-tier states, real estate sales activity tends to follow the habits of plants: with spring warmth comes activity—with the snow comes hibernation. Northern sellers know that buyers are few when the days grow short and the white stuff falls. The reverse is true in states such as Arizona and Florida. Boiling hot summers and wilting humidity motivate siestas rather than serious activity.

Financially, the best time to buy is when the weather is worst. Prices and interest rates tend to rise with strong sales activity. There is often a correlation between interest rates and election years. As national elections approach, politicians court voters with low interest rates and an infusion of federal (read your/my) money.

Time of Year
The ideal number of times to inspect property is four, in each of the seasons. That will be impractical unless you are living in the area and unless the owner of your dream property has Job-like patience. Realistically, determine what conditions are like during the worst times of the year: when it rains the most—when mud and flood enter each conversation, when it is the hottest and the coldest, when snow and ice cancel all travel. If you like a property during those conditions you will love it during better times.

My preference is to look at property after the school year begins. I struck the deal on my ideal country home in late September. Droughts most often occur in late summer and early autumn, so water supplies are most strained. Grass is brown. Sellers are more realistic about prices and terms as they look forward to winter in a place they no longer wish to be. Tourists have gone home and the community is most like what it is during the majority of the year. Local people have more time to talk.

Depending on the area, the inventory of available properties may be smallest in the fall and winter. One strategy is to find a place you like in the fall, then wait until spring when listings are most numerous, look at all the new listings and, unless you see one you like better, buy the one you found last fall. A plus is that you will have seen the property during two different seasons. The downside to this plan is having to resist the hungry real estate agent's sound logic that buying during the winter will likely get you the best price. Expect many phone calls. Worst, there is the chance that someone else may submit an offer while you are waiting.

Time of the Week

Weekday and weekend sounds and activities are often drastically different. The property that looks ideal on a quiet Saturday or Sunday afternoon will be awful on Monday through Friday when garbage trucks thunder by, stirring up clouds of dust on their way to the dump at the end of the road. That was exactly the case with friends of ours until they were able to sell. Conversely, the road that is quiet during the week may explode with weekend traffic heading for the local swimming hole, fishing stream, picnic spot. So once you find a property you like, make your second inspection when conditions are most likely to be different from when you first saw it.

Time of the Day

The action of the sun may make a cheery kitchen in the morning and create hot boxes of rooms exposed to the burning rays of afternoon. Again make your final inspection at a different time of day than your first visit.

Looking at Properties

Looking at country property requires attention to more details than when looking at city property. Without city streets, codes, ordinances, utilities, and services to insulate you from natural and human conditions you will want to consider essentially everything. Some of the material in this chapter has been covered earlier but is so important that it will be restated.

Make appointments with real estate agents a few days before you will see them. Help agents help you best by being open about your needs and your financial positions. Explain completely the type of property you are looking for. Show them your criteria list. Tell them your priorities. "We want a nice place in the woods that's not too expensive" just doesn't get it. To hold back pertinent information is to waste your time and the agent's time. Do not wait until after you've been shown several places to tell your agent that he or she is on the wrong track.

After an agent has shown you everything they have available, move on to the next agent. If there is not a local multiple listing service you will have to see several agents in each town to make sure you have seen everything. Repeat the process. Tell each agent the features of properties you have seen and what you did and did not like. Keep a scoresheet on each property.

If your agent tells you that there is nothing available that meets your requirements, move on to the next agent. If you get the same response from several agents, you may wish to rethink your demands.

How Many Places to Look At

In *Harrowsmith Country Life* (January/February 1992) Richard Todd explained "The Eleven Farm Theory." He wrote, "Look at ten farms. Buy none, but rank them in order of appeal. Then buy the next farm that you like better than the one you liked best."

Todd tried it. He made it nearly through the first ten before he fell in love with a place that—well, for the rest of the sad tale I refer you to that issue. Suffice it to say the theory might work for you. Don't feel guilty if you, too, fall in love before ten. It's as good a time to fall in love as any other.

If you find yourself confronted with too many places to look at, you may have given your agent only a general description of your target. Narrow your instructions down: "We want no fewer than X acres and no more than X. The house must face south or southeast. There must be at least X space open around the house. There must be at least X acres of hardwood forest for firewood. There must be live water within X feet of the house or house site." Like that. When you give specific information on items that are most important to you, the list of possible places gets shortened.

I found my ideal place on the third day of my search. It was tempting to make an immediate offer but I continued to look for many more days at dozens of additional properties, found nothing to match it, came back, looked at it again, and made an offer. If I had not looked at those extra dozens of places I might wonder if I missed something better. As it is, I know that I bought the place that was best for me out of everything available.

Make a Careful and Thorough Inspection

When inspecting homes, buyers are often shy about opening closets, cupboards, and drawers. Don't be. This is your potential home. Look at and into anything that will help you know that place. If you are not sure what you are seeing, ask. Do not be embarrassed about not understanding a pressure pump system, gravity-flow wood furnace, chicken-self-feeder, compost bin, or any of the countless other items often found with country homes.

Building Sites

Building site evaluation is similar whether the property has been improved with a house or the land is bare. Any building site must have stable soil and good drainage, especially in high-rainfall areas. A site slightly sloping to the south is ideal.

Waterways, side hollows, and other obvious drainage areas should be inspected for signs of flooding. Past flooding will have caused erosion and left leaves, weeds, pieces of bark, and other detritus in the low branches of trees and shrubs in the stream or drainage area. This evidence often will be found many feet above the ground.

If the land is flat, look for low spots that do not drain well. Flat land in high-rainfall areas often has drainage problems, especially where soil is heavy. Such conditions may make it difficult to have a good garden or orchard or install a septic tank and leach field system for waste disposal. If in doubt, a percolation test should be made a contract condition and performed after contract acceptance.

Ridgetop and Valley Pros and Cons

Ridgetops usually have superior views, freedom from flooding, good access, and good air flow. Disadvantages include well depth, dryness, susceptibility to fires (fires burn upward), rocky or thin soil, and exposure to high winds.

Valley advantages include springs and streams, plentiful groundwater, good soil, abundant trees, and other vegetation. Disadvantages include steep access roads, flooding, and a later sunrise and earlier sunset. Cold air drainage from above is a negative in wintertime and during late spring frosts at peach blossom time, but it is welcome during the summer.

Access

Ask your agent to verify the fact of legal ingress and egress rights. If the property does not front on a public road there should be a deeded easement for access purposes. If in doubt make that a condition in the contract.

Dependable year-round access requires a good road. South-facing slopes are drier and melt snow most quickly. During cold weather, north-facing slopes hold snow and ice, alternately thawing and freezing, making roads dangerous or even impassable. Unless built up with gravel, lowland and flatland roads are prone to rut, hold water, and grow mud after rain, which becomes ice in the winter.

Solar Exposure

The house site, garden site, pastures, and cropland will ideally have effective solar exposure. South slopes receive maximum solar exposure both summer and winter. Southwesterly exposure is warmer than southeasterly because afternoon sun is hotter than morning sun. For gardens I prefer southeasterly slopes because they receive first light, warm earlier in the spring and are protected from prevailing northwesterly winds.

During the growing season, the warmest land is that which is most perpendicular to the sun's rays. South-facing slopes are typically drier, sunnier, warmer—roses, grasses, tomatoes, oaks, and pines do well there with adequate rainfall. North-facing slopes are cooler and more moist—good for ferns, azaleas, rhododendron, blueberries, and fruit trees—to lessen the chance of premature bloom and late-freeze damage. North-facing slopes are preferred house sites in hot climates.

Utilities

The main consideration here is to ensure that electric and telephone service are installed or, if not, to determine what it will cost to bring them in versus the cost of an independent solar and generator-backup system. If you will be working with a computer you will want to discover conditions such as telephone line static, electrical voltage fluctuations, and historical frequency and duration of outages. If the agent or owners do not seem to be forthcoming about utility conditions, then talk to neighbors and others nearby.

Check with the phone company on the availability and cost of a private line.

Do not assume that neighbors will allow an easement across their property. If power lines must be brought in, make getting a legal easement a contract condition.

Views

While evaluating views, keep in mind that trees grow. If they are yours, you can trim them or cut them down and replace them with shorter varieties. If they are a neighbor's you will likely have to live with them. Many trees reach 100 or more feet at maturity. Conversely, if your enjoyment of the property is a forested area, consider that the trees may one day be cut down.

Wind

Learn wind directions and speeds. A home site exposed to persistent hot summer winds and cold winter winds can be a disaster. The exposed side and the lee side of a hill can be as two different worlds. Trees work well as a windbreak if they are large and thick enough.

If you are considering using wind to generate electricity, know that most wind plants require an average monthly wind speed of eight to fourteen miles per hour. Sites should be clear of upwind obstructions.

Use the Property Scoresheet

Some recommend using a property checklist. Yep, there's a house. Check house. Yep, there's a tree. Check tree. Garden? Check. Road? Check.

I prefer to use a property scoresheet. Let us not just make sure everything is there; let us decide what it is worth to us. So make copies of the property score- sheet and use one to rate each place you look at. It is the only way to effectively compare properties. After you have looked at ten to fifteen places, there is no other way you will remember the details of even several of them.

If you don't have a camera, borrow one. Take a picture or two of each place. Be sure to make a note on the scoresheet of some unique features shown in each picture so pictures can easily be matched with the correct property.

Learn how to make a final evaluation before making an offer to purchase.

To make looking at an area even more enjoyable, send for free information on Back Country Byways from our Bureau of Land Management. Ask for information relevant to your preferred state.

Headquarters office
C Street NW
MIB 5600
Washington, DC 20240
202-208-5717

PROPERTY SCORESHEET

Addresss_____

Contact person and phone_____

Acreage_____ Price_____ Terms_____

Occupancy conditions_____

Score 0 to 10 points for each item. Zero is nonexistent, 1 is poor, 10 is excellent. With multiple items, (spring, stream, well) circle what is found and assign score.

Water source: spring, stream, well_____ Supply system_____

Water quantity_____ Water quality_____

Solar exposure_____ Windbreak_____

Soil quality: garden_____ fields_____ woodlot_____

Woodlot_____ Orchard_____ Yard_____ Pasture_____

Fencing: garden_____ pasture_____ fields_____

Topography_____ Scenery_____

Drainage: road, house, garden, yard, woodlot, fields_____

Access road: surface material, width, well graded_____

Electricity_____ Telephone_____

Waste system: septic, outhouse, composting toilet_____

House size_____ Rooms_____ Layout_____ Quality_____ Roof_____

Foundation_____ Siding_____ Doors/windows _____

Heating_____ Plumbing_____ Electrical_____

Special features_____

Other buildings: garage, barn, shop, chicken coop_____

Notes_____

_____

_____

_____

_____

_____

~ 32 ~

Making a Final Evaluation Before Purchase

*"If decisions were a choice between alternatives,
decisions would come easy. Decision is the selection and
formulation of alternatives."*

—KENNETH BURKE, *Towards a Better Life* (1932)

Don't Fall in Love Until After the Marriage

Yes, I know. You have painstakingly developed your criteria, have researched the entire Northern Hemisphere, have looked at every place available in your chosen area and have found your absolutely perfect piece of property without which you will not be able to live. Congratulations. But calm down. Chill out. This is the time to keep your cool, maintain composure, evidence dignity and mature calculating discernment. You've come too far to blow it now.

Try harder.

Once you have seen the place that appears to be "it" you must return at another time to inspect it thoroughly. To not do so is to risk overlooking a condition you cannot live with. An equal risk is paying too much, which will brand you as a dumb city person and is the sort of thing for which newcomers are derided and talked about for decades.

You will already have filled out the property scoresheet when you first looked at the property. Review each item with a low score and decide if you can live with the condition, or determine what the cost will be to correct it. Such costs should be deducted from the price you would be willing to pay for the property if it were in top condition. You will need those dollars to correct the deficiencies.

Water

If you did not determine at the initial visit that water is both plentiful and of good quality, now is the time to do so. Water is a clearly understood necessity, so if there is a correctable problem you may be able to persuade the seller to fix it.

If water is supplied by a well, a good test for quantity is to fully open an outside faucet and let it run while continuing the property evaluation. It should be running just as strongly an hour after turning it on. If there is a problem with a well running dry, the seller will likely bring it up at this point and ask that the water be turned off to avoid a household shortage.

Look at the pressure system equipment and ask how old it is and what problems have been experienced. In cold weather areas the pressure tank and piping must be protected from freezing. Run each faucet to determine if flow is sufficient and steady. With most home water systems the strength of water flow and temperature fluctuate slightly as the pump motor cycles on and off. The better systems have a large pressure tank and three-quarter-inch or larger piping. With such a system, if the pressure switches are correctly adjusted, pressure fluctuation will be minimal. This is essential—especially adequately sized piping—to avoid the dangerous spectacle of a naked human being (you) doing the hula dance to avoid butt-burn in the shower.

With a small pressure tank, pressure fluctuation may not occur with a faucet wide open, as the pump may run continually. Turn the shower on and observe it. Flush the toilet and see if the pressure drops. While running faucets, observe how well drains work.

Water system problems in operating households are unlikely to be of great enough magnitude for you to reject the property, but you should be aware of them, as you may use them to affect the price and terms of purchase.

Quality may first be checked by tasting the water. Expect well water to taste different from the chlorinated city water to which you are accustomed, but it should not have an off taste. Toilets, shower heads, and faucet nozzles may show color or rust buildup, which indicates a high mineral content and can cause plumbing problems.

Houses

Structural and energy-efficiency inspections are typically made after contract acceptance. If you feel inspections are appropriate, make them a contract condition, with your disapproval adequate reason for the contract to be canceled. At this point you should satisfy yourself, by asking and by looking, as to the general condition of the house. Items to check include quality and condition of foundation or basement, siding, roofing, insulation, doors and windows, heating system, electrical and plumbing systems, appliances, and general overall condition. If you intend to work with a fax modem, listen to the telephone line noise. If snap, crackle, and pops are substantial, you should talk to the phone company to see if they are sensitive to your needs. Most house or utility deficiencies may be acceptable if they are reflected in the asking price.

New homes may have more problems than older homes that have been very well maintained. In *Crumbling Dreams*, Ruth S. Martin details personal and national problems with incompetent and sleazy builders.

Soil

If farming or market gardening is your intention, make your acceptance of soil tests a condition of the purchase contract. You can observe the general condition of the soil by what is growing well in the garden and in yards, fields, and woods. You may wish to review the material on soil quality in Chapter 10.

Property Lines

The only sure way to know what you are buying is to walk the property lines. Country property corners are usually identified by surveyors with monuments— pipes driven into the ground, or large stones or stone piles, often painted red. Property lines running through wooded land may be indicated by red surveyor's tape tied to branches—they will be close but are often somewhat off the line. Occasionally a tree will be blazed by cutting off the bark and marking the smooth wood with red paint. Here in the Ozarks, purple paint on trees is used by many property owners to mark their boundaries, to deflect deer and turkey hunters.

Fences and roads should not be relied upon as property line proof. For many reasons they may have been built within or beyond true property lines. One of the fences on our property is about thirty feet north of the line marked by surveyors.

Country surveyors are like people in other professions—they are limited by their training, experience, integrity. In some states they are not required to be certified or licensed. Additionally, large parcels of relatively inexpensive acreage have created an attitude of "it's not important to get the lines marked perfectly— a few feet one way or the other is of no consequence." And rough, hilly land is difficult to walk easily, let alone survey or carefully mark. A place originally surveyed "on the ground" may be deeded as "forty acres more or less." Surveyed using modern instruments, the same property may be many acres less. If in doubt, you may wish to make your offer based on dollars per acre, with acreage determined by a new survey, so you only pay for what you receive.

We have friends who built a house near what they believed was the edge of their land. Years later they discovered their house was on their neighbor's land. Such a situation is at least embarrassing, and could be very expensive to correct. Our friends were fortunate in having understanding neighbors, who sold them a few acres.

This is to alert you to the possibility of mismarked property lines. If the value of your target property is substantially affected by a feature—a building, spring, waterfall, cave, or a certain tree close to the property line—you may wish to hire a licensed surveyor to make a modern survey.

Take Your Time

Take plenty of time inspecting the property. Do not allow yourself to be hurried by the agent or the seller. Satisfy yourself that this is indeed your ideal country home. Make notes of all deficiencies that money can correct. Tell your agent to ask the seller to correct them, in writing, in your offer. Expect the seller to counteroffer. You may do the same. Once you have an accepted contract and are certain of your financing you can start falling in love.

You've come a long way. I sincerely hope you have enjoyed the journey. Happy country living!

"Believe nothing, no matter where you read it, or who said it—even if I have said it—unless it agrees with your own reason and your own common sense."

—THE BUDDHA

Appendix A: Resources

Note: With some exceptions, the following sources and resources are in addition to the items previously offered at the ends of the various chapters. To quickly locate a specific organization, agency, or publication within the chapters, please see Index for the page number.

United States Information Center: 800-688-9889

Federal Web Locator to find Web addresses for all federal agencies: http://www.law.vill.edu/fed-agency/fedwebloc.html

United States Government Printing Office
Superintendent of Documents
Washington, DC 20402
Phone: 202-512-1800; fax: 202-512-2250
For twenty-four-hour fax-on-demand service, dial U.S. Fax Watch at 202-512-1716.

State Government Information Centers

    Alabama...334-242-8000
    Arizona...602-542-4900
    Arkansas...501-682-3000; in AR only: 800-482-5850
    California...916-322-9900 north; 213-620-3030 south
    Colorado...303-866-5000
    Connecticut...860-566-2211; in CT only: 800-842-2220
    Delaware...302-739-4000
    Florida...904-488-1234
    Georgia...404-656-2000
    Idaho...208-334-2411
    Illinois...217-782-2000
    Indiana...317-232-3140; in IN only: 800-328-1563
    Iowa...515-281-5011
    Kansas...913-296-0111
    Kentucky...502-564-3130
    Louisiana...504-342-6600
    Maine...207-582-9500

Maryland...410-841-3000

Massachusetts...617-727-2121; in MA only: 800-392-6090

Michigan...517-373-1837

Minnesota...612-296-6013

Mississippi...601-359-1000

Missouri...314-751-2000

Montana...406-444-2511

Nebraska...402-471-2311

Nevada...702-687-5000; in NV only: 800-992-0900

New Hampshire...603-271-1110; in NH only: 800-852-3456

New Jersey...609-292-2121

New Mexico...505-827-4011

New York...518-474-2121

North Carolina...919-733-1110

North Dakota...701-328-2000

Ohio...614-466-2000

Oklahoma...405-521-2011; in OK only: 800-522-8555

Oregon...503-378-3131

Pennsylvania...717-787-2121

Rhode Island...401-277-2000; in RI only: 800-752-8088

South Carolina...803-734-1000; in SC only: 800-922-1367

South Dakota...605-733-3011

Tennessee...615-741-3011

Texas...512-463-4630

Utah...801-538-3000

Vermont...802-828-1110

Virginia...804-786-0000; in VA only: 800-422-2319

Washington...360-753-5000; in WA only: 800-321-2808

West Virginia...304-558-3456

Wisconsin...608-266-2211

Wyoming...307-777-7220

Newsletters

Rocky Mountain Institute Newsletter, published three times per year, is free, but a donation of $10 is requested. RMI, 1739 Snowmass Creek Road, Snowmass, CO 81654-9199. Phone: 970-927-3851; fax; 970-927-4178; e-mail: rmlomas@rmi.org

RMI is a nonprofit research and educational foundation, the child of Amory Lovins, a brilliant and caring physicist, and his lawyer-wife, Hunter. Lovins developed the theory of "negawatts," a concept by which utility companies make greater profits through energy conservation than through construction of new generating facilities. RMI's goal is to foster efficient and sustainable use of resources as a path to global security.

The Rural Network Advocate is a monthly newsletter of eight pages featuring letters from people (mostly singles, many looking for companions) who love the country life. $12/year subscription fee or $40/year for membership in Rural Network. 6236 Borden Road, Boscobel, WI 53805.

Rural Property Bulletin, P.O. Box 608, Valentine, NE 69201 Phone: 402-376-2617; e-mail: rural@valentine-ne.com Web site: http://www.cnweb.com/rural

Published monthly for over eighteen years by Bruce Weaver and Sandy Geib, good people who live in real country. Chris and I spent a night at their place and watched wood ducks come in to their pond. RPB contains ads for homes and businesses in small towns and rural areas all over the U.S. plus Canada. An independent publication not affiliated with any real estate agency. Subscriptions are $16 per year. New subscribers get a free ad.

Small-Scale Agriculture Today, available free but only if you send two typed, self-addressed gummed labels, including full nine-digit zip code (this is an understaffed office). Office for Small-Scale Agriculture, Ag Box 2244, Washington, DC 20250-2244; phone: 202-720-5245.

Magazines and Periodicals

American Demographics, 127 West State Street, Ithaca, NY 14850; phone: 800-529-7502. Monthly. $69/year. Primarily directed toward the business community, *AD* provides a lot of pertinent and timely information on what's happening with people and their money in the U.S. Much of the demographic information in this book was discovered there.

BackHome, P.O. Box 70, Hendersonville, NC 28793; phone: 800-992-2546. Quarterly. $17.97/one year; $31.97/two years. A magazine of basic independent family living. Owned and published by the former staff of *The Mother Earth News*, *Back Home* concentrates on independent energy, gardening, recycling, homeschooling, home business, home construction, and other rural life interests. Here is a list of article titles from past issues: Weed-Free Gardening, Shop for a Used Truck, Nontoxic House Construction, Living on Solar Power, Building Log Homes, Seed Starting Simplified, Make Water Pump Itself, Baking with Kids, Forming a Food-Buying Group, Homeschooling Methods, Aquafarming as a Business, Hand-Built Masonry Heaters, New Organic Pesticides, Cut Your Power Bills in Half, Household Rainwater System.

Backwoods Home magazine "is written for people who have a desire to pursue personal independence, self sufficiency, and their dreams. It offers 'how to' articles on owner-built housing, independent energy, gardening, health, self-employment, country living, and other topics related to an independent and self-reliant lifestyle." Straightforward information about food, building/tools/housing, independent energy, country skills, raising animals, gardening. Six issues per year for $19.95/one year; $35.95/two years. P.O. Box 40, Montague, CA 96064. Credit card orders: 800-835-2418; e-mail: editors@backwoodshome.com
Web site: http://www.backwoodshome.com

Countryside and Small Stock Journal, W 11564 Hwy 64, Withee, WI 54498. Bimonthly. $18/year; phone: 800-551-5691. *Small Stock* was founded in 1917, *Countryside* in 1969. Most of the editorial content is written by readers who are living on the land. This is the *Countryside* philosophy: "It's not a single idea, but many ideas and attitudes, including a reverence for nature and a preference for country life; a desire for maximum personal self-reliance and creative leisure; a concern for family nurture and community cohesion; a certain hostility toward luxury; a belief that the primary reward of work should be well-being rather than money; a certain nostalgia for the supposed simplicities of the past and an anxiety about the technological and bureaucratic complexities of the present and the future; and a taste for the plain and functional. *Countryside* reflects and supports the simple life, and calls its practitioners homesteaders."

Country Connections "is a project of EARTH ALERT, a nonprofit public benefit corporation which educates the public about sustainability and related issues." One year (six issues): $22.00 Sample copy: $4.00 Send check to 14431 Ventura Blvd. No. 407, Sherman Oaks, CA 91423.
Phone: 818-501-1896; fax: 818-501-1897;
e-mail: countryink@countryink.com
Web site: http://countryink.com

Country Journal is one of the few glossy, full-color magazines that offer useful information by real country experts issue after issue. In its twenty-fourth year, it covers the country spectrum from apples to zucchini, with equipment, ornamentals, and animals included. One year (six issues) for $14.95. P.O. Box 392, Mount Morris, IL 61054-9957; phone: 800-435-9610.

Mother Earth News, published by Sussex Publishers, 49 East 21st Street, 11th Floor, New York, NY 10010, is a bimonthly "dedicated to presenting information which will help readers become more self-sufficient, financially independent, and environmentally aware." $14.97/year; phone: 800-234-3368; e-mail: mearth@aol.com

The Natural Farmer is a publication of the Northeast Organic Farming Association. Useful articles on grains, soil, specific organic farms, book reviews, contact people, news reports on food producers who use poisons. Four issues per year for $10. 411 Sheldon Road, Barre, MA 01005; phone: 508-355-2853.

Organic Gardening, P.O. Box 7320, Red Oak, IA 51591-0320; phone: 800-666-2206. Nine issues per year for $16.97. Published by the Rodale people, who also put out a prodigious collection of gardening and country-skill books—at last count, we have about twenty of their titles, including the definitive *Organic Gardening Encyclopedia*.

Practical Homeschooling—*The Magazine That Makes You an Expert*. "In every issue we cover a variety of homeschooling methods, help for beginners, elementary and preschool resources, high school and college helps, reviews of the hottest new software and online opportunities, personal stories, lots of reviews." Christian orientation. Six issues for $19.95. P.O. Box 1250, Fenton, MO 63026-1850; phone: 800-346-6322.

Raise the Stakes is published two times per year by the Planet Drum Foundation, P.O. Box 31251, San Francisco, CA 94131, Shasta Bioregion. Phone: 415-285-6556. Planet Drum is "a voice for bioregional sustainability, education and culture." It asks the question: "What approach can people take to go beyond environmental protests and actually begin living sustainably wherever they are located?" Membership is $25/year, and includes two issues of *Raise the Stakes* and a 25 percent discount on all Planet Drum publications.

Small Farm Today—"The Original How-to Magazine of Alternative and Traditional Crops, Livestock, and Direct Marketing." A recent issue included the following articles: Why Red Angus?, Brangus—The Bonus Breed, Going to the Big Time Fair, On the Farm, Coping with Livestock Stress, Selling Chickens to an Ethnic Market, Boer Goats, Management-Intensive Grazing for Sheep. Bimonthly, $21/one year, $39/two years; $54/three years. Subscription Dept., 3903 West Ridge Trail Road, Clark, MO 65243-9525.

Book catalogues

Good Earth Publications has books about "conscious living, sustainable lifestyles," including some titles not easily found on the following subjects: gardening, farming, livestock, permaculture, health, self-improvement, environment. P.O. Box 160, Columbus, NC 28722; phone: 704-863-2288; e-mail: goodearth@igc.ape.org

Storey's Books for Country Living has books on everything from wildflower gardening to country businesses. Schoolhouse Road, Pownal, VT 05261; phone: 800-441-5700.

Alternative Technology

Jade Mountain, Appropriate Technology for Sustainable Living, P.O. Box 4616, Boulder, CO 80306; phone: 800-442-1972;
Web site: info@jademountain.com; http://www.jademountain.com/

"Over 5,000 products. Worldwide supply, design, sizing, installations, troubleshooting. Solar electric, micro-hydro, wind generators, composting toilets & greywater systems, super energy efficient appliances and much more."

Kansas Wind Power, 13569 214th Road, Holton, KS 66436; phone: 913-364-4407. KWP's catalogue ($4) offers independent power systems and energy-saving devices, including solar electric modules, batteries, DC equipment and supplies, ram pumps, refrigerators, and composting toilets.

Real Goods, 555 Leslie Street, Ukaih, CA 95482-5507; phone: 707-468-9292; orders: 800-762-7325. Real Goods publishes the *Real Goods Catalog* and the *Solar Living Sourcebook* ($23), the latter a combination catalogue and primer on home electric generation systems, energy-efficient lighting, water pumps and purification systems, nontoxic household products, and recycling products and aids.

Sunelco, The Sun Electric Company, 100 Skeel Street, P.O. Box 787, Hamilton, MT 59804-0787; phone: 406-363-6924; orders: 800-338-6844; e-mail: sunelco@montana.com
Web site: http://www.sunelco.com

Their *Planning Guide and Product Catalog* offers a lot of information and assumes you know nothing about solar power or electricity.

Appendix B: State Maps

The state maps on the following pages are provided to help you identify areas of low population density. Shaded areas are general indicators only; some areas are growing rapidly. The state flower and tree are included, as vegetation indicates soil and climate conditions. The percentage of wooded area is also included. Trees absorb carbon dioxide and generate oxygen, the stuff that keeps our blood happy. Trees are good. Live among trees and plant more.

ALABAMA

Shaded area: 50 or fewer
people per square mile.
State average: 81.5 ppsm.
Camellia
Southern pine
68% wooded

Montgomery

ARIZONA

Shaded area: 50 or fewer
people per square mile.
State average: 33.7 ppsm.
Saguaro cactus blossom
Paloverde
27% wooded

Phoenix

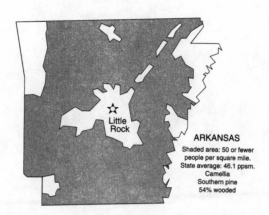

ARKANSAS

Shaded area: 50 or fewer
people per square mile.
State average: 46.1 ppsm.
Camellia
Southern pine
54% wooded

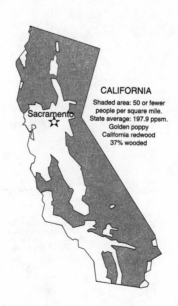

CALIFORNIA

Shaded area: 50 or fewer
people per square mile.
State average: 197.9 ppsm.
Golden poppy
California redwood
37% wooded

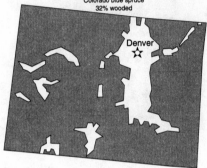

COLORADO

Shaded area: 10 or fewer
people per square mile.
State average: 33.5 ppsm.
Rocky Mountain columbine
Colorado blue spruce
32% wooded

CONNECTICUT

No area of 50 or fewer
people per square mile.
State average: 677.2 ppsm.
Mountain laurel
White oak
59% wooded

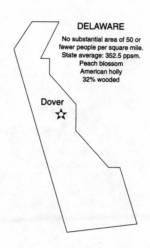

DELAWARE

No substantial area of 50 or
fewer people per square mile.
State average: 352.5 ppsm.
Peach blossom
American holly
32% wooded

Dover
☆

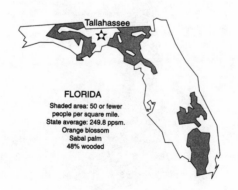

Tallahassee
☆

FLORIDA

Shaded area: 50 or fewer
people per square mile.
State average: 249.8 ppsm.
Orange blossom
Sabal palm
48% wooded

GEORGIA

Shaded area: 50 or fewer
people per square mile.
State average: 116.6 ppsm.
Azalea
Live oak
65% wooded

Atlanta

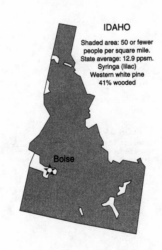

IDAHO

Shaded area: 50 or fewer
people per square mile.
State average: 12.9 ppsm.
Syringa (lilac)
Western white pine
41% wooded

Boise

ILLINOIS
Shaded area: 50 or fewer
people per square mile.
State average: 209.2 ppsm.
Native violet
White oak
12% or less wooded

INDIANA
Shaded area: 50 or fewer
people per square mile.
State average: 157.8 ppsm.
Peony
Tulip tree
19% wooded

IOWA

Shaded area: 50 or fewer
people per square mile.
State average: 50.3 ppsm.
Wild rose
Oak
6% wooded

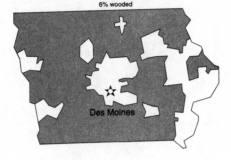

Des Moines

KANSAS

Shaded area: 50 or fewer
people per square mile.
State average: 30.8 ppsm.
Sunflower
Cottonwood
3% wooded

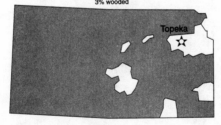

Topeka

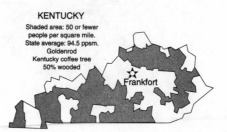

KENTUCKY

Shaded area: 50 or fewer
people per square mile.
State average: 94.5 ppsm.
Goldenrod
Kentucky coffee tree
50% wooded

Frankfort

LOUISIANA

Shaded area: 50 or fewer
people per square mile.
State average: 98.4 ppsm.
Magnolia
Bald cypress
50% wooded

Baton Rouge

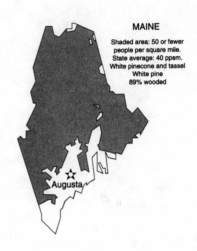

MAINE

Shaded area: 50 or fewer
people per square mile.
State average: 40 ppsm.
White pinecone and tassel
White pine
89% wooded

Augusta

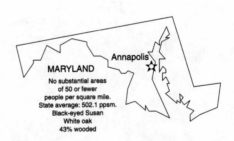

MARYLAND

No substantial areas
of 50 or fewer
people per square mile.
State average: 502.1 ppsm.
Black-eyed Susan
White oak
43% wooded

Annapolis

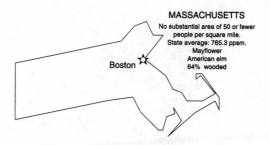

MASSACHUSETTS

No substantial area of 50 or fewer
people per square mile.
State average: 765.3 ppsm.
Mayflower
American elm
64% wooded

Boston

MICHIGAN

Shaded area: 50 or fewer
people per square mile.
State average: 166.1 ppsm.
Apple blossom
White pine
50% wooded

Lansing

MINNESOTA

Shaded area: 50 or fewer
people per square mile.
State average: 56.3 ppsm.
Shadowy lady's slipper
Red (Norway) pine
33% wooded

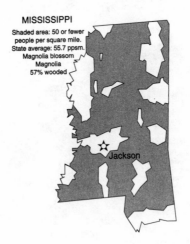

MISSISSIPPI

Shaded area: 50 or fewer
people per square mile.
State average: 55.7 ppsm.
Magnolia blossom
Magnolia
57% wooded

MISSOURI

Shaded area: 50 or fewer
people per square mile.
State average: 75.4 ppsm.
Hawthorn
Dogwood
32% wooded

Jefferson City

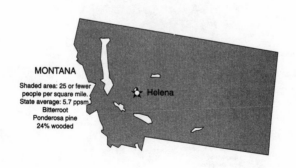

MONTANA

Shaded area: 25 or fewer
people per square mile.
State average: 5.7 ppsm
Bitterroot
Ponderosa pine
24% wooded

Helena

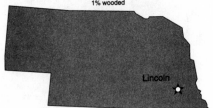

NEBRASKA

Entire state is sparsely
populated other than towns.
State average: 20.9 ppsm.
Goldenrod
Cottonwood
1% wooded

Lincoln

Carson City

NEVADA

Shaded area:
25 or fewer
people per square mile.
State average: 12.1 ppsm.
Sagebrush
Single-leaf pinon
13% wooded

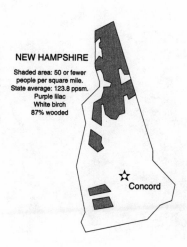

NEW HAMPSHIRE

Shaded area: 50 or fewer
people per square mile.
State average: 123.8 ppsm.
Purple lilac
White birch
87% wooded

☆ Concord

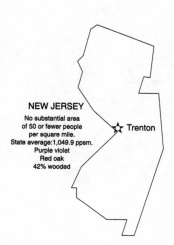

NEW JERSEY

No substantial area
of 50 or fewer people
per square mile.
State average:1,049.9 ppsm.
Purple violet
Red oak
42% wooded

☆ Trenton

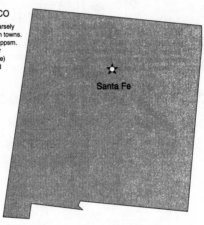

NEW MEXICO

Entire state is sparsely
populated other than towns.
State average: 13 ppsm.
Yucca flower
Pinon (nut pine)
20% wooded

Santa Fe

NEW YORK

Shaded area: 50 or fewer
people per square mile.
State average: 383.7 ppsm.
Rose
Sugar maple
62% wooded

Albany

NORTH CAROLINA

Shaded area: 50 or fewer
people per square mile.
State average: 140.5 ppsm.
Flowering dogwood
Pine
62% wooded

☆
Raleigh

NORTH DAKOTA

Shaded area: 25 or fewer
people per square mile.
State average: 9.2 ppsm.
Wild prairie rose
American elm
2% wooded

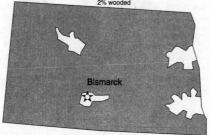

Bismarck

357

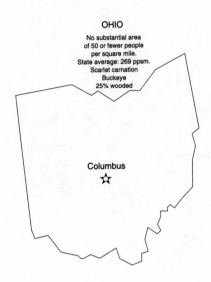

OHIO

No substantial area
of 50 or fewer people
per square mile.
State average: 269 ppsm.
Scarlet carnation
Buckeye
25% wooded

Columbus
☆

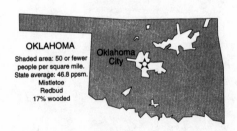

OKLAHOMA

Shaded area: 50 or fewer
people per square mile.
State average: 46.8 ppsm.
Mistletoe
Redbud
17% wooded

Oklahoma
City

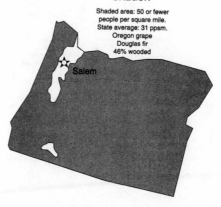

OREGON

Shaded area: 50 or fewer
people per square mile.
State average: 31 ppsm.
Oregon grape
Douglas fir
46% wooded

Salem

PENNSYLVANIA

Shaded area: 50 or fewer
people per square mile.
State average: 267.9 ppsm.
Mountain laurel
Eastern hemlock
59% wooded

Harrisburg

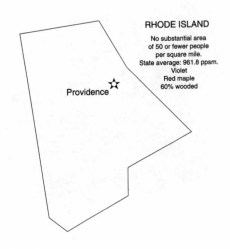

RHODE ISLAND

No substantial area
of 50 or fewer people
per square mile.
State average: 961.8 ppsm.
Violet
Red maple
60% wooded

Providence

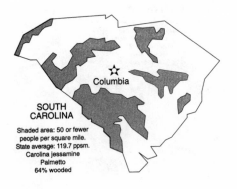

Columbia

**SOUTH
CAROLINA**

Shaded area: 50 or fewer
people per square mile.
State average: 119.7 ppsm.
Carolina jessamine
Palmetto
64% wooded

SOUTH DAKOTA

Shaded area: 25 or fewer
people per square mile.
State average: 9.37 ppsm.
American pasqueflower
Black Hills spruce
3% wooded

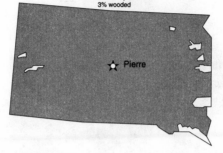

☆ Pierre

TENNESSEE

Shaded area: 50 or fewer
people per square mile.
State average: 121.9 ppsm.
Passionflower
Tulip poplar
52% wooded

☆
Nashville

361

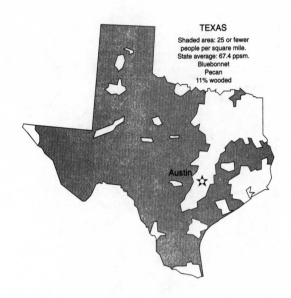

TEXAS

Shaded area: 25 or fewer
people per square mile.
State average: 67.4 ppsm.
Bluebonnet
Pecan
11% wooded

Austin

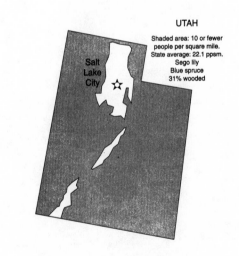

UTAH

Shaded area: 10 or fewer
people per square mile.
State average: 22.1 ppsm.
Sego lily
Blue spruce
31% wooded

Salt
Lake
City

VERMONT

Shaded area: 50 or fewer
people per square mile.
State average: 61.6 ppsm.
Red clover
Sugar maple
77% wooded

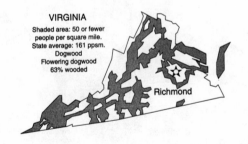

VIRGINIA

Shaded area: 50 or fewer
people per square mile.
State average: 161 ppsm.
Dogwood
Flowering dogwood
63% wooded

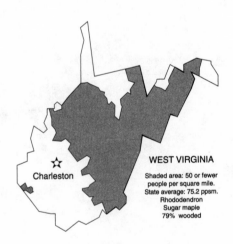

WASHINGTON

Shaded area: 25 or fewer
people per square mile.
State average: 77.1 ppsm.
Coast rhododendron
Western hemlock
48% wooded

☆
Olympia

☆
Charleston

WEST VIRGINIA

Shaded area: 50 or fewer
people per square mile.
State average: 75.2 ppsm.
Rhododendron
Sugar maple
79% wooded

WISCONSIN

Shaded area: 50 or fewer
people per square mile.
State average: 92.2 ppsm.
Wood violet
Sugar maple
45% wooded

☆
Madison

WYOMING

Shaded area: 50 or fewer
people per square mile.
State average: 4.8 ppsm.
Indian paintbrush
Plains cottonwood
16% wooded

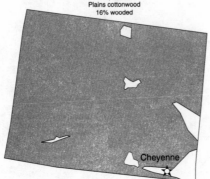

Cheyenne
☆

Glossary

abstract of title: A chronological summary of all recorded documents that affect title to a property, usually going back to a government patent or Spanish land grant. Often simply called an abstract. Old abstracts were often bound in leather, like a little book.

acceleration clause: A condition in a *security instrument* that accelerates the time of final payment, for instance, nonpayment of taxes, nonmaintenance of improvements, or failure to make payments. Usually allows the lender to demand immediate payment.

adjustable rate mortgage: See *ARM*.

adverse possession: A legal condition allowing a stranger to a real estate title to gain title by performing certain acts for a prescribed period of time, most notably being in possession of the property contrary to the interests of the owner.

agent: In real estate law, one who acts for another and owes a *fiduciary* duty to perform. A real estate broker is usually the agent of a seller (a seller is the agent's *principal*) through a listing agreement. She may also be the agent of a buyer through an agreement. She may not be an agent of both buyer and seller at the same time without full disclosure and agreement by the principals. A real estate salesman acting for the broker is an agent of the broker and a sub-agent of the seller. Another real estate broker working through a multiple listing authority is a sub-agent of the seller.

agency: The legal relationship whereby one (the agent) may act on behalf of another (the *principal*).

appraisal: An estimate of value, usually by a licensed appraiser.

appraiser: One who investigates and evaluates real property. Appraiser licensing laws vary from state to state.

APR: Annual percentage rate, as defined by the Truth-in-Lending Act: the total finance charge expressed as an interest rate.

arbitration: A nonjudicial process by which a monetary dispute is heard and decided. Although there may be only one arbitrator, typically the plaintiff and defendant each select one arbitrator and then those two agree on a third, who acts as the chairman or chief arbitrator at the proceedings. Realtor® boards offer arbitration, often at no cost to members of the public who have legitimate disputes with Realtors. Usually three board members, who have no relationship with the defendant, comprise the arbitration panel. Contrary to what one might think, Realtors tend to deal harshly with their peers who injure the public. Most courts uphold and enforce the decision of an arbitration panel.

ARM: Adjustable rate mortgage. The interest rate rises and falls with changes in certain published indexes, such as CDs or treasury notes. ARMs can be good under certain circumstances but disastrous under others. Ask for a blank copy of the note and deed of trust you will be required to sign so you can read it at your leisure. Make sure you understand how fast and how much the interest rate can rise.

assessed value: County tax assessors place a value on property that is usually well below market value. The tax rate multiplied against the assessed value (usually per hundred) determines the tax liability.

assessment: An assessment is a lien for a special purpose, for instance to pay off water or sewer bonds, and usually means special taxes are due to some agency on a regular basis.

bioregion: A term so new it is not in my dictionaries. A bioregion is a definable natural area containing distinct climate, topography, minerals, plants, and animals. Bioregions have natural boundaries, as contrasted with the artificial boundaries of states and counties. A bioregion is often defined by a watershed.

broker: A licensed real estate agent who may or may not be a Realtor®. A broker associate has a broker's license but works as a salesman for another broker.

broker-salesperson: A real estate agent qualified as a broker but working as the salesperson of another broker.

buyer's agent: A real estate broker who works solely for a buyer, by contract, as opposed to the norm, in which the broker works for the seller.

caveat emptor: Let the buyer beware. But of course you already knew that. Well, just in case you've led a sheltered life.

CC&Rs: Covenants, conditions, and restrictions. These are encumbrances on the property usually placed by a subdivider to protect the economic integrity of the subdivision. A typical covenant is that the owner will not conduct a business on the property. A condition may require that any building plans be approved by a committee before construction will be allowed. Get a copy of the CC&Rs and read them carefully to be sure you will not be prevented from doing as you wish with the property. If you are an insomniac, reading CC&Rs will be less expensive and less injurious to your body than sleeping pills.

closing: The act of completing a transaction, where the buyer gets title to the property and the seller gets the purchase price. If you hear "closing escrow," it means the same thing. Some areas still use the word "settlement."

closing instructions and statements: The escrow agent prepares instructions according to the orders of the buyer, seller, and lender, including monetary demands by persons such as termite inspectors, appraisers, and insurance agents. The instructions list all monies and documents to be given and to be received. Instructions usually contain estimates, such as for interest and insurance pro-rations. After closing, the escrow agent prepares buyer's, seller's, and lender's statements reflecting final disbursements.

contract of sale: An uncertain, confusing term. Some use the term to mean an offer to purchase, which, if accepted, becomes a legally enforceable contract. Also known as contract *for* sale, land contract, contract for deed, and installment land contract. Is sometimes used instead of a mortgage or note and deed of trust to act as a security instrument, typically for sellers who carry the financing on the sale of their property. Potentially dangerous for buyers, as the contract often allows the seller to easily regain the property if the buyers fails to perform any condition on time, with the buyer losing all deposits, down payments, and payments on the contract. See *installment land sales contract*.

country: In this book, country means a place outside the obvious influence of a city. Country places don't have parking meters or traffic congestion. They do have store clerks and bank tellers who smile, address you by your name, ask how you're doing—and listen to your answer. Country is—well, you'll know it when you feel it.

covenants, conditions, and restrictions: See *CC&Rs*.

deed: A deed is a written instrument by which a seller transfers legal interest to a buyer. Examples of common deed types follow.

> **grant deed:** Typically, a warranty deed that limits warranties to two: 1) the grantor has good title and the power to convey, and 2) there are no encumbrances on the property that would harm the grantee.

quitclaim deed: The grantor gives the grantee all the interest that he has in the property. This may be little or none as there are no implied warranties. Quitclaim deeds are useful in clearing clouds on title, such as the potential claim of an ex-spouse. Perhaps it will be helpful to your understanding of this deed if I tell you that it would be perfectly legal for me to give you a quitclaim deed to the Tower of Pisa. Stand back!

sheriff's deed: In some counties, when properties are sold for back taxes or to settle a disputed estate, the sheriff conducts the sale (usually an auction) and a sheriff's deed is given to the purchaser. If the sheriff is bona fide, the deed most likely is also.

trustee's deed: In states using deeds of trust to evidence a security interest in property, a trustee's deed is given in a foreclosure.

warranty deed: The grantor warrants to the grantee that the title is clear of encumbrances and he will defend the grantee's title against all other claims. Various states include other warranties.

deed of trust: A deed of trust creates a security interest for a lender and spells out the conditions of default, for instance, if the buyer does not make payments, fails to maintain the property in good condition, or fails to provide fire insurance; and the method the trustee may use to effect the foreclosure.

deposit receipt: Much more than a receipt for money, "DRs" are binding purchase contracts if certain conditions are met.

earnest money deposit: Cash, promissory note, check, or other item of value given by a buyer with a purchase contract. Not legally required, but shows serious intent to a seller. Amount is negotiable between buyer and seller. Most contracts call for forfeiture of deposits to the seller upon buyer default or, if seller defaults, deposit returns to buyer.

easement: A right to use someone else's land as a right-of-way, or for some other legal purpose.

ecosystem: A system of interaction of organisms with their environment. Modernly used to depict a distinct geographic area, as the Greater Yellowstone ecosystem.

eminent domain: The power of government to take property for the public good. An eminent domain proceeding is the legal process for determining if the taking is proper, and what shall constitute fair compensation. The power may also be used to use your property to gain access to a nearby property.

encumbrance: A claim, lien, charge, or liability attached to and binding on real property. Includes mortgages, assessments, leases and easements.

escrow: A neutral depository of funds and documents.

escrow agent: Also called escrow officer. A person who accepts and holds escrow funds and documents, and takes instructions for closing the sale: recording the appropriate documents, delivering them to the proper parties, and disbursing funds in agreement with the signed instructions of the parties, typically the buyer, seller, and lender. Depending on the area, escrow agents may be real estate brokers, lawyers, employees of title insurance companies, or independent escrow agents. Escrow officers are much like Santa Claus, but they require that you pay in advance for your present.

escrow instructions: See *closing instructions.*

estimated purchase cost sheet: Prepared by real estate agents for buyers so there are no financial surprises at closing. Shows all anticipated costs of purchase, including down payment, escrow fee, title insurance policy fee, recording fees, loan fee, appraisal fee, termite inspection fee, property insurance premium, and prorations of taxes, insurance, and interest if appropriate.

ethics hearing: A hearing conducted by a board of Realtors to decide if a member has violated the Code of Ethics of the National Association of Realtors®. The hearing may be initiated by a Realtor or a member of the public. Monetary disputes are resolved through an *arbitration.*

exclusive listing or exclusive right to sell: A listing agreement in which the seller agrees to pay a commission to the broker in the agreement no matter who provides the buyer, even if the seller finds the buyer.

FHA: Federal Housing Administration, which insures loans.

fiduciary: Sometimes used synonymously with agent. An agent has a fiduciary obligation to his principal—a very high degree of confidence and trust.

foreclosure: The procedure by which a property is taken from an owner who has failed to meet certain conditions of a mortgage.

forty: Originally a square parcel of land containing approximately forty acres, one quarter mile per side, and being one-sixteenth of a section. Now used loosely to describe any parcel containing forty acres.

grantor: The party that grants a real property interest—i.e., the owner-seller.

grantee: The party that receives the interest, usually the buyer, and usually in the form of a deed. You would be a happy grantee if your Aunt Mabel left her country estate to you as a small part of your inheritance.

GRI: Graduate of Realtor's Institute. A designation awarded upon completion of a prescribed course of study.

homestead: May refer to property obtained by the Homestead Act of 1862. The last of such programs ended in 1977. Homestead exemptions may be recorded in some states, protecting one's primary residence from foreclosure for certain reasons, but not from default on a security device. Also used loosely to describe a country home place with garden, orchard, chickens—that sort of thing.

installment land sales contract: Also known as land contract, conditional sales contract, contract for deed, and agreement of sale. A contract that calls for the deed to be given to the buyer only after all payments have been completed. You don't want this, because if you miss one payment the seller can keep the property plus all monies you have paid. Also, if the contract is not recorded, the seller may use the property as collateral for loans. Sellers who carry the financing like this contract because, in case of default, they need not to go through a foreclosure proceeding to regain title to the property. See *contract of sale*.

lawyer's title opinion: See *title opinion*.

lien: A legal encumbrance on land, ensuring payment of a debt, obligation, or duty.

lis pendens: A legal notice that a lawsuit is pending, the outcome of which could affect real estate title.

listing agreement: A contract between a property owner and a real estate broker, providing a commission to the broker if he procures an acceptable buyer—but see *open listing* and *exclusive listing*.

MAI: Member of Appraisal Institute. The MAI designation is awarded only upon successful completion of various classes and after substantial experience.

maintenance agreement: Generally for upkeep of a private road used by two or more parties. Also used in subdivisions that contain common areas used by the various owners.

marketable title: Title that is free from encumbrances and third-party rights or interests incompatible with the use, enjoyment, and ownership of the title holder. Not perfect title but considered reasonably free of potential legal challenges.

mechanic's lien or materialmen's lien: A lien against real property available to those who have provided services or materials used to improve real property. These are the responsibility of the seller; make sure they are paid before you take title.

metropolitan area: In 1970, Standard Metropolitan Statistical Areas were designated by the Census Bureau wherever there was an urban center of 50,000 or more people. Neighboring commuter counties of metropolitan character were also included in these areas, to the county borders. All other counties were non-metropolitan. In 1980 the designation was changed. It is now simply a thickly populated county or counties of at least 50,000 population. Peripheral counties are included if they meet certain criteria. "Both rural and urban areas are found in metropolitan and nonmetropolitan sectors of the country" (Fuguitt, Brown, Beale, *Rural and Small Town America, 1989*). These changing and confusing designations have made the statistics of metropolitan-nonmetropolitan-rural migration patterns less meaningful. Who cares—we know where we're going, even if the statisticians don't.

metropolitan statistical area: See *metropolitan area.*

microclimate: A pocket of localized climate different from nearby or sur-rounding areas. The lee side of hills, valleys, and large bodies of water create microclimates.

monument: A permanent physical object marking the corner point of a land survey, as an iron pipe driven into the ground, or a pile of rocks, sometimes marked with red paint.

mortgage: Commonly used as a term to describe a loan made with property as security, a mortgage is a document which makes property security for the repayment of a debt.

note: Also called a promissory note. A document evidencing a debt, typically stating the amount, the interest rate, and the terms of repayment. Usually secured by a deed of trust or a mortgage, otherwise it is simply a promise to pay. Some states use a bond for the same purpose.

offer to purchase: The first step in a real estate sale. The buyer makes a written offer to the seller, which if accepted, becomes a contract. The term also is used to reference a document used for this purpose. See *purchase agreement.*

open listing: A nonexclusive listing given by a seller to many real estate brokers; a commission is paid only to the broker procuring a buyer. The seller reserves the right to sell the property without incurring a commission liability.

personal property: All property that is not real property.

point: Each point charged by a lender is equivalent to one percent of the loan amount.

prepayment penalty: A lender's charge to a borrower when the loan is paid off before the maturity date. This can be a very painful surprise—shop for your loan carefully and ask if there will be such a penalty.

principal: In a real estate sale, the primary principal is generally the seller, who employs the real estate broker as his agent. An increasingly common arrangement is the *buyer's agent*, where a buyer is the principal of the agent who represents him.

purchase agreement: Also known as purchase contract, deposit receipt, offer and acceptance, purchase offer, and purchase and sales agreement. Four key parts: (1) receipt of the buyer's deposit; (2) terms of the buyer's offer; (3) provision for the seller's acceptance; (4) provision for payment of the broker's commission. Usually preprinted forms; specific wording and clauses vary from state to state.

radon: A colorless, odorless, tasteless, naturally occurring radioactive gas formed by radium decay.

real estate broker: One licensed to sell, rent, or buy property and collect a commission. Especially in the country, may not be a Realtor®.

real estate salesperson: A person licensed to perform real estate activities, but must work under the authority of a broker.

real property: Land and that which is affixed to it, including buildings, vegetation, and minerals. A tree purchased at a nursery is personal property; once planted, it becomes real property.

Realtor®: A licensed real estate broker who is a member of the National Association of Realtors, which membership includes a pledge to adhere to a strict Code of Ethics.

Realtor® Associate: A licensed real estate salesperson who is a member of the National Association of Realtors and works for a Realtor.

recording: The process of placing important documents such as deeds and deeds of trust into the public record. Serves as constructive notice to the public.

right-of-way: The right to use the land of another for a certain purpose, typically as a roadway or for utility lines. This is very handy if it's the only way to access your property but a real nuisance if someone else has one over your land.

riparian rights: Water rights of a property owner whose property touches the water. The extent of riparian rights varies from state to state.

rural: The Bureau of the Census defines rural as the population outside incorporated or unincorporated places with more than 2,500 people and/or outside urbanized areas, the latter being defined as a central city or cities which together with surrounding closely settled territory (density of more than 1,000 persons per square mile) has a minimum population of 50,000.

sales associate: A real estate salesperson who works for a broker.

second mortgage or lien: Also simply called a second. A lien that is in a junior position. Sellers often "take back a second" if the buyer does not have all of the down payment required by the first lender.

section: A square parcel of land surveyed according to the United States rectangular survey system, containing approximately 640 acres and being approximately one mile on each side.

security instrument or device: Notes, deeds of trust, mortgages, and other agreements that pledge property as security for a loan.

settlement: In some places this term is used synonymously with *closing*.

SRA: Senior Residential Appraiser.

subdivision: Division of land into smaller parcels. In many counties, a subdivider must comply with various state and county regulations as to roads, utilities, minimum lot size, and others. If the subdivision map has not been accepted and recorded, no building permits will be issued. Subdivision lands sold through interstate commerce must comply with federal regulations.

subordination: A clause that allows a lien to be moved into a junior position, as when a seller finances the sale but allows the buyer to obtain a bank loan for house construction. The bank will insist on being in first position: this will only be possible if the initial first loan contains the subordination clause.

taxes: The rent that the king (or governor) charges you for using his property.

title: The right to or ownership of property. The evidence of ownership, as a deed.

title insurance: For a one-time fee, a title insurance company issues to a property buyer a policy indemnifying loss against any factor listed in the policy occurring before the purchase. I dislike insurance on general principles, but I have a high regard for title insurance. Title insurance contributes to peaceful sleep.

title opinion: Also called lawyer's title opinion. A lawyer's written statement of the quality and condition of real property title. Lawyers usually issue a statement that they have studied the abstract of title and, in their opinion, the seller has clear and marketable title. Among other potential problems, examining an abstract does not reveal forgeries—and the lawyer is not responsible for same. If a lawyer makes a mistake he or she may be liable but unable to pay your loss. And if lawyers are not honest they may squeeze out of liability. You will have much more protection if you buy title insurance.

trustee: The person or company that will take your property away from you if you fail to meet your payments or other requirements of the lender.

truth in lending: An indecipherable rule decreed by Big Brother to make sure we aren't fooled into paying more for our loans than we thought we were. Gave birth to *APR*—annual percentage rate, by which charges other than interest are calculated to determine the true cost of a loan to a borrower.

VA: Veteran's Administration. Helps veterans obtain loans by *guaranteeing* payment of the loan to the lender. Differs from the FHA, which is available to all citizens, and which *insures* loans.

VIR: Variable interest rate. The note contains provisions for increasing the interest rate that you will pay. Make sure you understand the terms of any loan before agreeing to it.

watershed: The total land area from which rainfall drains into a stream. Extends from ridgetop to ridgetop. Watersheds are often *bioregions*.

wrap-around mortgage: A mortgage that includes an existing smaller mortgage. We used "wraps" during the early period of rising interest rates, to keep assumable low-interest-rate loans alive. Many lenders refuse to allow their loans to be wrapped and, if they discover the transaction (often through insurance policies), will demand immediate payoff. This can create a most awkward situation, especially if the borrower cannot quickly obtain another loan.

You'ns and us'ns oughta get together sometime: Mid-south country version of "Let's do lunch." More likely to be sincere than city version.

Essential Country Skill #101: using a pig to discover mushrooms

Instructions: Buy a trained pig and follow him.

Bibliography

Arden, Lynie. *The Work-at-Home Sourcebook*. Sixth edition. Boulder, CO: Live Oak Publications, 1996.

Bailey, Liberty Hyde. *The Outlook to Nature*. New York: Macmillan, 1924.

Bennett, Hal Zina, and Susan J. Sparrow. *Follow Your Bliss*. New York: Avon, 1990.

Berry, Wendell. *Sex, Economy, Freedom, and Community*. New York: Pantheon, 1993.

———. *The Unsettling of America: Culture and Agriculture*. San Francisco: Sierra Club Books, 1977.

Bowman, Thomas F.: George A. Giuliani, and M. Ronald Minge. *Finding Your Best Place to Live in America*. New York: Red Lion Books, 1981.

Brabec, Barbara. *Homemade Money: The Definitive Guide to Success in a Homebased Business*. White Hall, VA: Betterway Publications, 1989.

Bromfield, Louis. *Pleasant Valley*. New York: Harper & Brothers, 1945.

Brown, Lester R. *State of the World 1996*. New York: W.W. Norton, 1996.

———. *State of the World 1998*. New York: W.W. Norton, 1998.

Campbell, Carlos C. *New Towns: Another Way to Live*. Reston, VA: Reston Publishing Company, 1976.

Castle, Emery N., editor. *The Changing American Countryside: Rural People and Places*. Lawrence University Press of Kansas, 1995.

Celente, Gerald. *Trends 2000*. New York: Warner Books, 1997.

Conway, H. McKinley, and Linda L. Liston. *The Weather Handbook*. Atlanta: Conway Research, 1974.

Crampton, Norman. *The 100 Best Small Towns in America*. New York: Macmillan, 1995.

Danbom, David B. *Born in The Country: A History of Rural America*. Baltimore: Johns Hopkins University Press, 1995.

Davidson, Osha Gray. *Broken Heartland: The Rise of America's Rural Ghetto.* New York: The Free Press, 1990.

Dickerman, Pat. *Farm, Ranch and Country Vacations.* New York: Farm and Ranch Vacations, 1983.

Dickinson, Peter A. *Retirement Edens Outside the Sunbelt.* Glenview, IL: Scott, Foresman, 1987.

Downing, Joan, project editor. *America the Beautiful* (separate book for each state in the set). Chicago: Children's Press, 1987–1992.

Doyle, Rodger. *Atlas of Contemporary America: Portrait of a Nation—Politics, Economy, Environment, Ethnic and Religious Diversity, Health Issues, Demographic Patterns, Quality of Life, Crime, Personal Freedoms.* New York: Facts on File, 1994.

Dychtwald, Ken. *Age Wave.* Los Angeles: Jeremy Tarcher, 1989.

Easterbrook, Gregg. *A Moment on the Earth: The Coming Age of Environmental Optimism.* New York: Viking, 1995.

Etzioni, Amitai. *The Spirit of Community: The Reinvention of American Society.* New York: Simon & Schuster, 1993.

Famighetti, Robert, editor. *The World Almanac and Book of Facts 1996.* Mahwah, NJ: Funk & Wagnalls, 1996.

Ford, Norman. *The 50 Healthiest Places to Live and Retire in the United States.* Bedford, MA: Mills & Sanderson, 1991.

Garreau, Joel. *Edge City: Life on the New Frontier.* New York: Doubleday, 1991.

Germer, Jerry. *Country Careers: Successful Ways to Live and Work in the Country.* New York: John Wiley & Sons, 1993.

Gilligan, Gerald S. *A Price Guide for Buying and Selling Rural Acreage.* Stamford, CT: Gerald S. Gilligan & Associates, 1974.

Goldman, Benjamin A. *The Truth About Where You Live: An Atlas for Action on Toxins and Mortality.* New York: Times Books, 1991.

Graves, William, editor. *National Geographic Special Edition: Water: The Power, Promise, and Turmoil of North America's Fresh Water.* Washington, DC: National Geographic Society, 1993.

Gusewelle, C. W. *Far from Any Coast: Pieces of America's Heartland.* Columbia: University of Missouri Press, 1989.

Hall, Bob, and Mary Lee Kerr. *1991–1992 Green Index: A State-by-State Guide to the Nation's Environmental Health.* Washington, DC: Island Press, 1991.

Haywood, Julie, and Ken Spooner. *Goodbye City Hello Country.* Grand Junction, CO: Highland Books, 1985.

Healy, Robert G., and James L. Short. *The Market for Rural Land: Trends, Issues, Policies.* Washington, DC: Conservation Foundation, 1981.

Heenan, David A. *The New Corporate Frontier: The Big Move to Small Town, USA.* New York: McGraw-Hill, 1991.

Herbers, John. *The New Heartland: America's Flight Beyond the Suburbs and How It Is Changing Our Future.* New York: Times Books, 1986.

Hiss, Tony. *The Experience of Place.* New York: Alfred A. Knopf, 1990.

Jacob, Jeffrey. *New Pioneers.* University Park: Pennsylvania State University Press, 1997.

Joseph, Stanley, and Lynn Karlin. *Maine Farm.* New York: Smallwood & Stewart, 1991.

Kimble, George H. T. *Our American Weather.* New York: McGraw-Hill, 1955.

LaFavore, Michael. *Radon: The Invisible Threat.* Emmaus, PA: Rodale Press, 1987.

Lessinger, Jack. *Penturbia.* Bow, WA: Socio-Economics, 1991.

———. *Regions of Opportunity: A Bold New Strategy for Real Estate Investment with Forecasts to the Year 2010.* New York: Times Books, 1986.

Levering, Frank, and Wanda Urbanska. *Simple Living: One Couple's Search for a Better Life.* New York: Viking, 1992.

Little, Charles E. *Louise Bromfield at Malabar: Writings on Farming and Country Life*. Baltimore: Johns Hopkins University Press, 1988.

Logsdon, Gene. *At Nature's Pace*. New York: Pantheon, 1994.

————. *The Contrary Farmer*. Post Mills, VT: Chelsea Green Publishing, 1993.

Long, Charles. *Life After the City: A Harrowsmith Guide to Rural Living*. Camden East, Ontario: Camden House Publishing, 1989.

Longino, Charles F. Jr. *Retirement Migration in America*. Houston: Vacation Publications, 1995.

Martin, Ruth S. *Crumbling Dreams: What You Must Know Before Building or Buying a New House (or Condo)*. Cleveland: Lakeside Press, 1993.

McCaig, Donald. *An American Homeplace*. New York: Crown, 1992.

McGill, Robert. *Moving to the Country*. Reeds Spring, MO: White Oak Press, 1987.

McPhee, John. *Basin and Range*. New York: Farrar, Straus & Giroux, 1981.

McWilliams, Peter. *Do It! Let's Get Off Our Buts*. Los Angeles: Prelude Press, 1991.

Mitchell, John Hanson. *Living at the End of Time*. Boston: Houghton Mifflin, 1990.

Morrison, Peter A., editor. *A Taste of the Country: A Collection of Calvin Beale's Writings*. University Park: Pennsylvania State University Press, 1990.

Nader, Ralph, and John Abbotts. *The Menace of Atomic Energy*. New York: W.W. Norton, 1977.

Naisbitt, John. *Megatrends*. New York: Warner Books, 1982.

Naisbitt, John, and Patricia Aburdene. *Megatrends 2000: Ten New Directions for the 1990's*. New York: William Morrow, 1990.

Nearing, Helen, and Scott Nearing. *Continuing the Good Life: Half a Century of Homesteading*. New York: Schocken, 1979.

————. *Living the Good Life: How to Live Sanely and Simply in a Troubled World*. New York: Schocken, 1970.

Norwood, Ken, and Kathleen Smith. *Rebuilding Community in America: Housing for Ecological Living, Personal Empowerment, and the New Extended Family.* Berkeley, CA: Shared Living Resource Center, 1995.

Popcorn, Faith. *The Popcorn Report.* New York: Doubleday, 1991.

Powers, Ron. *Far from Home: Life and Loss in Two American Towns.* New York: Random House, 1991.

Ringholz, Raye, C. *Little Town Blues: Voices from the Changing West.* Layton, UT: Gibbs Smith, 1992.

Robbins, Jim. *The Last Refuge: The Environmental Showdown in Yellowstone and the American West.* New York: William Morrow, 1993.

Rosenberg, Lee, and Saralee Rosenberg. *50 Fabulous Places to Raise Your Family.* Hawthorne, NJ: Career Press, 1993.

———. *50 Fabulous Places to Retire in America.* Hawthorne, NJ: Career Press, 1991.

Ross, Tom and Marilyn Ross. *Country Bound!* Buena Vista, CO: Communication Creativity, 1992.

Rossiter, Phyllis. *A Living History of the Ozarks.* Gretna, LA: Pelican Publishing Company, 1992.

Ruegg, Frank, and Paul Bianchina. *You Can't Plant Tomatoes in Central Park.* Far Hills, NJ: New Horizon Press, 1990.

Rybczynski, Witold. *City Life.* New York: Scribner, 1995.

Sale, Kirkpatrick. *Dwellers in the Land: The Bioregional Vision.* San Francisco: Sierra Club Books, 1985.

Savageau, David. *Places Rated Almanac.* New York: Macmillan, 1997.

———. *Retirement Places Rated: All You Need to Plan Your Retirement or Select Your Second Home.* New York: Prentice Hall, 1990.

Schaeffer, John, editor. *Solar Living Sourcebook. Eighth edition.* White River Junction, VT: Chelsea Green Publishing, 1994.

Schama, Simon. *Landscape and Memory.* New York: Alfred A. Knopf, 1995.

Scher, Les, and Carol Scher. *Finding and Buying Your Place in the Country.* Chicago: Dearborn Financial Publishing, 1992.

Setterberg, Fred, and Lonny Shavelson. *Toxic Nation: The Fight to Save Our Communities from Chemical Contamination.* New York: John Wiley & Sons, 1993.

Shattuck, Alfred. *The Greener Pastures Relocation Guide: Finding the Best State in the United States for You.* Englewood Cliffs, NJ: Prentice Hall, 1984.

Steila, Donald. *The Geography of Soils.* Englewood Cliffs, NJ: Prentice Hall, 1976.

Teaford, Jon C. *Cities of the Heartland: The Rise and Fall of the Industrial Midwest.* Indianapolis: Indiana University Press, 1993.

Thomas, G. Scott. *The Rating Guide to Life in America's Small Cities.* Buffalo, NY: Prometheus Books, 1990.

———. *Where to Make Money: A Rating Guide to Opportunities in America's Metro Areas.* Buffalo, NY: Prometheus Books, 1993.

Toffler, Alvin. *Future Shock.* New York: Random House, 1970.

———. *Power Shift.* New York: Bantam, 1990

———. *The Third Wave.* New York: Bantam, 1980.

Vinz, Mark, and Thom Tammaro, editors. *Common Ground: A Gathering of Poems on Rural Life.* Moorhead, MN: Dacotah Territory Press, 1988.

Whatley, Booker T. *Booker T. Whatley's Handbook on How to Make $100,000 Farming 25 Acres.* Emmaus, PA: Regenerative Agriculture Association, 1987.

Index

About the Author

Gene GeRue has lived in a town and on a farm in Wisconsin, in Japan, in Seattle, in San Francisco, and other California cities of varying size. He has worked as a draftsman, laborer, welder, marketing director, technical writer, graphics designer, and editor. The longest he ever stayed with one thing was fifteen years as a real estate broker and instructor in the San Francisco Bay Area. He finally got his act together and found and moved to his ideal country home in the Ozarks, where he now does what he likes most: writing, designing, gardening, woodworking, building, hiking, and trying to make the world's thickest perfect pizza.